T0396551

Contemporary Gulf Studies

Series Editors
Steven Wright, College of Humanities and Social Sciences, Hamad bin
Khalifa University, Doha, Qatar
Abdullah Baabood, School of International Liberal Studies, Waseda
University, Tokyo, Japan

Salient Features:

- The Gulf lies at the intersection of regional conflicts and the competing interests of global powers and therefore publications in the series reflect this complex environment.
- The series will see publication on the dynamic nature of how the Gulf region has been undergoing enormous changes attracting regional and international interests.

Aims and Scope:
This series offer a platform from which scholarly work on the most pressing issues within the Gulf region will be examined. The scope of the book series will encompass work being done on the member states of the Gulf Cooperation Council (GCC): Saudi Arabia, Oman, United Arab Emirates, Qatar, Bahrain, Kuwait in addition to Iraq, Iran and Yemen. The series will focus on three types of volumes: Single and jointly authored monograph; Thematic edited books; Course text books. The scope of the series will include publications relating to the countries of focus, in terms of the following themes which will allow for interdisciplinary and multidisciplinary inquiry on the Gulf region to flourish:

- Politics and political development
- Regional and international relations
- Regional cooperation and integration
- Defense and security
- Economics and development
- Food and water security
- Energy and environment
- Civil society and the private sector
- Identity, migration, youth, gender and employment
- Health and education
- Media, literature, arts & culture

Ali A. Alkandari

The Muslim Brotherhood in Kuwait

1941–1991

Ali A. Alkandari
Kuwait University
Kuwait City, Kuwait

ISSN 2662-320X   ISSN 2662-3218 (electronic)
Contemporary Gulf Studies
ISBN 978-981-99-3049-4   ISBN 978-981-99-3050-0   (eBook)
https://doi.org/10.1007/978-981-99-3050-0

Cover image: Fernando Tatay, shutterstock.com
Cover design by eStudio Calamar

This Palgrave Macmillan imprint is published by the registered company Springer Nature
Singapore Pte Ltd.
The registered company address is: 152 Beach Road, #21-01/04 Gateway East, Singapore
189721, Singapore

PREFACE

This is the first focused study of the Society of the Muslim Brotherhood, the most influential and organised social and political movement in Kuwait, from its beginnings in 1946 up to 2000. It focuses on the circumstances surrounding the emergence and development of the Muslim Brotherhood as part of a general Islamic revival in Kuwait. It argues that the Muslim Brotherhood was driven first and foremost by cultural considerations and that Kuwaiti secularists regarded it as a challenge to their growing influence in both the political domain (traditionally controlled by the ruling family) and the social domain (historically under the control of the religious establishment). The resulting conflict with secularists over the social domain posed a serious threat to the Muslim Brotherhood who considered themselves an extension of the traditional religious establishment. They also viewed the secularists' attempts to reshape Kuwaiti identity as a threat to Kuwait's Islamic identity. This prompted the Muslim Brotherhood to channel all their social, educational and political efforts towards reclaiming the social domain.

This study focuses also on the mechanisms adopted by the Muslim Brotherhood, ones which combined Islamic values with modern mobilisation strategies producing a dynamic Islamist movement seeking to revive the golden age of Islam through modern means. The movement maintained a pyramid hierarchy, and it refashioned modern economic theory to make it more compatible with Islamic teachings. It also established a Muslim Boy Scouts movement and an Islamic press, while it reformed other organisations to make them compatible with Islamic values. All this was done in an effort to implement Hasan al-Banna's vision of fashioning a pious Muslim individual, a virtuous family and, finally, a true Muslim state. The Muslim Brotherhood's comprehensive and sweeping agenda seeks the complete transformation of social conditions. The Muslim Brotherhood in Kuwait was not very different from its mother organisation in Egypt. It played a pioneering role in revising Islamic banking, developing charity work and challenging secularism. The Kuwaiti political system supported the Muslim Brotherhood in its struggle against secularists, but the Muslim Brotherhood nonetheless stayed out of politics, focusing on rehabilitating the social domain, in the interests of maintaining on good terms with the ruling family.

Kuwait City, Kuwait   Ali A. Alkandari

CONTENTS

NOTES ON TRANSLITERATION

The standard transliteration of the *International Journal of Middle Eastern Studies* (IJMES) has been adopted for transliterating Arabic words. Arabic words and titles quoted from different sources are written as in the original where they are printed in italics and followed by their English translation for explanatory purposes. Some words have been written in as they appeared in the word list of IJMES such as Shiᶜa, shariᶜa and daᶜwah.

Some exceptions have been made such as the name Rashīd which is different than Rashid.

ABBREVIATIONS

Al-Irshad	*Jam'iyyatal-Irshad al-Islami* (The Society of Islamic Guidance)
Al-Islah	*Jam'iyyatal-Islahal-Ijtima'i* (Social Reform Society)
ICM	Islamic Constitutional Movement
NUKS	National Union of Kuwaiti Students
RMT	Resource Mobilization Theory
USDS	U.S. Department of State
Usra	Organizational Cell

CHAPTER 1

Introduction

OVERVIEW

The modern Islamist movement in Kuwait today traces its roots back to the 1940s, when ʿAbdulʿaziz al-Mutawwaʿ became a member of the Muslim Brotherhood in 1941 and later imported this ideology and the organisational structure of the Muslim Brotherhood in Egypt to Kuwait in 1946. During the early years of the Muslim Brotherhood in Kuwait, al-Mutawwaʿ applied the Egyptian Muslim Brotherhood's method of mobilising the masses to promote an Islamic revival in Kuwait. Al-Mutawwaʿ called the new organisation *Jamʿiyyat al-Irshad al-Islami* [The Society of Islamic Guidance] that established in 1952. Its purpose was to spread the message of Islam to the wider Kuwaiti public. Al-Irshad, as the founders called it, succeeded in recruiting large numbers of young people and adults within few years. However, this success did not last for long because of internal disagreements between the founders and a negative public opinion towards the movement in Kuwait that resulted directly from Nasser's attack on the Muslim Brotherhood in Egypt. Al-Irshad gradually diminished in size until it was eventually closed down in February 1959, when all societies and clubs were ordered to close by an Emiri decree immediately after the UAR anniversary celebrations at Shuwaikh School in Kuwait City. From 1958 to 1968, the members of the Muslim Brotherhood splintered into small groups in the wake of

A. A. Alkandari, *The Muslim Brotherhood in Kuwait*, Contemporary Gulf Studies, https://doi.org/10.1007/978-981-99-3050-0_1

pressure from the Nationalists and Nasserites, forcing them to go underground to practice their religious and organisational activities secretly. During this period, number of Islamists including former members of al-Irshad established *Jam'iyyat al-Islah al-Ijtima'i* [Social Reform Society] in 1963 which enabled members of the Muslim Brotherhood working in society in Kuwait. These years (1958 to 1968) were a transitional period for the Muslim Brotherhood to rebuild its organisation and reshape many of its ideas. Nasser's defeat in the 1967 War by Israel provided the Muslim Brotherhood with a much-needed reprieve and reenergised their organisation in the Arab world. In 1968, a small number of Kuwaiti members of the Muslim Brotherhood re-established the organisation on the same basis as before, but with different people and newer methods. This new organisation of Muslim Brotherhood in Kuwait was influenced by the Iraqi Muslim Brotherhood's organisational method, which was clandestine, cautious and entailed a long spiritual and organisational training for its members. This strict method and the lengthy training period built a cohesive generation of Muslim Brotherhood that was more numerous and better organised than its predecessor, a tradition that continues to the present day.

The branches of the Muslim Brotherhood in Egypt and Palestine have been studied at length. Research on the Muslim Brotherhood in other countries, however, has received little or no attention. As a result, the experiences of the Muslim Brotherhood in other countries were greatly influenced and even dominated by the Egyptian experience, which greatly impacted the general perception of the Muslim Brotherhood and writings thereon. The Muslim Brotherhood in the Gulf has received the least attention, with almost nothing written about its origins, development, ideology, organisational structure, mobilisation and influence on the society. The experience of the Muslim Brotherhood in this part of the world remains understudied and misunderstood.

This study unearths the story of the Muslim Brotherhood in Kuwait, filling a very specific gap in the literature on Islamist movements. Special attention has been paid to the gradual development of the Muslim Brotherhood in Kuwait and the different phases it went through from the late 1940s until the end of the twentieth century. Its focuses mainly on the quest to win back the control over the social domain after it was taken over by the seculars during the 1950s and 1960s. Historically, the study argues, traditional Muslim societies have been split into two main domains: political and social. Traditionally, the social domain was controlled by the religious establishment. The rise of the secular powers in Kuwait, however, that domain was gradually dominated by them which made the religious establishment, including Islamist Movements, feels threaten because of the loss of the domain it had controlled for a very long time. The study also applies Social Movement Theory to this case study to enhance our understanding of how Islamist movements in the Middle East progress on different levels (political, social, economic, etc.). It explains why and how different branches of the same movement act and react according to socio-political circumstances. The case of the Kuwaiti branch of the Muslim Brotherhood shows important differences that differentiate it from the mother organisation in Egypt where the former does not have a real problem with the existing political system while in Egypt the movement aims to change the whole system.

Research Framework

This book is an examination of the Muslim Brotherhood in Kuwait as both a local movement and a regional movement with a special focus on the Kuwaiti context in which it developed. Understanding this phenomenon requires analysing its origins, objectives and the historical context in which it was born. In examining its origins, the research focuses on the emergence of the movement as a direct cultural and intellectual response to the Western colonial presence in Kuwait and the region. The book also addresses the reaction of various sectors of Kuwaiti society, especially the merchant class, to the shift from *shura* to dictatorship in Kuwait with the blessing of the British government, a state of affairs that also elicited a lot of animosity towards Western cultural influence represented by missionaries operating in Kuwait. The early reaction in Kuwait by Islamic figures such as Muhammad al-Shanqiti and Hafiz Wahba in early twentieth century marked the beginning of the reaction to Western cultural and political intervention. However, the repression by the ruling family at that time forced Islamist figures to work on protecting the identity of the society through establishing modern Islamic education as evident from the efforts of Yousif bin Isa and Abduaziz al-Rushaid. Yet, the Muslim Brotherhood members believed at the time that with the rise of secular forces in Kuwait, Islamists faced a new cultural challenge. Islamists represented by the Muslim Brotherhood and supported by a number of Islamist figures clashed with secularists who were very influential in some government institutions such as education and the media.

The rise of nationalist and Nasserite socio-political movements in the Arab world gave secularists in Kuwait a great boost in the 1950s, 1960s and 1970s. Islamist movements struggled to emphasise society's Islamic identity in the face of secularists, be they the liberals, the nationalists or left-wing parties.

The Islamist revivalist movement in the Muslim world, of which Kuwait is a part, was a reaction to the lack of progress of Muslim nations and the Western political and cultural superiority and hegemony over the Muslim world. Esposito explains that the reason behind Islamic revivalism is the "quest for identity, authenticity, and community, and a desire to establish meaning and order in both personal life and society."[1] This quest starts by shaping a solid Muslim personality and ends with the Muslim Nation or umma. This quest is a response triggered by the religio-cultural threat coming from the West, whether they are referred to as the new Crusades or atheist secularism. Hrair Dekmejian also argues that Islamic revivalism occurred as a response to the faltering conditions of the Muslim world and called for the return to true Islamic teachings.[2] The role model that revivalism aims to emulate is the golden age of Islam, the period of the first four Rightly Guided Caliphs (rashidun), on all levels: economic, social and political. Salwa Ismail argues that "subjugation is presented [by Islamists] as 'intellectual' (subjugation of Islamic concepts to Western concepts)."[3] After the Islamic golden age, the political domain was taken away from religious institutions, though the social and cultural domain remained under their control for centuries. With Western colonisation of the Muslim world, the authority of religious institutions over the social domain was challenged by westernised forces, particularly by the nationalists and secularists. As far as religious establishment was concerned, imperialism and colonialism introduced a new system of beliefs and way of life into the Muslim world.

---

[1] John L. Esposito and Emad El-Din Shahin, *Islam and Politics Around the World* (Oxford: Oxford University Press, 2018), 1.

[2] R. Hrair Dekmejian, *Islam in Revolution: Fundamentalism in the Arab World* (New York: Syracuse University Press, 1995), 8–19.

[3] Ismail, Salwa. "Confronting the Other: Identity, Culture, Politics, and Conservative Islamism in Egypt," *International Journal of Middle East Studies*, 30, No. 2 (1998) 24.

The Context

Islamist movements such as the Muslim Brotherhood are a continuation and an implementation of al-Afghani's, ʿAbdu's and Rida's Islamic revivalist project. The rise of Islamist movements in the Arab world in general and the Muslim Brotherhood in Egypt in particular has been the subject of many studies which seek to examine the reasons for this religious revivalism. Researchers usually describe this rise as a cultural response to the secularist Westernisation of Muslim societies, especially those under foreign occupation.

The reformist Islamist movement was the brainchild of Jamal al-Din al-Afghani (1938–1993), Muhammad ʿAbduh (1849–1905) and Muhammad Rashīd Rida (1865–1935) who challenged the secularist literature's contention that Islam was the reason Muslim societies remained backward and incapable of progress. Secularists compared Islam to the Catholic Church, usually blamed for Europe's Dark Ages. The three thinkers defended Islam against these accusations and argued that Islam by its nature encourages the pursuit of knowledge, thus leading to the creation of one of the greatest human civilisations. Their work provided the framework for the rise of many Islamist movements, including the Muslim Brotherhood who aspired to translate these thinkers' vision into a reality that would combat the secularist efforts of the colonial project and, later, the indigenous secularists who carried these efforts forward during the post-independence era. This marked the beginning of a long struggle between reformist Islamist movements and secularists over all aspects of economic, political and cultural life.

The twentieth century in the Arab world witnessed major changes on all political, economic, intellectual and cultural levels. Anti-colonial liberation movements gained increasing momentum with a considerable degree of success, especially in the aftermath of the Second World War which saw the decline of France and Britain in the Middle East, and their displacement by the new superpowers, the United States and the Soviet Union. The United States epitomised the spirit of capitalism, a legacy of European colonial power, while the USSR promoted a communist ideology. With the British and French Empires declining, the two new superpowers rushed in to take their piece of the pie, with a particular interest in controlling traditional centres of power in Egypt and the Levant, in addition to the newly-emerging oil-rich centres of economic power in the Gulf and Iraq.

According to Hourani, as a reaction to Western control over many parts of the Muslim world, Islamic Intellectuals and activists called for the unification of the Islamic world, a movement that was founded by al-Afghani who proposed the establishment of an Islamic League and vociferously defended the legitimacy of Ottoman rule. Fearful of the rising Pan-Arabist and Turanist sentiments in the late nineteenth century, the Ottoman government encouraged this approach, which was also adopted later by al-Afghani's friend and student Muhammad ʿAbduh. ʿAbduh advocated a reconciliatory intellectual approach between Islamic traditions and Western modernity that would preserve aspects of Islamic identity in the Arab and Muslim world while incorporating Western elements of progress. Muhammad Rashīd Rida also adopted this reconciliatory approach and, through his widely-circulated journal, *al-Manar*, helped to disseminate its basic tenets which combined modernity with Islamic Salafi tradition.

Albert Hourani argues that the spread of the reconciliatory approach was constrained by the rise of the Kemalists who turned their backs on the collapsing Ottoman Empire and who, through a plethora of legal, intellectual and political writings calling for the separation of state and religion, validated the establishment of a secular state. The First Wold War proponents of the reconciliatory approach were torn apart by internal conflicts which eventually divided them into Islamists and secularists, particularly since this approach had not fully matured, especially on a political level. Scholars and thinkers such as Shaikh Ali ʿAbdulraziq (1885–1966) and Taha Hussain (1889–1973) favoured a Kemalist approach, albeit in a less extreme form, but such secularist tendencies were challenged by Islamists like Shaikh Mustafa Sabri (1869–1954) and Rashīd Rida (1865–1955). Political life in Egypt was greatly influenced by this intellectual conflict which saw the establishment of the Nationalist Wafd Party in 1919 and the secularist Liberal Constitutionalist Party in 1922, both of which announced themselves as the true representatives of the school of Muhammad ʿAbduh.[4]

Arab Nationalism may have spread rapidly from the time of the Great Arab Revolt (1916–1918) and liberation movements in Egypt, the Levant, Iraq and other Arab countries, yet its sources were varied. Some branches of nationalism were inspired by Islamic civilisation's offering of

---

[4] See Rashid Rida in Albert Hourani, *Arabic Thought in the Liberal Age 1798–1939* (Cambridge: Cambridge University Press, 1983), 222–244.

a vision where Islam and Arab Nationalism were two faces of the same coin, while other liberal and secularist branches of Arab Nationalism were derived from European nationalism which had freed political life from church control and liberated the individual from the influence of priests. The success of the 1917 Bolshevik Revolution and calls for rebelling against the powers of capitalism and imperialism played a huge part in shifting Arab Nationalism, which found the notions of liberation from the colonial West and its control of Arab resources very appealing, to the far Left.

Notwithstanding the wide right-left spectrum of Arab Nationalism, its several Islamist, Liberal and left-wing branches were able to co-exist peacefully for a while. A number of organisations, in the style of Turkish reformist parties such as the Young Turks (1902–1918) and reflecting various ideologies, became increasingly active. Despite the plethora of parties and political organisations, the most prominent was the movement of the Muslim Brotherhood which was born in 1928 out of the Islamist nationalist school of thought. The movement which originated in Egypt rose to prominence there and spread to a number of Arab countries.[5] Other left-wing organisations soon followed but did not gain a very strong foothold until Jamal ʿAbdulnasser seized power in Egypt in 1952. There was naturally a battle between these organisations over the hearts and minds of the masses and to attract as many followers as possible, a fact which did not bode well for the newly-independent Arab countries since it soon became evident that it would be impossible to apply all these conflicting thoughts, programmes and schemes to these countries once a certain party was in power. Former comrades on the battlefield became arch enemies fighting over political and intellectual power, keen to influence and direct public opinion. In Egypt, for example, a fierce confrontation between the Muslim Brotherhood and Nasser resulted in Nasser proclaiming the Muslim Brotherhood traitors in 1954; very soon open war was being waged by Nasser and the leftists, against the Muslim Brotherhood in particular and the Islamists in general.[6]

---

[5] Mufid Al-Zubaidi, *Al-Tayyarat al-fikriyyah fi al-Khalij al-ʿArabi 1938–1971* [Intellectual Trends in the Arabian Gulf 1938–1971] (Beirut: Markaz Dirasat al-Wihdah al-Arabiyya, 2000), 247–248.

[6] Barbara H. E. Zollner, *The Muslim Brotherhood: Hasan al-Hudaybi and Ideology* (London: Routledge, 2009), 25–35.

The Muslim Brotherhood's reformist and revivalist project emphasised the superiority of Islam with its long history and rich heritage, especially its ability to lead the world. The Muslim Brotherhood devised their own unique discourse to respond to secularist ideologies which sought to undermine Islam as a leading social force. A number of slogans were born: "Islam as a way of life," "Islam encourages the pursuit of knowledge" and the most famous "Islam is the Solution." The Muslim Brotherhood used these slogans to emphasise their conviction that all of the modern Muslim world's economic, religious, political and social problems can be solved with a return to true Islam as introduced by the Prophet and the Rightly Guided Caliphs (the golden age of Islam which lasted only for half a century). This emphasis on the superiority of Islam was aimed at increasing Muslims' faith in the Muslim Brotherhood's project which represented a true effort to challenge secularist and nationalist ideologies in the political, economic and social domains. The confrontation was not easy due to the strength of the secularist project which was supported by foreign colonial powers. A good portion of decision-makers in the Arab world were lured by secularist ideology and began to use their positions to spread its values. With help from political parties, armies fashioned after their Western counterparts and government officials, these secularists succeeded in gaining full control over the political life of Muslim societies. They worked tirelessly to refashion social identities by exercising control over a number of institutions such as schools where Western-influenced curricula were introduced. Traditionally, schools had been the domain of influence of religious scholars and institutions. Natural sciences replaced religious studies, and secularist approaches to human sciences replaced religious ones. The judiciary replaced shariᶜa laws with civil codes, especially the French legal system. Secular judges replaced shariᶜa ones. In addition to education and the judiciary, secularists controlled media outlets. In essence, religious institutions lost all control they had over cultural and social media.[7]

As a part of the Muslim world and Arab world, Kuwait witnessed the same cultural challenges and reacted to them in the same way. The early Western presence from the first two decades of the twentieth century was political (in the form of British Political Agents) and social (symbolised by the medical and educational missionary activities of the Arabian

---

[7] Ira M. Lapidus, "State and Religion in Islamic Societies," *Past & Present*, 151, No. 1 (May 1996), 3–27.

Mission of the Dutch Reformed Church of America), both of which were a direct threat to Kuwait's Islamic-Arab identity. Although they provoked the reformist movement (both Islamist and nationalist groups) in Kuwait, in reality neither of these Western institutions in Kuwait had a great influence on the conservative and generally closed Kuwaiti society. The reformist movement, which was comprised of Islamists and nationalists, focused on political and social reform. The early political reform reached its peak with the 1921 and 1938 *Majlis* movements, whose main goal was reviving the principle of *shura* that had been practised before Shaikh Mubarak seized power in 1896. However, the new demands were more modern with the call for the instatement of legislative councils in 1921 and 1938, respectively. Yet when the political crisis reached its peak in 1938 between the reformist movement and the ruling family, the Islamists represented by Yusif al-Qinaʿi took a stance more supportive of the ruling family. This can be explained by the fact that the main objective of the Islamists was dominating and reforming the social domain as opposed to the political domain. This goal of dominating and reforming the social domain, in addition to the good relationship between the ruling family and the Islamists, continued with the student of al-Qinaʿi, ʿAbdulʿaziz al-Mutawwaʿ, who later established the branch of the Muslim Brotherhood in Kuwait. The 1938 incident was the beginning of the split among the reformist movement between the two main groups, Islamists and nationalists, who both adopted the Islamic-nationalist ideas of Rida, the role model for both. However, the emergence of the more radical and secular nationalist activists such as Ahmad al-Khatib, who shifted the movement to be secular, and the conflict between the Muslim Brotherhood and Nasser totally ruined the relationship between the nationalist and Islamist groups.

The implications of these events spread to most of the Arab world, including Kuwait where both the Muslim Brotherhood and the Arab Nationalists were very active. In the early 1950s, and immediately after Shaikh Abdullah al-Salim al-Subah (1895–1965) had come to power in 1950—an era marked by democratic liberalisation—a number of Arab expatriates, heavily influenced by Arab Nationalist trends, mobilised to establish nationalist groups whose initial aim was to support the Palestinians and their cause. Ahmad al-Khatib (1927–...), a young physician who had just graduated from the American University in Beirut (AUB), co-founded the Arab Nationalist movement in Kuwait with George Habash, and before long became its leader. Along with Jasem al-Qatami

(1929–2012), al-Khatib and other nationalist pioneers established a number of nationalist networks, clubs and societies, such as the Nationalist Cultural Club founded in 1952 which served as the movement's headquarters. The Nationalists' demands centred on resisting colonial powers, supporting liberation movements and Arab unity in addition to the Palestinian cause. They also demanded the nationalisation of various government bodies, including the oil company. The movement utilised relatively new platforms, such as clubs and students' unions like the National Union of Kuwaiti Students (NUKS) in Cairo. The National Union for Kuwaiti Students, established in 1964, served as a very influential platform for the movement from which they broadcast their ideas and messages to students and the wider society.

The Arab Nationalist movement was also very active in the political domain through its demands for increased freedoms and democratic change. In the 1950s, the movement's leaders had called upon the government of the Emir Abdullah al-Salim to adopt a democratic system of government. In February 1959, on the first anniversary of the 1958 union between Egypt and Syria, Ahmad al-Khatib and Jasim al-Qatami delivered speeches before a large audience that included few members of the ruling family, in which they criticised the backward system of rule embodied in the ruling al-Subah family. This inflammatory speech did not go down well and the ruling family responded by closing down the Nationalists' clubs and societies in addition to al-Irshad. All societies and clubs remained banned by the government until Kuwait's independence in 1961, at which time the ruling family became aware of the importance of the socio-political support for its regional and international legitimacy, especially in the light of some movements far-reaching influence of some movements such as the Nationalists, in a region dominated by nationalist governments, such as Egypt.

New ideas and trends spread in the 1950s and 1960s by a new class of educated Kuwaitis who had studied in Lebanon, Egypt and Iraq where they were exposed to new intellectual and social trends in these more advanced countries. They brought these ideas back with them and contributed to their dissemination in Kuwait. Each group was influenced by whichever ideology was prevalent in their country of study—Nasserism in Egypt, Nationalism in Lebanon and Ba'thism in Iraq—and established new societies accordingly, the most prominent of which was the Arab

Nationalist movement.[8] In fact, none of these organisations and movements with their secularist overtones would have gained such success in the conservative Kuwaiti society without the oil money that helped fund students' studies abroad. Oil was destined to play a central role in the transformation of society as economic gains brought with them new social, cultural and political realities.

Theory of Domains

Equally important is a careful consideration of the historical context in which Islamist movements developed; the book adopts insights from the theory of domains to shed light on how a Muslim society is sometimes divided into a social and political domain, each of which is controlled by certain forces. Lacroix employs a theory of domains to describe the division of the social, the political and the religious in Saʿudi Arabia.[9] Lacroix argues that al-Saʿud ruling family controls the political domain while the cultural domain is dominated by liberal secularists, with the religious domain being the share of the al-Saʿud's allies the Salafis, the most prominent of whom are the al-Shaikh, the descendants of Muhammad bin ʿAbdulwahab. The same approach will be applied to the Kuwaiti experience but with the religious and cultural domains merged into one since culture, religion, education and the judiciary system existed under one domain of influence.

The term "religious establishment" shall be used to refer to the convergence of different actors in the social domain such as religious scholars, judges, teachers and Sufis. The religious establishment is mix of different religious actors who instil Islamic teachings in society where Islam is the dominant source of identity of the state and society. Lapidus argues that historically, the religious establishment controlled the social domain in addition to the political domain since the first Islamic state but with the rise to power of the Umayyads, the political and social domains parted ways. Ruling families from the Umayyads through the Abbasids and subsequent dynasties controlled the political domain in various Muslim

---

[8] Al-Zubaidi, *Al-Tayyarat al-fikriyyah*, 178–179.

[9] Stéphane Lacroix, *Awakening Islam: The Politics of Religious Dissent in Contemporary Saʿudi Arabia* (Cambridge, MA: Harvard University Press, 2011).

regions while the social domain remained in the hands of religious establishment, which gradually lost their ambitions to regain control of the political domain. Thus, two distinct domains emerged in Muslim societies, each controlled by an independent party. The situation persisted until colonial powers followed by dictatorial military secularists changed the division of power.[10] Despite the fact that the political system in Gulf States remained the same with ruling families controlling the political domain, secularists succeeded in having a great impact on the social domain with the spread of nationalist anti-Muslim Brotherhood ideology inspired primarily by Nasserism. The religious establishment in the Sunni World during the late nineteenth and early twentieth centuries was fluid and did not represent a solid institution except for some examples such as al-Azhar in Egypt. What would be recognised as a religious establishment in the modern era is the same as previous eras where various religious actors such as Islamic figures, families (e.g. al-Shaikh in Saudi), judges (e.g. al-ʿAdsani family in Kuwait), teachers, Muftis, Sufis, preachers and every cultural and religious producer whether it was a person or an institution make up the religious establishment. In his description of opinion makers in Egypt in the 1920s, al-Banna explains the source of opinion in society "(1) the *ulama*; (2) the shaikhs of the Sufi orders; (3) the 'elders,' by which he meant the leading families and groups in the broadest sense; and (4) the 'clubs' (social and religious societies)."[11] However, the new challenges posed by Western powers and the secular movement put the religious establishment in a difficult position. Consequently, the Muslim Brotherhood came to fill the gap of the scattered and fluid religious establishment which was weakened by Western intervention and also the new socio-political non-Islamic forces and regimes. The Muslim Brotherhood and other Islamist movements emerged as new actors and part of the religious establishment. Soon they rose to become the leaders of the religious establishment because of their high level of organisation, strong leadership and clear goals. The boundaries between the political and social domains in Kuwait have been defined, yet, since the emergence of the seculars the boundaries became blurred because of the interposition of the seculars in both domains. However, the political domain is more defined than

---

[10] Lapidus, "State and Religion in Islamic Societies."

[11] Richard P. Mitchell, *The Society of the Muslim Brothers* (Oxford: Oxford University Press, 1993), 7.

the social one because of the structured institution of the ruling family in contrast to the fluid structure of the social domain. As a result, it was easier for seculars to intervene in the social domain more than the political one.

The Muslim Brotherhood was secretly founded in Kuwait in the late 1940s and, a few years later, *Jamᶜiyyat al-Irshad al-Islami* was launched as a front for the movement. Al-Irshad, however, was banned in 1959 and, a few years later, Islamists launched *Jamᶜiyyat al-Islah al-Ijtimaᶜi* and carried on with the Islamist project of reforming society. The ideology, strategies and tactics of the organisation were adopted from the mother organisation in Egypt. However, political views on domestic issues differed from the Muslim Brotherhood in Egypt. The Kuwaiti context has always been different from the Egyptian one because in Kuwait a good relationship between the religious establishment and the ruling family exists. Moreover, the religious establishment in Kuwait, including the Muslim Brotherhood, did not see any threat posed by the ruling family to the social domain they controlled. The real threat was posed by the secularists, be they communists, liberals or nationalists, who called for a new moral code and way of life. The secularists competed with the religious establishment over control of the social domain. This conflict began in the 1950s and continues until this day. The competition manifested itself on many occasions such as the call for banning alcohol in Kuwait, gender segregation at Kuwait University and the ongoing battle since Kuwait's independence in 1961 over the second article of the Constitution. Islamist movements in Kuwait, especially the Muslim Brotherhood, inherited the religious establishment's authority over the social domain using new methods of control. These methods developed over time, and the shift in the socio-political context in Kuwait is a good example of employing the political opportunity theory. The Muslim Brotherhood profited from contextual shifts, raising the ceiling of their demands and increasing their control over the social domain. Major turning points such as the 1967 Arab–Israeli War, the 1979 Islamic Revolution in Iran and the 1990–1991 Iraqi occupation of Kuwait helped the Muslim Brotherhood gain more social influence in Kuwait. By time, Islamists movements became the leaders of the religious establishment where they succeeded in controlling Islamic discourse by producing religious scholars, founding Islamic schools and bookshops, establishing Islamic financial institutions, producing Islamic art, etc.

Although the Kuwaiti branch of the Muslim Brotherhood traces its origins to the mother organisation in Egypt and was heavily influenced by the Iraqi branch, the leaders of the Muslim Brotherhood state that the movement has its own distinctive characteristics. While most branches of the Muslim Brotherhood have had to survive under authoritarian regimes and were under constant attack from seculars, the Kuwaiti branch of the Muslim Brotherhood has operated in a more democratic political environment where people can express their opinions freely. The political system in Kuwait permits people to freely elect their representatives while most Arab countries have little or no parliamentary traditions. The Muslim Brotherhood allied with the ruling family against the seculars for a long time in contrast to Egypt, Iraq, Syria and most Arab countries. As a result, the Muslim Brotherhood in Kuwait never represented a challenge to the ruling family, and in return, the ruling family was very tolerant of the Muslim Brotherhood and allowed them to operate freely in the social domain. The boundaries between the two domains were to some extent clear and allowed the ruling family and the religious establishment, particularly the Muslim Brotherhood, to enjoy a harmonious relationship. Yet, the religious establishment never quite won back the kind of control it used to exercise over the social domain before the intervention of seculars.

THEORETICAL FRAMEWORK AND OUTLINE OF THE STUDY

The Muslim Brotherhood in Kuwait is part of the global Muslim Brotherhood movement, reflecting its ideology and structures along the same organisational lines. Nonetheless, the movement in Kuwait has many unique characteristics and differs from the mother movement in Egypt. This study focuses on the complexity of the Muslim Brotherhood in Kuwait, which is a combination of the external imported ideology and structure, and internal social and political factors. The book also argues that the main objective of the Muslim Brotherhood in Kuwait is maintaining the control over the social domain. Religious establishment and its various actors, which used to dominate social and intellectual discourses and domains were over controlled by the new ideological Islamist movements (the Muslim Brotherhood and the Salafis) who were heir to the religious establishment along with other actors such as independent religious figures. The Muslim Brotherhood seized the political opportunity post-1967 Six Day War when Arabs lost this war to spread its influence over the social space via different means, such as targeting youth by organising social and cultural activities, distributing religious lectures and sermons on cassettes, establishing charitable organisations, involvement in professional syndicates and participating in elections and the parliament. However, the Muslim Brotherhood in Kuwait does not have a clear political project similar to other Muslim Brotherhood branches such as Egypt or Iraq for several reasons. First, the Muslim Brotherhood in Kuwait as an extension of Islamic institutions in Kuwait aims mainly to control the social domain. Second, the Muslim Brotherhood in Kuwait believes that the ruling family's main objective is maintaining total control over the political domain and, as such, has no interest in competing with the Muslim Brotherhood over control of the social domain, while the secularists are the real competitors for the political and social domains. Third, the Muslim Brotherhood helped forge good relations between religious institutions and the ruling family. The study will analyse the history of the origins, structures and cultural spaces and the mixture of activities (socio-cultural, political, etc.) of the Muslim Brotherhood in Kuwait.

The argument of this book adopts a theoretical framework of several interrelated themes:

1. A holistic approach towards the complex phenomenon: The Muslim Brotherhood is a multidimensional phenomenon, not a simple socio-cultural or political reaction to social or political contingencies. The multifaceted activities of the Muslim Brotherhood (economic, cultural, social, and political) should be studied together. The Muslim Brotherhood as an ideology and a movement is a comprehensive reaction to the multidimensional challenges facing Muslim societies: political, social, cultural, economic and so on. The ideal model of society, which the Muslim Brotherhood seeks to emulate, is what the group views as the golden age of Prophet Mohammad and his Companions in Islamic history. Therefore, by reviving the values of early pristine Islam, Muslims will regain the spiritual and material power they enjoyed during the golden age. Studying this holistic vision is crucial to understanding the ideology and reality of the Muslim Brotherhood in Kuwait.

2. Protecting the social domain: although the Muslim Brotherhood is a holistic phenomenon, the movement in Kuwait focuses on protecting the socio-cultural domain that had been traditionally controlled by the religious establishment. Religious scholars in different fields used to shape culture, intellectual discourse, and

social norms in various ways: through *fiqh* (Islamic Jurisprudence), which regulates the life of people by codifying the legal system; through *tarbiyyah* (the development process conforms to Islamic guidelines and standards) and *tasawwuf* (Islamic Mysticism), which instil in the Muslim individual self-improvement and spirituality with a focus on the relationship with God; and through *ʿaqida*, which determines the religious belief system. However, the secular dominance over culture supported by the West or by the Arab nationalist movement in other Arab states threatens the domain of the religious establishment. The Muslim Brotherhood in Kuwait focuses mainly on controlling the socio-cultural domain. The political domain in Kuwait is traditionally controlled by the ruling family, which enjoys good relations with religious establishment. The absence of a political agenda by the Muslim Brotherhood in Kuwait and the control of the ruling family of the political domain have meant that the Muslim Brotherhood took a marginal interest in politics in its beginnings until the end of twentieth century.

3. By applying an empirical methodology, this book will examine what could be referred to as "the anthropology of the movement" by studying its agents. The members of the Muslim Brotherhood mobilised as social agents in the traditional society of Kuwait with its different local networks, sources of power, and interests. The agents of the movement were affected by micro-level elements such as kinship and social groups and the state. These, in turn, interact on a macro-level with regional and international events and the broad Islamic reaction to them. This interaction forms the discourse in which the agents comprehend the development and reality of the movement. This methodology fills the gaps in other social movement theories that lack to explain the process of mobilisation and the incentives of it.

Focusing on these themes, the book will seek to study the origins, development, ideology, organisational structure, mobilisation and social influence of the Muslim Brotherhood in Kuwait. To do so, this study will rely on extensive interviews and primary sources in Kuwait, some of which will be examined for the first time.

PRIMARY SOURCES

The covert nature of the Muslim Brotherhood in Kuwait is the main reason for the scarce literature on the movement. However, the significant role of the movement during the Iraqi occupation of 1990–1991 built trust between the movement, society and the government. During the post-liberation period in 1991, the Muslim Brotherhood declared the establishment of its political wing, the Islamic Constitutional Movement (ICM). It also became more open about its aims and objectives. As a result, the movement's literature became more accessible and the leaders more cooperative with researchers.

This study draws on six types of primary sources:

1. Writings by members of the Muslim Brotherhood in Kuwait. This includes the memoirs of the leaders of the Muslim Brotherhood such as Abdullah al-Mutawwa, statements on political and social events, ideological and theological debate with nationalists and other Islamist groups, published and unpublished studies by members of the movement, the rhetoric of the Muslim Brotherhood figures and *fatwas* issued by the movement's ʿulama such as Shaikh Ajeel al-Nashmi, Khalid al-Mathkour and Jassim Muhalhal al-Yassin, published in newspapers or otherwise circled among the members of the Muslim Brotherhood, and *al-Mujtamaʿ* Journal, the official publication of the Muslim Brotherhood in Kuwait.
2. Writings by other Islamist groups and authors, such as studies of the Muslim Brotherhood in Egypt and elsewhere, and the writings and magazines of other Islamist groups in Kuwait, such as the magazines of *Al-Furqan* and *Al-Bayan*.
3. Contemporary journalism and travellers' accounts of Kuwait: Kuwaiti newspapers (i.e. *Al-Qabas*, *Al-Watan*, *Al-Aan*, etc.) and magazines (i.e. *Al-Biʿthah*, *Al-Raʾid*, etc.) campaign literature, periodicals, as well as the writings of outside observers.
4. Interviews. With the relatively new open environment of the Muslim Brotherhood, interviews have been easy to obtain and have become a rich source of information.
5. British and American government records: the records and correspondence of British and American diplomats in Kuwait provide

insights into the history of the movement. However, British and American government records give very limited information about the Muslim Brotherhood in Kuwait due to the secret nature of the movement.

CHAPTER 2

The Beginnings of Reformist Movement in Kuwait and the Rise of the Muslim Brotherhood in the Arab World

INTRODUCTION

Before examining the history of the Muslim Brotherhood in Kuwait, it is important to provide an overview of the origins of Kuwait's reformist movement which preceded the Muslim Brotherhood by almost four decades. It is equally important to examine the roots of the Muslim Brotherhood from its point of origin in Egypt before it spread to the rest of the Arab world. From the time it was launched in the early years of the twentieth century and for the next 50 years, the reformist movement in Kuwait was characterised by its uniformity. The reformist ideas of Jamal al-Din al-Afghani, Muhammad ʿAbduh and Muhammad Rashīd Rida, were at the heart of all demands for reform in the Arab and Muslim world, especially in the struggle against colonisation. The Arab and Islamic components of identity were deemed essential in the struggle to protect Arab countries from Westernisation and secularism.

These calls for reforms were very positively received in various parts of the Arab world, and paved the way for a number of reform movements in various Muslim countries, including Kuwait. A number of young Kuwaiti intellectuals mobilised against British interests in the country and challenged the cultural and religious activities of missionaries, especially American ones. These movements continued to grow and succeeded in changing the cultural landscape of Kuwait society in relation to a number of political and social issues.

A. A. Alkandari, *The Muslim Brotherhood in Kuwait*, Contemporary Gulf Studies, https://doi.org/10.1007/978-981-99-3050-0_2

The reformist movement in Kuwait represented an Islamic national project where Arabism and Islam were perceived as two faces of the same coin. Nationalists did not contest the Islamic component of the Kuwaiti identity, while Islamists considered freedom from the West part of their religious creed. The two sides worked together very closely for a while, until signs of disagreement began to emerge over a number of political and social issues and how best to tackle matters related to the structure of the state and the old society. Political and social structures in Kuwait were a continuation of an old system that had persisted for centuries in various parts of the Islamic world, where the state was divided into two domains controlled by two groups: the social and political domains. The realm of politics included the daily affairs of the state, foreign relations, taxes and other matters related to the monarchy, the army and the merchant class. The social domain included education, the judiciary, culture and religious *waqf* and was usually the domain of religious institutions.

The system in Kuwait was not much different except for the participation of the merchant class and its great influence on politics, especially during the period when merchants considered themselves more or less equal to the ruling family—whose main source of funding was these same merchants, most of whom, similar to al-Sabah ruling family, traced their origins to Najd. After Mubarak al-Sabah came to power, having killed his two brothers who had ruled Kuwait, he imposed his political will and vision on the country. The merchant class felt it had lost most of its political power but had no choice except, reluctantly, to embrace the new reality.[1]

The new reformist thinking spread rapidly among many merchants and religious scholars and the parties created a very strong and extremely influential reformist movement. Through its conflict with the rulers of Kuwait, the merchant class planned to recover some of its traditional power. The reformists also struggled against the rising influence of traditional jurists and succeeded in imposing a new reality on society through reformist thought. In 1939 the political project of the merchant class clashed with the social project of the religious scholars to such an extent that many feared an armed confrontation between the merchants and the ruling family. These reformist movements were the harbinger for many

---

[1] Al-Rushaid, *Tarikh al-Kuwait*, 136–150.

other later reform projects, including the Muslim Brotherhood which considered itself an extension of the reformist religious scholars.[2]

The Muslim Brotherhood in Egypt was established according to the same principles of the reformist movement in Kuwait. Indeed, the Muslim Brotherhood is considered an extension of the reformist thought of al-Afghani, ʿAbduh and Rashīd Rida, followed by Hasan al-Banna who worked as an editor et al.-*Manar* Journal while a student under Rashīd Rida. Al-Banna transformed reformist thinking from theory into practice and sought to establish a strong movement that could successfully implement the reformist project within both the state and society. At that time, movements and political parties were widespread in Egypt, Turkey and Greater Syria, and included, for example, the Young Egypt Party, the National Party, the Wafd Party and others. However, despite the existence of a wide variety of liberal, nationalist and leftist ideologies, there were no Islamist movements. The Muslim Brotherhood was the first movement to succeed in surpassing the influence of most other parties in just a few years. The success of the Brotherhood in Egypt encouraged al-Banna to begin holding meetings during Hajj seasons, with Arabs from other countries in order to invite them to form similar movements. It was during one of these trips that he met and inspired the founder of the Kuwaiti Muslim Brotherhood ʿAbdulʿaziz al-ʿAli al-Mutawwaʿ.

Reformist Ideas Enter Kuwait

On the eve of the twentieth century, Kuwait was a country still in thrall to its local concerns.[3] The intellectual and cultural mood at that time was not conducive to a greater degree of openness; thus religious issues were restricted to matters related to the daily rituals of prayer, ablution and family laws. Geographically, Kuwait's contact with the outside world did not extend beyond the few bordering towns and villages such as Zubair and al-Hasa, and whatever little Wahhabi doctrines trickled in

---

[2] Aman, interview.

[3] The first population census in Kuwait was conducted in 1957, but before that date there is no clear data about Kuwait's population, although some foreign travellers gave estimates. The Central Statistics Office estimates the 1910 population at about 35,000. See "Happened in this Day in Kuwait," 28 February 2008.

Also: ʿAbdulʿaziz Al-Mansour, *Kuwait and its Relationship with Arabistan and Basra 1896–1915* (1980), 24.

with merchants and immigrants to Kuwait. The main religious influence resulted from the conservative religious movements in the nearby al-Hasa region of Saʿudi Arabia.[4] Some merchants went beyond the nearby towns for business, to Basra, Zanzibar and India since trade was very strong with these parts of the world. Like many coastal emirates on the Gulf, Kuwait persisted in this traditional and rigid environment, detached from the rest of the Arab and Islamic world and disconnected from the intellectual and political debates surrounding democracy and modernism which were being explored in Egypt and the Levant at that time.

Intellectual reform in the Gulf in general, and in Kuwait in particular, saw its first stirrings in the early twentieth century with the arrival of Pan-Arabist and Islamist publications, such as *al-Hilal*, *al-Muqattam* and *al-Manar* which had a wide readership.[5] Newspapers and intellectual journals were circulated by middle and upper-class readers who could afford to buy them, and they would often be read and debated at *diwaniyya*.[6] With a fresh focus on Arab and Islamic issues, a new atmosphere of cultural and political interests was born that was a far cry from the traditional religious knowledge and folklore to which the country had been accustomed. A new breed of intellectuals had heated discussions about colonialism, Arab and Islamic identity, liberal modernism and women's emancipation. Al-Khudair, a prominent Kuwaiti family which had subscriptions to a number of well-known Egyptian, Iraqi and Syrian publications, was usually the first stop for these publications. Zaid and ʿAbdulrazzaq al-Khalid al-Khudair subscribed to *al-Manar* and *al-Muʾayyad* in 1902 and would read them every night at their shops in

---

[4] This explains why people in Kuwait were not influenced by the Wahhabi intellectual movement.

[5] ʿAbdulʿaziz Al-Rushaid, Tarikh al-Kuwait (Baghdad: al-Matbaʿah al-ʿAsriyyah, 1926), 353.

[6] *Diwaniyya* is a designated reception room in many houses where people gather to talk about various issues of daily life. The diwaniyya can be formal or casual, for family gatherings or friends and so on, however, it functions more generally as a town hall. These social events usually take place in the evening and are found on every street and neighbourhood and became a fundamental part and the generator of Kuwait's political, intellectual and social life in. See Muhammad al-Jassar, "Constancy and Change in Contemporary Kuwait City: The Socio-Cultural Dimensions of the Kuwait Courtyard and Diwaniyya" (PhD diss., University of Wisconsin, 2009).

the presence of friends and acquaintances.[7] The publications would then make their way to other places and gatherings such as the *diwaniyya* of al-Naqib family. Yusif bin ʿIsa al-Qinaʿi[8] recalls the impact of these publications on his intellectual and cultural development,

> I grew up in Kuwait and, like many others, I was raised in an extremely rigid and unyielding environment dominated by myths and falsehoods. The works of bin Taymiyyah and bin alQayyim, and journals such as *al-Manar* dispelled many of these myths while my moderation could be attributed to journals such as *al-Hilal, al-Muqattam* and others.[9]

A number of young men, labelled by ʿAbdulʿaziz al-Rushaid "the pioneers of renaissance in Kuwait,"[10] formed the core of the first generation to embrace the modern intellectual movement in Kuwait and included Hamad al-Khalid, Mishʿan al-Khudair al-Khalid, Ali and Sultan al-Kulaib, Hamed al-Naqib, Marzuq al-Bader and certainly Shaikh Yusif bin ʿIsaal-Qinaʿi and Shaikh ʿAbdulʿaziz al-Rushaid in addition to others.[11] This process was further strengthened by visits from leading Arab and Islamic intellectuals sponsored by Kuwaiti businessmen such as Qasim al-Ibrahim, who invited Muhammad Rashīd Rida to visit Kuwait following their meeting in India. As a token of gratitude for al-Ibrahim's efforts in supporting the establishment in Egypt of *Dar al-ʿUlum*, a project proposed by Rida, Rida accepted the invitation. Several other thinkers, most importantly ʿAbdulʿazizalThaʿalibi and Amin al-Rihani, visited Kuwait, but the greatest influence exerted on the nascent intellectual movement in Kuwait was undoubtedly that of Shaikh Muhammad al-Shanqiti and Shaikh Hafiz Wahba. Being able to interact with the leading figures for change in the Arab and Islamic world meant that debates were carried from the world of books into the arena of direct

---

[7] ʿAbdullah al-Nuri, *Qissat al-Taʿlim fi al-Kuwait fi Nisf Qarn* (Kuwait: That al-Salasil, no date), 37.

[8] Yusif bin ʾIsa al-Qinaʿi (1879–1973) is the most famous religious Shaikh in Kuwait and was a prominent figure in Kuwait's political and intellectual history. See ʿAbdulʿaziz al-Rushaid, "Shaikh Yusif bin ʾIsa al-Qinaʿi: Muslih al-Kuwait," Kuwait Journal (January–February 1930), 330–332.

[9] Ibid.

[10] Al-Rushaid, *Tarikh al-Kuwait*, 315.

[11] Ibid.

engagement. These new cultural trends reached their peak in the form of intellectual and political movements at the hands of Yusif bin ʿIsa al-Qinaʿi, ʿAbdulʿaziz al-Rushaid, Muhammad al-Shanqiti and Shaikh Hafiz Wahba.

The reformist movement in Kuwait was built on the religio-nationalist principles of the school of the leading figures: al-Afghani, ʿAbduh and Rashīd Rida. This school differed from the nationalist movement developed in the Levant by Christian Arab Nationalists which excluded Islamic principles from social life and treated it in the way new secular nationalist European states treated Christianity. Secular Arab Nationalists looked on Islamic history as a period of glory that had influenced human civilisation positively in such fields as philosophy and science. However, this positive influence diminished over the centuries, and a new era based on secular nationalism began to emerge. The reformist school also differed from the Salafi school of Muhammad ʿAbdulwahab that based its teachings on reviving orthodox Islamic values and purifying it from innovations. Wahhabism also implemented a strict Islamic system based on Hanbali School of *fiqh* with the support of al-Saʿud, the ruling family in Saʿudi Arabia. The alliance between the ruling family and the Wahhabis drew a clear division between the political domain and the socio-religious domain with the former controlling the political domain and the latter dominating the socio-religious domain.

The reformist school of Rashīd Rida dealt with both domains, political and social, but focused more on the social domain in order to protect the identity of Muslim societies. The political demands were a reaction to the West's imperial and colonial intrusion in the Muslim world, since this political intervention carried a social and cultural project that challenged domains that had traditionally been controlled by the religious establishment. In Islamic history, the Golden Age (632–661 CE) of the Four Guided Caliphs (Abu Bakir, ʿUmar binal-Khattab, ʿUthmanbin ʿAffan and ʿAli bin Abi Talib) represented for Sunni Muslims the role model for all aspects of life. The four Caliphs were religious scholars as well as political leaders, as were their advisers. Politics and society both followed Islamic values and the head of the state, or Caliphate, was also the leader of the religion, the Imam.

Under the Umayyad dynasty, the political domain separated from the religio-social domain, with the former controlled by the ruling dynasties and the latter by scholars, clerks and religious judges (or what could be referred to as the "religious establishment"). As the ruling dynasties in the

Muslim world waned and the superiority of Western powers increased, the latter's intervention in the Muslim world was inevitable. However, Western intervention in the Muslim world carried an unfavourable social and cultural project that threatened the heart of the social domain. Therefore, fighting the Imperial West became a sacred obligation to protect both state and identity.[12]

REFORMISTS AND THE SOCIAL DOMAIN

The religio-nationalist trend of al-Afghani, ʿAbdu and Rida worked on fighting Western intervention and reforming Islamic societies against the socio-cultural and political project of the West. In Kuwait, these teachings met the requirements of the Islamist Reformists who saw the Western presence as a social more than a political threat. The best way to protect the society was by spreading awareness of reformist ideas among Kuwaitis, through education, literature and the press. Islamist Reformists also worked on controlling the social domain and taking it from the hands of traditional conservative Islamists who obstructed reformist activities and did not like the idea of losing control over the religious establishment to the new Islamists.

Reforming the Educational System

The first step in this reform was the educational system which witnessed significant transformations. Rather than being based exclusively on Qurʾanic schools, British government records indicate that education gradually became the domain of modern schooling systems with the establishment, encouraged by Rida,[13] of al-Mubarakiyyah School. Al-Mubarakiyyah was partly a response to the classes that had been organised in the same year by Mr and Mrs Calverley, who were American missionaries. Fearing their children would be converted to Christianity, local families were initially reluctant to send their children to these classes, but Calverley reacted to their hesitation by visiting *diwaniyyas* to convince parents of the benefits to be gained from attending thee lessons, and did

[12] Hourani, *Arabic Thought*, 222–244.

[13] "Administration Report for the Political Agency, Kuwait, 1912," in the *Annual Report of the Persian Gulf Political Residency for 1911*, IOR: R/15/1/711/2 (London: British Library), 113–119.

succeed in attracting a few children (none of whom was influenced by the Christian teachings).[14]

Shaikh Yusif bin ʿIsa al-Qinaʿi recalled how the idea for the al-Mubarakiyyah school was first proposed during the ceremonies held on 12 April 1911 to celebrate Prophet Muhammad's birthday. The sermon in the mosque was delivered by Shaikh Yasin al-Tabtabaʾi who concluded by saying,

> The purpose behind celebrating the birth of the Prophet (Peace Be Upon Him) does not simply lie in reading verses from the Qurʾan but in following in the Prophet's (PBUH) footsteps and we cannot do that without knowledge of his life and achievements. Such knowledge can only be attained from books and good schooling.[15]

Shaikh Yusif bin ʿIsa al-Qinaʿi was inspired by this, since it resonated with his earlier writings on the importance of education and knowledge. He, therefore, embarked on a concerted effort to collect donations from members of the ruling family (Naser al-Subah and Salem al-Subah), and businessmen (Ibrahim bin Mudaf, al-Khalid al-Khudiar, Hilal al-Mutairi, Qassim and Yusif al-Ibrahim), whose contributions went towards building the new school. Named al-Mubarakiyyah after the Ruler of Kuwait at the time, Shaikh Mubarak al-Subah, the school opened on 22 December 1912, Shaikh Yusif bin ʿIsa al-Qinaʿi was appointed its first principal, and Hamad al-Khalid al-Khudair, Shamlan bin Ali bin Saif and Ahmad al-Humaidi became members of its first council.

Al-Mubarakiyyah put an end to the traditional forms of teaching where a *mulla* sitting on a bench taught students in his own house, without supervision or curricula. A school now occupied a separate building, was subject to rules and regulations, and followed a strict curriculum. Despite these changes, subjects remained fundamentally traditional and did not venture beyond the teaching of Arabic, the Qurʾan, and rudimentary mathematics, until 1915 when ʿUmar Asim al-Azmiri became principal. He overhauled the system and introduced a more modern school curriculum based on what was being taught in Iraq at the time.[16]

---

[14] *History of Education in Kuwait: Documentary Study* (Kuwait: The Center for Research and Studies on Kuwait CRSK, 2002).

[15] Yusif al-Qinaʿi, *Safahat min Tarikh al-Kuwait* (Kuwait: No Publisher, 1960), 43–45.

[16] Al-Nuri, *Qisat*, 47.

However, al-Mubarakiyyah was destined to remain ensnared by an inflexible curriculum, since despite many attempts, the school administration failed to introduce the teaching of foreign languages, as was the practice at the more advanced Arab schools at the time. This situation was due mainly to the extreme views of certain uncompromising religious scholars who considered that the teaching and learning of foreign languages and modern sciences were sinful, and the school's main financial supporters were either influenced by these views or wished to spare themselves the unsavoury task of confronting the religious scholars. ʿAbdulʿaziz al-Rushaid's solution to this dilemma was to establish a new school that would have more freedom to manoeuvre.

Shaikh Yusif bin ʿIsa al-Qinaʿi recounted the story of how al-Ahmadiyyah school was founded,

> When shaikh Ahmad al-Jaber al-Subah came to power, he entrusted me with the task of tackling some of the pressing issues et al.-Mubarakiyyah where subjects were limited to teaching the Qurʾan, reading, basic arithmetic and Islamic jurisprudence. My only condition was that I be allowed to work without interference from teachers who were very difficult to deal with when I worked there as principal. Shaikh al-Subah instructed me to discuss my vision for the curricula with them, so I offered to introduce modern sciences and English but they were vehemently opposed to the idea. Loath to have another confrontation with them, I abandoned al-Mubarakiyyah. During subsequent meetings at Khalaf al-Naqib's shop, ʿAbdulʿaziz al-Rushaid proposed that we leave al-Mubarakiyyah to its current format and establish a new school that would reflect our own educational vision. The idea was met with great enthusiasm by everyone.[17]

Al-Ahmadiyyah school opened in May 1921, with the moral and financial support of Shaikh Ahmad al-Jaber and reformist merchants such as al-Khalid family. Away from the influence of the conservatives, Yusif bin ʿIsa al-Qinaʿi became simultaneously al-Ahmadiyyah's President and a teacher, and successfully introduced foreign languages as well as science into the curriculum. As a result, many students left al-Mubarakiyyah to join al-Ahmadiyyah, which clearly showed how reformist ideas had penetrated the society.

---

[17] Yusif al-Qinaʿi, *Al-Multaqatat* (Kuwait: Kuwait Government Press, no date), 228–229.

The Cultural Reaction to the Missionaries Presence in Kuwait

Reforms were not limited simply to education, which was propelled from its traditional modes into some very modern structures of learning. Cultural and intellectual life was greatly influenced by the reform movement led by Rashīd Rida, as indicated by his visit in 1912 that further cemented his status among the burgeoning intellectual classes. Commenting on that visit, ʿAbdulʿaziz al-Rushaid noted that,

> The first to sow the seeds of intellectual revival was the great scholar Muhammad Rashīd Rida. People flocked to the main mosque where he delivered his great sermons. Many Kuwaitis who had previously doubted him were left in awe. There was renewed interest in knowledge and science and the number of subscribers to his journal increased exponentially.[18]

Chief among Rida's concerns was the danger to Muslim culture and identity posed by Christian missionaries in Islamic countries, a threat he warned against constantly as part of the imperial goal of the Western powers. Rida mentioned his visit to Kuwait in an article in *al-Manar* entitled "Our Indian-Arab Trip: A Public Expression of Gratitude to the people of Oman and Kuwait," but did not elaborate on the intellectual and cultural aspects of the trip. However, Captain Shakespeare, the British Political Agent in Kuwait, included details of the visit in his annual report of 1912,

> [Rashīd Rida] arrived in Kuwait on the 9th May and the next day delivered a lecture attended by shaikhs Jabir and Nasir (Shaikh Mubarak's sons) and some 1,000 Arabs of all classes. He lectured on the rites and the propagation of the Islamic faith, and in the course of it warned his hearers against foreign missionaries and others like them who endeavoured to obtain a footing in Muhammadan countries. The lecture was not actively anti-European or anti-Christian, but its tone undoubtedly indicated that foreigners should be discouraged. Though the Saiyid [Rida] remained more than a month in Kuwait, his subsequent lectures were confined strictly to interpretation and elucidation of the Koran and Hadaya

---

[18] Al-Rushaid, *Tarikh*, 353, and as British Government Record show.

[Guidance], possibly on a hint from Shaikh Mubarak, whose guest he was.[19]

Establishing the *Al-Jam‘iyyah Al-Khairiyyah Al-‘Arabiyyah [Arab Charity Society] in 1913*

The visit of Rida encouraged a group of Kuwaitis to move more seriously against Christian missionary efforts. In addition to al-Mubarakiyyah school, these efforts culminated in the establishment in 1913 of *al-Jam‘iyyah al-Khairiyyah al-‘Arabiyyah* [the Arab Charity Society] by young Kuwaitis, such as Farhan al-Khalid al-Khudair, influenced by the new intellectual trends. The Society directed its efforts against Christian missionaries in Kuwait as epitomised by the American Hospital.[20] Rida received an anonymous letter—widely believed to have been written by the founder of the society himself, Farhan al-Khudair—in which he concurred with Rida about the dangers posed to Kuwait by the growing numbers of Christian missionaries in Bahrain and Kuwait, and emphasised the importance of stemming the tide of these missionary efforts.[21]

The Society was established with the help and financial support of Farhan's family and a number of prominent figures in Kuwait such as Shaikh Abdullah al-Khalaf al-Dehayyan and Shaikh Nasser al-Mubarak al-Subah. Most of the founding members, including the founder himself, were quite young (the oldest was 35), clearly indicating the youthful nature of the movement that was inspired by the intellectual revival sweeping through the Arab and Islamic world. Captain Shakespeare attests to this in his 1913 report: "… with the blessings of Shaikh Nasser bin Mubarak, a number of young Arab men with purported aspirations for progress established a charity organisation in February."[22] According

---

[19] "Administration Report for the Political Agency, Kuwait, 1912" in the *Annual Report of the Persian Gulf Political Residency for 1911*, IOR: R/15/1/711/2 (London: British Library), 113.

[20] Extract from the *Majallat al-Manar* of Cairo, Vol. 15, Part 7, dated Rajab 1330 (14 July 1913), 559, in IOR: 15/5/62 (London: British Library), 32.

[21] Sa'ih Nasih, "Christianity Missionaries in Bahrain and Arab Land," *Majallat Al-Manar*, No. 5 (May 1913), 379–383.

[22] "Administration Report for the Political Agency, Kuwait, 1913" in the *Annual Report of the Persian Gulf Political Residency for 1912*, IOR: R/15/1/712/2 (London: British Library), 126.

to its initial statement, the Society was founded to serve society and indirectly to oppose the role of missionaries and foreigners in Kuwait:

The purposes of our Society are to:

1. Send students on scholarships to study at Islamic universities in distinguished Arab countries.
2. Appoint a pious speaker to deliver lectures and act as a spiritual guide for the people.
3. Appoint a doctor and a pharmacist to treat the poor and the impoverished.
4. The distribution of clean water is one of our most important priorities.
5. Fund the burial of the poor and those visiting from out of town.[23]

These objectives were set forth in response to Christian missionary activities and the presence of the American Hospital. A Turkish doctor, Assad Efendi, and a Turkish pharmacist were appointed to run the newly-established local clinic, and medicines and surgical equipment were imported from Bombay.[24] A library set up in the Society's headquarters was supported by local people who donated books, journals and newspapers; later it subscribed to several journals and purchased books from abroad. Shaikh Muhammad Amin al-Shanqiti, at the time a resident of Zubair, was invited to join the Society, and delivered various lectures on religious and intellectual issues in a style that was considered a long way from traditional modes of religious indoctrination. The Society also kept its promise to provide clean drinking water—not the easiest of feats—and played an important role in funding burials, in addition to its other charity activities.[25]

However, the Society was not destined to survive beyond its first year. At the end of 1913 it was dissolved, the clinic was closed down, and both the doctor and the pharmacist were let go. There have been conflicting reports about the reasons for its closure. Some attributed it

---

[23] Al-Nuri, *Qisat*, 58.

[24] "Administration Report for the Political Agency, Kuwait, 1913," 126–127.

[25] Bader Al-Mutairi, *Al-Jamʿiyyah al-Khairiyyah al-ʿArabiyyah* (Kuwait: The Center for Research and Studies on Kuwait CRSK, 1998), 80–83.

to the death of its founder Farhan al-Khalid,[26] others to the reluctance of the local community to embrace the Society's vision and aspirations,[27] while yet another group blamed its demise on the clash between the Society's reformist efforts which favoured the Islamic Ottoman government, and the political leanings of Shaikh Mubarak al-Subah who preferred to accommodate the British presence despite the associated Anglo-American missionary activities.[28] These factors probably all contributed to the Society's downfall, but the most important reason was the pressure of the foreign political presence (represented by the British Political Agent), the foreign cultural presence (represented by the American Hospital and Christian missionaries), and Shaikh Mubarak, who regarded the Society as a threat to his relations with Britain.

Those reasons aside, the Society's importance lay in its being the first cultural and political project with a reformist agenda, thereby paving the way for several secular and religious movements geared towards reform. The seeds of change survived long after the Society had closed its doors, and as many political and cultural events would later show, a number of its young members carried on its message. Shaikh Yusif bin ʿIsa al-Qinaʿi and Shaikh ʿAbdulʿaziz al-Rushaid were among the most prominent figures who spread the reformist message. Although both came from a religious scholarly background and had originally acquired their knowledge through traditional routes, such as attending the sessions of renowned religious scholars at the time in Zubair, al-Hasa and Medina, they deviated from the norm by choosing instead to keep abreast of the latest political and cultural developments in the Arab and Islamic worlds and to inject some of these ideas into Kuwaiti society. Al-Mubarakiyyah and al-Ahmadiyyah schools were established according to the latest trends in education and, in the case of al-Ahmadiyyah, English was taught as a subject, despite fierce opposition from traditional conservative forces within the Kuwaiti society.[29]

[26] Al-Nuri, *Qisat*, 58.

[27] Charles Mylrea and Stanley Gerland, *Kuwait before Oil: Memoirs of Dr. C. Stanley G. Mylrea, Pioneer. Medical Missionary of the Arabian Mission, Reformed Church in America*, trans. Muhammad al-Rumaihi (Kuwait: Dar Qirtas, 1997), 143. Also: Mary Allison, *Doctor Mary in Arabia* (Houston: University of Texas Press, 1994), 38–43.

[28] Al-Nuri, *Qisat*, 58–60.

[29] Al-Mutairi, *Al-Jamʿiyyah al-Khairiyyah al-ʿArabiyyah*, 55.

While Shaikh Yusif bin ʿIsa al-Qinaʿi was busy with the school, Shaikh ʿAbdulʿaziz al-Rushaid turned his attention to the world of journalism. Journals and newspapers took their place in the reformist movement's "awareness project." ʿAbdulʿaziz al-Rushaid was in fact the founding father of journalism in Kuwait, having published the first journal in Kuwait, *al-Kuwait* Journal. He wrote in the first issue that publishing a journal for Kuwaitis by Kuwaitis was one of their highest aspirations.[30] The topics covered in the Journal were varied and the journal included sections dedicated to religious issues, ethics, literature, language and biographies. However, its "History" and its "Old and New" sections were the most revolutionary, since al-Rushaid adopted a scientifically-sound method for presenting Kuwait's history that was an unequivocal departure from traditional methods of documenting history on the basis of oral narratives. Later, his book, *Tarikh al-Kuwait* [History of Kuwait], adopted a similar method for narrating the history of the country.

In the section entitled "*Qadim wa Jadid*" [Old and New], al-Rushaid examined the latest burning topics, chief among which were modernism, civil society, gender issues from a religious perspective and a number of other themes that resulted directly from the clash between the cultures of the coloniser and the colonised. These topics were meant to protect the pure Kuwaiti society from the Western cultural intervention that other Muslim societies had witnessed. Al-Rushaid adopted the reformist ideas of Jamal al-Din al-Afghani, Muhammed ʿAbduh and Rashīd Rida who maintained that there was no conflict between Islam and science, and encouraged Muslims and Arabs to learn from Western civilisation and acknowledge the role of women in society, since none of this jeopardised religious and moral values or threatened the family unit that was considered the corner stone of society, even though this view contradicted Western culture's emphasis on individualism.[31]

In addition to the two important figures of al-Qinaʿi and al-Rushaid, Shaikh Muhammad al-Shanqiti and Shaikh Hafiz Wahba played an equally important role in spreading the message of reform, even after the Society, of which they were founding members, had closed down. It would not be an exaggeration to claim that these four men had a tremendous influence as the driving force behind the education of a whole generation of young

---

[30] ʿAbdulʿaziz al-Rushaid, "Introduction," *al-Kuwait Journal*, 1 (1928), 3.

[31] Ibid, 17–18.

people, a mission that would eventually lead them to clash with British interests in the region.

Islamists and Social Reforms

There was relatively little in the way of political reform, compared with the social and cultural reform that was initiated by the reformists, especially Islamists. During the 1920s, the pioneers of reform, mainly Yusif bin ʿIsa al-Qinaʿi and ʿAbdulʿaziz al-Rushaid, continued to exert efforts in many domains of life, with a particular emphasis on cultural activities. Al-Ahmadiyyah School, as noted above, surpassed al-Mubarakiyyah by introducing subjects like English language and natural sciences, while students were encouraged to take part in cultural activities, such as acting, which sometimes formed part of the final assessment of the student's performance in school. ʿAbdulʿaziz al-Rushaid's influence was discernible in the production of a school play called "A Reformist Dialogue" which he wrote and directed, and which was performed by students as part of their final exams and end-of-year celebrations.

In addition to progress made in the field of education, cultural reforms were extended to other domains of life; a national library was established in 1922 on the metaphorical ruins of *Al-Jamʿiyyah al-Khairiyyah al-ʿArabiyyah's* own library. Yusif bin ʿIsa who, with Sultan al-Kulaib and ʿAbdulhamid al-Saniʿ, was one of the founders of the national library, joined the Muslim Brotherhood later. The library, which grew in size over the years, became a meeting place for writers and intellectuals who converged upon it to debate issues in *fiqh*, literature and politics.

A literary club was established by Khalid al-ʿAdsani in 1924, which in turn helped create a venue for those interested in discussing literary, political and scientific topics. Poets like Saqiral-Shabib, Ahmad al-Bishr al-Rumi and several others honed their talents at the club, as explained by al-ʿAdsani,

> A period of active cultural and political engagement led to the establishment of the Literary Club whose idea was first proposed by the author of these lines. A member of the ruling family was invited to become an honorary president. Within a few years, the club was a cultural force to be reckoned with among young people. More than a hundred members joined its ranks and the scientific and literary lectures delivered on its

podium resonated with developments in both Kuwait and neighbouring countries.[32]

Islamist Reformists and Their Opponents

However, these reforms had as many opponents as supporters. Conflict arose mainly over control of the social domain; this had previously been regulated by other forces, mainly traditional conservatives who had viewed the reforms with great suspicion and often equated them with heresy. Figures like ʿAbdulʿaziz al-ʿAlj and Ahmad al-Farisi had a big following from all classes, including several very influential people who lent their support to al-Mubarakiyyah. The conservative forces generally had very strict views about teaching foreign languages and natural sciences, and allowing girls to attend schools. In addition, they had strong views on other issues like the spherical nature of the earth, the use of printers to publish religious books, and reading journals like *al-Manar*, since, along with Rashīd Rida, they were considered a very bad influence on young people. Al-ʿAli and al-Farisi blocked the introduction of certain subjects (foreign languages and modern sciences) into the school curricula et al.-Mubarakiyyah through their influence on some of the school's main financial supporters, such as Hamad al-Saqir and Ibrahim bin Mudaf; it was this setback that prompted Yusif bin ʿIsa and ʿAbdulʿaziz al-Rushaid to leave al-Mubarakiyyah and establish al-Ahmadiyyah away from the dominance of al-ʿAlj and al-Farisi. Nor could al-Ahmadiyyah escape the criticisms levelled by the conservatives, who often described it as a Christian school.

Nevertheless, Ahmad al-Jaber, a Kuwaiti prince, was instrumental at the time in keeping the conservatives at bay by lending both moral and financial support to al-Ahmadiyyah because of his special relationship with Yusif bin ʿIsa. This enabled the school to introduce modern curricula and attract teachers from more advanced countries, such as Iraq, the Levant and Egypt. The school also emphasised the importance of extra-curricular activities such as debates, speeches and the theatre. The conflict between the conservatives and the proponents of reform was showcased in al-Rushaid's play "*Muhawarah Islahiyya*" [A Reformist Dialogue], which

---

[32] Khalid al-ʿAdsani, "*Tarikh al-Harakah al-Fikriyyah fi al-Kuwait*" (Sijil al-Kuwait al-Yawm, no date), 1417.

took the form of a dialogue between an enlightened student and a narrow-minded ultra-religious man, and was performed at the end of the school year in 1924, before a huge audience. In the introduction to the play, which he later published in a small booklet, al-Rushaid mentions that the play was based on an imaginary dialogue between a turbaned shaikh and his brother who wished to consult him about enrolling in a modern school. The shaikh provided a long list of reasons why these schools had a corrupting influence, whereupon another student hastened to refute the shaikh's entire claim with solid evidence and logical argument,

> Shaikh: Isn't it true that these modern schools like al-Ahmadiyyah teach geography, history and English. And can anyone dispute the corrupting power of these subjects? Wasn't it the scientists of geography who claimed the earth was round and that rain was no more than steam rising from the earth and other sacrilegious allegations? I warn my dear brother against enrolling in this school.
>
> Student: Don't be swayed by him, brother, for his tongue does not speak the truth of his mind. And soon he will be exposed for what he is. I once heard him tell his group of his companions that "We are in an age where the young have overtaken us with the power of knowledge and now competing with us for jobs."[33]

From the student's point of view, the real reason the conservatives opposed the tide of reform and fought it tooth and nail lay in the perceived loss of social and religious status that they would incur. Yet, the influence of the conservatives gradually declined as increasing numbers of young people joined the ranks of the reformers, along with the political and social developments that occurred during the 1930s and dramatically reduced the impact of the conservative element on the minds of the youth.

REFORMISTS AND THE POLITICAL DOMAIN

Nationalist reformers were more interested in politics than the Islamists, who focused more on the social domain. Nationalist reformers strove to give more power to the people in general, and in particular to the merchant class to which many belonged. The reformist movement worked

---

[33] Khalifa al-Wuqayyan, *Al-Thaqafah fi al-Kuwait: Bidayat, Ittijahat, Riyadat* (Kuwait: al-Faisal Press, 2010), 370–374.

over the years to spread political and cultural awareness, but their efforts were restricted to urban centres in which Sunni Arabs resided. This was construed by urban Shi'as, Kuwaitis of Persian origin, and tribes, as a form of exclusion from a movement that considered them second-class citizens. As a result, they rushed to form an alliance with the ruling family in its struggle against the reformists, especially in 1938 and 1939 when matters came to a head. The conflict between the nationalist reformers and the ruling family led to rifts in the reformist movement, especially when the Islamists refused to antagonise the ruling family (being not very interested in politics, the Islamists thought that the nationalists had gone too far in their demands).[34]

The reformist movement undoubtedly contributed to the creation and spread of a fresh kind of political culture. The reformists introduced the notions of *shura*, democracy and political participation in a society where *shura* had previously been limited to those close to the ruler, while democracy and political participation were virtually non-existence in Kuwaiti political life. The reformist movement also introduced successful administrative experiences from neighbouring countries such as Bahrain's municipalities experiment. In 1938 and 1939, there were clashes between reformists and the ruler and his supporters, when the Emir and his followers realised how much was at stake in the success of the reformists who were gradually usurping some of their traditional powers. The Emir managed, however, to marginalise the reformists and to steer the country back onto its traditional track, and the discovery of oil and the resulting flow of revenues from 1949 served only to concentrate more power in the hands of Kuwait's rulers, who no longer needed support from the merchants.

The Beginnings of Political Opposition and the Role of the Islamists

The early seeds of opposition in Kuwait were political and against the ruler, although opposition sometimes took an economic shape. When Shaikh Mubarak al-Subah ascended the throne through fratricide, having killed his two half-brothers, Jarrah and Muhammad in a political move unprecedented in the history of Kuwait, Yusifal-Ibrahim, the brother-in-law of Jarrah and Muhammad, who was a prominent merchant and

---

[34] Al-'Adsani, *Muthakkarat*, 75.

a powerful personality, objected to the coup and roused public opinion against Shaikh Mubarak. Mubarak had meanwhile prevailed upon several of Kuwait's major figures to sign a letter addressed to the Ottoman Porte in Istanbul claiming that it was Yusifal-Ibrahim who had murdered the ruler and his brother.[35] Some of these individuals refused to sign the letter.[36]

Al-Ibrahim then intensified his political opposition to Mubarak at both the local and regional level by striking up an alliance with Mubarak's arch-enemy, ʿAbdulʿaziz bin Rashīd, the ruler of Haʾil, as well as with the Ottoman government which was opposed to the British and, by default, to their ally Shaikh Mubarak. Given this level of internal and external animosity, Mubarak was forced to improve his standing with the people of Kuwait and especially with its influential figures. Such flattery was to last ten years until 1906, when bin Rashīd was killed, and until the death of al-Ibrahim in 1907, after which Mubarak finally felt free to sever all ties with the local opposition, which consisted of al-Ibrahim's allies and a considerable number of influential Kuwaiti figures.[37]

Since numerous battles had exhausted his coffers, Mubarak was also in desperate need of money, and therefore imposed hefty taxes on the population in general, and on the merchants in particular, in order to fund more of his war efforts.[38] Pearl fishers were banned from diving for the precious stones at a time when pearl diving was one of the pillars of the Kuwaiti economy and sustained the livelihood of most Kuwaiti families. Unable to handle the ramifications, major pearl merchants such as

---

[35] Muhammad bin Subah (1831–1896): the sixth ruler of Kuwait. He came to power in 1892 with the support of his brother Jarrah who helped him in ruling the emirate. Muhammad ruled between 1892 and 1896 during which he held the title of Pasha from the Ottoman government. Both Muhammad and Jarrah were religious and preferred an alliance with the Ottoman Empire rather than with Great Britain. Their ambitious brother, Mubarak, who disagreed with their internal and external policies, eventually Mubarak killed Muhammad and Jarrah and seized power on 18 May 1896. See al-Rushaid, *Tarikh*, 235; also, Hussain Khaz'al, *Tarikh al-Kuwait al-Siyasi* (Beirut: Dar al-Hilal, 1962), 3:148.

[36] Al-Rushaid, *Tarikh*, 247.

[37] Khaz'al, *Tarikh al-Kuwait al-Siyasi*, 2:67.

[38] Saif Shamlan, *Min Tarikh al-Kuwait* (Kuwait: That al-Salasil, 1986), 151.

Hilal Fajhan al-Mutairi,[39] Shamlan bin ʿAli,[40] and Ibrahim bin Mudaf,[41] reacted by leaving the country and heading to Bahrain, departing in secret for fear of the shaikh's retaliation. Mubarak's rule clearly could not have survived the economic implications of this boycott and he was forced to send a delegation armed with a letter of apology in an attempt to persuade them to return but to no avail. On the pretext of visiting the Emir of Bahrain, Shaikh ʿIsa al-Khalīfa, Mubarak then visited Bahrain himself and, having no choice but to comply with all the conditions laid down by the pearl merchants, he managed eventually to win them back.[42] This incident represented the first real opposition moves against the ruler in Kuwait, but it was merely political opposition via economic means; this explains why the Islamists neither participated in, nor even commented about it, since it was so far from their social domain.

The Political Role of Muhammad Al-Shanqiti and Hafiz Wahba

During the early years of the twentieth century, Shaikh Muhammad al-Shanqiti travelled from the extreme west of the Maghreb to the eastern part of the Arab world in a search for knowledge that took him to Egypt, Medina, Mecca, India, Oman and al-ʃasa. He eventually settled in Zubair, in southern Iraq, at the request of one of his mentors who asked him to stay and teach at the school that had been established by Mezʾil Pasha Saʿdun. Despite the focus of al-Shanqiti's studies on Maliki *fiqh*, he was more influenced by the views of bin-Taymiyyah and bin al-Qayyem (the two main Hanbali scholars), especially concerning contrivances such as pleading with the righteous, the construction of shrines and similar practices that should be eradicated. Al-Shanqiti remained in Zubair for four years (1909–1913) during which time his reputation as a learned scholar reached as far as Basra and Kuwait. As noted above, when the Arab

---

[39] Hilal al-Mutairi: the most famous merchant in Kuwait at the beginning of the twentieth century. Hilal, who was born and raised in a poor family and had worked in trade since his early years and, died of the biggest as one of the wealthiest men in wealth in the Gulf at that time. See, al-Qinaʿi, *Safahat*, 44–67.

[40] Shamlan bin Ali: one of the biggest pearl merchants during Mubaraks's time. Ibid.

[41] ʿIbrahīm bin Mudhaf: from the famous al-Mudhaf family, and the wealthiest of them. Ibid.

[42] ʿAbdulrahman al-Ibrahim, "Development of the Constitutional Movement in Kuwait between 1938–1961" (MA Thesis, University of Sharjah, 2011), 18–21.

Charity Society was established, al-Shanqiti was invited to lecture and deliver sermons in Kuwait, where his charm, skilled oratory and modern Islamic views coincided with the reformist zeal of the time.

Al-Shanqiti's colleague Hafiz Wahba, a graduate of al-Azhar in Cairo, had travelled extensively between the urban centres of the Islamic world such as Istanbul and the Levant, before receiving an invitation from Yusif bin ʿIsa al-Qinaʿi to teach et al.-Mubarakiyyah, a job he combined with lecturing and, outside school hours, with awareness-raising activities. Together Wahba and al-Shanqiti were a reforming duo, alongside Yusif bin ʿIsa al-Qinaʿi and al-Rushaid. The teachings of al-Shanqiti and Wahba educated a whole generation of young people who in turn sought to articulate a reformist vision that reconciled Islamic, Pan-Arabist, social and political aspirations. An inevitable clash ensued between these aspirations, on the one hand, and British interests and traditional conservative forces, on the other (as is discussed later in the book).

The establishment of the Arab Charity Society marked the beginning of this cultural conflict, since the Society's declared goals of combating missionary efforts in Kuwait were frowned upon by the British. When the Society closed down, they were very relieved as was Shaikh Mubarak who agreed with them that the Society's ambitions were simply too big and too dangerous. However, calls for reforms did not end with the demise of the Society but continued unabated at mosques, *diwaniyyas*, and, to some extent, et al.-Mubarakiyyah. Things came to a head when Mubarak called upon Kuwaitis to support his friend, the ruler of Muhammara, Shaikh Kazʾal, a staunch ally of the British, in his battle against pro-Ottoman rebels. The Kuwaitis, spurred by al-Shanqiti and Wahba, have rejected Mubarak's orders. Al-Rushaid recalls,

When the Kuwaitis learned they were being asked to fight against their brothers [the rebels rising against Kaz'al], they resorted to civil strife and vociferously rejected Mubarak's calls, especially since al-Shanqiti and Hafez Wahba were touring the city warning people against obeying Mubarak, arguing that it constituted a sin to fight their brothers. Their words were met with great enthusiasm and emboldened the masses further. When Jaber bin Mubarak ordered them to march, they said, "We don't hear nor shall we obey." Jaber, taken aback, asked them for their reasons. They replied, "We cannot obey that which angers Allah."[43]

[43] Al-Rushaid, *Tarikh*, 175.

The religious impetus of the political activities of al-Shanqiti and Wahba is obvious in their reaction to Mubarak in that they saw this war against Ottomans as a "sin" by empowering a non-Muslim state over a Muslim state.

In 1914, al-Shanqiti and Wahba played an important role in recruiting youth and mobilising people under the Islamic principle of supporting the Muslim Ottoman state against the non-Muslim state of Britain. An angry Mubarak returned to Kuwait and immediately summoned al-Shanqiti and Wahba to chastise them for turning public opinion against him and the British,

> I am an Ottoman Muslim who jealously guards his religion and his country and I don't like those who want to harm either one of them. But I have reached an agreement with the British over something which I believe is of great benefit to my country and I will not tolerate any opposition to that decision, despite the fact that I don't like the British and acknowledge that their religion is very different from mine. Children in schools and out on the streets are cursing the British and praising the German. I am sure they are too young to make up their own minds and they are just repeating what is being taught to them.[44]

Following this incident and fearing retaliation or exile, both al-Shanqiti and Wahba felt compelled to leave Kuwait. The former took up a teaching post in Zubair, while the latter accepted an invitation to teach in Bahrain. This act of civil strife was unprecedented and came on the heels of al-Ibrahim's political opposition and the decision of the three merchants to engage in economic boycott. It thus formed the seeds of intensive political and cultural activism which, in turn, transformed domestic social and political issues into matters with wider regional, Arab and Islamic implications.

The Ruling Family and the Reformists

The ruling family's reaction to the reforms fluctuated, according to the matter at hand and the ruler in power. Shaikh Mubarak al-Subah was very interested in expanding the base of his power in the region and struck several alliances with British allies such as Shaikh Khazʿal and tribes that

---

[44] Ibid, 176.

were hostile to the pro-Ottoman bin-Rashīd who wielded absolute power in the heart of the Arab Peninsula. This inevitably put Mubarak on a collision course with public opinion which was sympathetic to the Ottoman Empire and regarded it as the protestor of Islam in the face of European greed. Mubarak's brutal rule also left people little space to manoeuvre and express their opinions. Although Mubarak was out of the country when al-Shanqiti and Wahba spearheaded an opposition movement in Kuwait, both had to leave Kuwait when he returned.

Mubarak's close friendship with Shaikh Khazʿal, infamous for his decadent lifestyle, introduced him to a life of luxury and opulence he attempted to mimic in his own household. This, in addition to Mubarak's dictatorial style of rule, prevented any reform movement from flourishing. The fact that reforms were being pushed by religious scholars who supported the Muslim Ottoman government in its struggle against Mubarak's European-backed ally and called for religious values in their versions of reform made them Mubarak's worst enemy.

Mubarak's son Jaber (1860–1917) ruled for a short period during which he revoked some of his father's policies vis-à-vis Kuwait's elders and improved his relations with them, and also repealed some of the taxes his father had imposed, but he did not live long enough to effect any significant changes. When his conservative, traditionalist brother Salem (1864–1921) ascended the throne in 1917, conservative scholars found themselves once more in fashion. A believer in old-fashioned methods of rule, Salem, was loath to consult anyone and intensely disliked the kind of political change pushed by the reformers. He took advice (mainly social and economic) from Kuwait's prominent figures infrequently and on specific occasions, such as al-Jahra' incident when he sought their guidance as to whether or not to negotiate with Faisal al-Duish's envoy after al-Duish found himself under siege by the British forces in Kuwait. Salem was advised not to accept al-Duish's conditions which he did.

Salem had inherited his father's legacy of despotism, but unlike his father who had lived a life of luxury and extravagance, this power was contained by his religiousness and predilection for all that was traditional. When al-Shanqiti returned to Kuwait to visit his family, Salem admonished him for this unexpected visit for which he had not sought prior permission. Pushed by the traditional conservatives, Salem found the visit quite disconcerting due to al-Shanqiti's history with his father and his reformist views, and his nervousness over the visit became quite evident when he had al-Shanqiti put under surveillance. Even after al-Shanqiti had left Kuwait to return to Zubair, Salem tracked him, and even sent a letter to the British-appointed Governor of Basra (since Zubair was under the Basra's jurisdiction), warning him that al-Shanqiti was agitating the masses against the British government in the name of religion.[45]

The Governor of Basra wanted to keep al-Shanqiti under control and questioned Shaikh Ibrahim, who was hosting al-Shanqiti in his house, about al-Shanqiti's activities. In return, Ibrahim assured the Governor that al-Shanqiti no longer regarded the war against the British as a religious one but as a purely political one, and that he had left Kuwait not for political reasons but because of disagreements with some students. However, the real reason behind Salem's opinion of al-Shanqiti and Wahba was their intervention in the political domain in the name of religion, which threatened the legitimacy of the ruler in the society.[46]

Islamists and Socio-Political Reform After Shaikh Mubarak

Yusif bin ʿIsa al-Qinaʿi and ʿAbdulʿaziz al-Rushaid entered the reformist arena following the departure of al-Shanqiti and Wahba in 1914, but maintained a low profile until Mubarak's death. During his rule, they were very busy with al-Mubarakiyyah and also feared his persecution and that of his son, Salem, the successor to Jaber who had ruled only briefly. Whispers of the need for reform began to circulate during the rule of Shaikh Salem who had also inherited his father's uncompromising attitude,[47] but talk of political change remained subdued and sporadic until late 1920 and early 1921, when several Kuwaiti figures stressed the importance of involving the general population in the process of decision-making. They proposed to pressure Shaikh Salem into forming a council of six members from the local community—including Shaikh Ahmad al-Jaber—to act as permanent advisers, a step that they believed would secure a lasting social peace.[48]

---

[45] Abdullatif al-Khaldi, *Min Aʿalam al-Fikr al-Islami fi al-Basra: Muhammad Amin al-Shanqiti* (Baghdad: Awqaf Ministry, 1981), 122–125.

[46] Ibid.

[47] Jabir succeeded Mubarak in 1915 and ruled only for 14 months, and after him Salem son of Mubarak came to power and ruled from a1917 to 1921.

[48] Bader Aldin Khusousi, *Maʿrakat al-Jahraʾ: Dirasa Tawthiqiyyah* (Kuwait: That al-Salasil, 1983), 113 and 319.

No sooner had Shaikh Salem died, then they seized the opportunity to demand a bigger piece of the political pie, especially in the absence of Shaikh Ahmad al-Jaber, the man who was considered most likely to succeed Salem (at the time al-Jaber was away, negotiating with ᶜAbdulᶜaziz bin Saᶜud et al.-ᶜUqair Conference). A group of men met at the home of Nasser al-Bader on the day Salem of Salem's death and drafted a political manifesto that was published by Saif al-Shamlan in his book *The History of Kuwait*. This version differs slightly in language and considerably with regard to names from the version reproduced in Khalīfa al-Wuqayyan's book *Culture in Kuwait: Beginnings, Trends and Pioneers*. The document contained demands that would have been deemed virtually impossible during Mubarak's reign six years earlier. Al-Wuqayyan's version was as follows,

> In the name of Allah, the Most Beneficent, the Most Merciful We the undersigned have agreed on the following:
> 1. Reform the House of Subah to avoid disagreements over the line of succession.
> 2. The three candidates for the throne are Shaikh Ahmad al-Jaber, Shaikh Hamad al-Mubarak and Shaikh Abdullah al-Salem.
> 3. If the Subah family reaches a consensus on one of the candidates or if the government chooses one of them, we shall accept the decision in both cases.
> 4. The appointed ruler shall be the president of the Shura Council.
> 5. Several members of the Subah family and Kuwaiti people shall be elected to run the country on the basis of fairness and justice.[49]

Yusif bin ᶜIsa al-Qinaᶜi was one of the signatories on the al-Wuqayyan version of the document, in addition to being a member of the twelve representatives on the advisory council as recommended by the negotiations between a number of Kuwaiti figures and Shaikh Ahmadal-Jaber on board his ship upon his return from al-ᶜUqair Conference.

Al-Rushaid was also a member of the council which did not survive for long. Suleiman al-ᶜAdsani records in his memoirs that court advisers encouraged the Shaikh to agree to the delegation's demand because they were deeply convinced that disagreements among council members would

---

[49] Khalifa Al-Wuqayyan, *Al-Thaqafahfi al-*Kuwait, 275.

soon spell the end of the Council. Sure enough, the council did not survive longer than six months due to irreconcilable differences between its members over policy issues and future plans, and the intrigues perpetrated by court staff.[50] In this incident, the Islamists represented by Yusif bin ʿIsa and ʿAbdulʿaziz al-Rushaid did not, for several reasons, play a crucial role. First, the Islamists had had a bad experience with Mubarak and Salem before al-Shanqiti and Wahba had been expelled from Kuwait. Second, Yusif bin ʿIsa and al-Rushaid were still young and had not reached the point of being able to lead the traditional merchant families and other influential figures. Finally, and most importantly, although Islamists were part of the reformist movement, they did not consider this political demand as a priority because their real focus was the social more than the political domain.

Despite being short-lived and small, and with its membership being limited to certain classes, mainly merchants and religious scholars, the 1921 Council was the first experience of its kind in the modern history of Kuwait and the Gulf, in that its principles were guided by the notions of democracy, as understood by Islamic *shura*, even though the people did not directly elect their representatives. The absence of a culture of democracy also contributed to the 1921 Council's rapid downfall, nor was fresh elections called to form a new council. Arab society in general and the Gulf in particular were still governed by tribal and familial ties.

The fact that the pioneers of reform had proposed such revolutionary ideas and had attempted to realise them in the form of the council soon became an inspiration, albeit a rather romanticised one, for all those who aspired to introduce democracy into the Arab Gulf. The 1921 Council represented a historical moment when the people forced the ruling family to accept their demands. The 1921 Council was also presided over by a commoner, and despite its simplistic nature, its manifesto regulated the line of succession to prevent future disputes. All these achievements in 1921 paved the way for a culture of democracy that would inspire later generations to demand bigger political reforms.

Shaikh Ahmad al-Jaber al-Subah ruled for 20 years during which time the country underwent significant periods of political, social and economic transformation, chief among which was the discovery of oil and

---

[50] Khalid al-'Adsani, *Mudhakarat Khalid Sulaiman al-ʿAdsani* (Printed by a typewriter, unpublished. no date), 8.

the awarding of the first oil concession agreements to British and American companies. The ruling family increased its political and economic power through direct control of all oil resources. Shaikh Ahmad's relationship with the proponents of reform was fullet al. of friction from the moment of Shaikh Salem's death (while Shaikh Ahmad was -ʿUqair Conference negotiating over borders with ʿAbdulʿaziz bin Saʿud). A number of Kuwait's elders then decided to amend the laws of autocratic rule that Mubarak, Jaber and Salem had followed in order to make them more democratic and more oriented towards Shura. Despite the short lifespan of the Shura Council, the reformers persisted in their cultural and intellectual efforts during the 1920s, and the notion of re-establishing the council surfaced again the 1930s, when several reform leaders such as Shaikh Yusif bin ʿIsa al-Qinaʿi, Suleiman al-ʿAdsani, Sayyid ʿAli Sayyid Suleiman and others suggested establishing an elected municipal council that would be entrusted with the task of keeping Kuwait's streets clean. The council would be funded by an increase from 4 to 4.5 per cent on taxes on imported goods. Shaikh Ahmad al-Jaber liked the idea, especially as it cost the government practically nothing while simultaneously functioning as a form of financial control to limit cases of corruption in some government agencies.[51]

Despite Ahmad al-Jaber's approval, several parties that had long benefited, financially, socially and politically, from the old arrangements were deeply opposed to the municipal council. An open conflict ensued between the old guard and members of the council whose twelve members were elected by 50 of Kuwait's prominent figures. Council members included: Yusif bin ʿIsa, Mishʿan al-Khudair, Suleiman al-ʿAdsani, Sayyid ʿAli Sayyid Suleiman, Muhammad Ahmad al-Ghanim and Nisf Yusif al-Nisf. Sulaiman al-ʿAdsani was elected as the president of the council, while Shaikh Ahmad al-Jaber's brother, Abdullah al-Jaber, was appointed the honorary president of the first municipal council,[52] which was elected for two years, after which the number of prominent figures eligible to vote increased to 200. Most of the same members were re-elected for the council's second session, with al-ʿAdsani as president for the second time running.

---

[51] Al-Ibrahim, 58–60.

[52] Khalid al-'Adsani, *Mudhakarat*, 8.

There was a sharp conflict of interest between the reformists and several figures, close to Ahmad al-Jaber's court, who had taken advantage of their positions for personal gain. The most prominent of these was Saleh al-Mulla who, since the days of Shaikh Mubarak al-Subah, had occupied what in modern times would be equivalent to the position of prime minister. Saleh al-Mulla had gained much authority and influence over the years by the simple expedient of being increasingly invested with a wider range of powers by a succession of rulers. He was thus authorised to write letters in the name of the ruler and held all the official seals. Al-Mulla also had an entourage of like-minded sycophants who benefited greatly from their relationship with him—or were simply too afraid that he would hamper their interests.

This affected group attempted to stem the tide of reformist ambitions and when it was time to elect the third council, they succeeded in their attempt. Saleh al-Mulla used the official seals to issue letters in the name of the emir, banning certain reformist figures from running as candidates. They also put up their own candidates and pressured people to vote for them (at the time the small size of the electorate allowed for such power). Al-Mulla also revoked the membership of several winners, such as Zaid Sayyid Muhammad, on the pretext that he held dual nationality (Kuwaiti and Iraqi), despite the fact that at the time it was common practice for merchants to hold other nationalities to facilitate travelling and their business deals. The reformists then felt compelled to boycott the council, with Yusif bin ʿIsa describing the elections as "rigged." Suleiman al-ʿAdsani was also removed from the presidency when al-Mullah's men voted him out.[53]

Despite these setbacks, the reformists maintained the same zeal. After the incident of forgery, two young Kuwaitis from prominent merchant families, Abdullah Hamad al-Saqir and Muhammad Ahmad al-Ghanim, worked on founding the Education Council to advance cultural and educational causes. Al-Saqir and al-Ghanim, and a number of Kuwaiti figures proposed to Shaikh Ahmad al-Jaber that a 0.5 per cent increase in customs duties could be introduced to support the Education Council. Ahmad al-Jaber welcomed the proposal, especially as it did not dip into his coffers, but on condition that the merchants agreed to the idea—which they did. Members of the Education Council were elected away from the

---

[53] Ibid, 13–14.

negative influence of Saleh al-Mulla who was kept at arm's length.[54] The elections followed the same format as that of the Municipal Council.[55]

The first Education Council was founded in 1936, was headed by Abdullah al-Jaber and had twelve members, including Yusif bin 'Isa, since most were reformists, this created a very harmonious environment in which to achieve the council's goals of developing the field of education and school curricula.[56] Saleh al-Mulla was once again deeply disconcerted by the presence of so many reformers on the Education Council since it threatened his own interests. The elected Education Council was, therefore, dissolved in 1937, one year after it had been set up, in order to get rid of the reformists and appoint pro-establishment members. Elections were again rigged, and results were tampered with. The reformists were left with no choice but to resign and to regroup in secret to avoid Saleh al-Mulla and his cohorts.[57]

The National Bloc
Until the dissolution of the Municipal and Education Councils, reformists, Islamists and nationalists, worked as one entity. However, in the aftermath of the Municipal and Educational Councils fiasco perpetrated by Saleh al-Mullah, most reformists opted to withdraw from the two councils and began to hold secret meetings to address some of the more pressing political issues and work out how to put an end to Saleh al-Mullah's glaring interferences. Three of their most enthusiastic nationalist members, Abdullah Hamad al-Saqir, 'Abdulatif al-Ghanim and Khalid Suleiman al-Adsani (general secretary of the two councils), met and formed the core of the National Bloc which called for an elected legislative council with comprehensive powers to govern the emirate, in other words, a legislative rather than an advisory or *shura* council.[58]

During the 1930s, the Arab world witnessed a surge in Western-style secular Pan-Arabist ideologies which, surprisingly enough, did not clash

---

[54] Najat al-Jasem, *Baladiyyat al-Kuwait fi Khamsin 'Aman* (Kuwait: Baladiyyat al-Kuwait, 1980), 30–37.

[55] 'Abdul'aziz Hussain, *Arab Society in Kuwait* (Kuwait: Dar Qirtas, 1994), 107.

[56] Saleh Shihab, *Tarikh al-Ta'limfi al-Kuwait* (Kuwait: Kuwait Government Press, 1984), 54–56.

[57] Abdulmehsin Jamal, *Political Opposition in Kuwait* (Kuwait: Dar Qirtas, 2007), 99.

[58] Khalid al-'Adsani, *Mudhakarat*, 24–28.

with Islamic schools of thoughts since both shared similar views regarding colonialism and imperialism and called for the advancement of the Arab and Islamic nations. These trends were spearheaded by a new generation of young Arab scholars influenced by secular Pan-Arabist thinkers like Sati᷄ al-Husari[59] more than they were influenced by Islamic intellectuals such as Muhammad ᶜAbduh and Rashīd Rida.

These schools of thoughts brought with them clandestine organisations such as the Pan-Arabist, communist and other underground movements whose ideologies were channelled from Iraq via newspapers, journals and meetings between the Iraqi and Kuwaiti intelligentsia. Al-Saqir and al-Ghanim also opened channels of communication with several cultural and intellectual centres with Pan-Arabist orientations in Iraq and the Levant. These two, along with al-ᶜAdsani, joined the Secret Arab Movement and obtained ranks within it.[60] The inspiration for the National Bloc came from these secret organisations, which extended invitation to other reformists to join them; Shaikh Yusif Bin ᶜIsa gave them his blessing, but did not join them.[61] The National Bloc published its reform programme in the Iraqi newspaper *al-Zaman*. The programme included various demands, such as establishing more schools and ending the emigration of Iranians to Kuwait to preserve the demographic balance. A number of articles were published in 1938 in Iraqi, Egyptian and Syrian newspapers that criticised the ruling family and expressed sympathy with the demands of the National Bloc. Qasr al-Zuhur, the Iraqi radio station,

---

[59] Sati' al-Husari (1882–1968): A Secular Nationalist Syrian thinker. He adopted the European model of Nationalism and applied it to Arab Nationalism which was originally correlated with Islam. He believed Arab Nationalism should be based on Arabic language and culture, rather than on religious loyalties or regional dialects, and definitely not on the Ottoman *millet* system. Al-Husari worked throughout his life on propagating a secular Arab Nationalism through educational curricula in Syria, Egypt and Iraq (where he died). See William Cleveland, *The Making of an Arab Nationalist: Ottomanism and Arabism in the Life and Thought of Sati' al-Husari* (New Jersey: Princeton, 1971).

[60] In 1940, al-Saqir, al-ᶜAdsani and al-Ghanim became members of the Arab Club in Damascus and al-Muthanna Club in Baghdad, where al-Saqir obtained the rank of *worker* which was considered the highest rank in these societies. Al-ᶜAdsani and al-Ghanim also obtained high ranks. See, Shafiq Juha, *Al-Harakah al-ᶜArabiyyah al-Sirriyya* [The Secret Arabic Movement] (Beirut: al-Furat, 2004), 49–51. Also, "Administration Report for the Political Agency, Kuwait, 1941" in the *Annual Report of the Persian Gulf Political Residency for 1940*, IOR: R/15/5/206/135 (London: British Library), 135.

[61] ᶜAbdulridha Asiri, *Political System in Kuwait* (Kuwait: al-Watan Prints, 1996), 192.

allocated segments of its programmes to promoting the demands of the National Bloc.[62]

The First Legislative Council 1938

The pressures exerted by Iraqi newspapers and Qasr al-Zuhur, in addition to the disagreements between Shaikh Ahmad al-Jaber and the British Political Agent, proved quite opportune for the National Bloc, whose members took the opportunity to present their demands to Shaikh Jaber through the respected businessman Muhammad Thnian al-Ghanim who supported the National Bloc's mission. Shaikh Yusif bin ʿIsa al-Qinaʿi blessed the move, although he did not participate, and the British Political Agent's tacit approval of the demands gave further support. The following letter was presented to Shaikh Ahmad al-Jaber,

> Your Highness, the nation swore its allegiance to you on the day you ascended the throne on the understanding that the principles of your rule would rest on the notions of Shura which Islam decreed and was adopted by the four Righteous Caliphs but these notions have been quickly forgotten by both sides in Kuwait due to the unique circumstances the country has endured. This has prompted several of your subjects to offer their advice and counsel to redress the situation and spare you and themselves the vagaries of time and the unpredictability of circumstances and safeguard our country and its sovereignty and independence. They seek to remove the roots of discontent through dialogue and have, therefore, decided to propose the establishment of a legislative council to run the country's affairs. We have authorised the bearers of this letter to discuss the matter with you. We beseech Allah to guide us onto the path of all that is good and righteous.
>
> 30 Rabi' al-Awwal, 1357 Hijri (31 May 1938).[63]

Al-Ghanim duly met Shaikh Ahmad al-Jaber in the presence of Shaikh Abdullah al-Salem al-Subah, who was second in line to the Kuwaiti throne, and a cousin of Shaikh Ahmad. Abdullah, who was sympathetic to the National Bloc's demands, advised his cousin to accept the demands

---

[62] Muhammad Al-Rumaihi, "The 1939 Reformist Movement in Kuwait, Bahrain, and Dubai," *Journal of Gulf and Arab Peninsula Studies*, 1, No. 4 (1985), 34.

[63] Al-'Adsani, *Mudhakarat*, 27.

lest the Bloc should resort to violence,[64] and also recommended that elections be brought forward before further foreign immigrants arrived, particularly in the absence of any official records of electorates.[65] Ahmad al-Jaber approved all the demands and a committee was formed to supervise the elections that included Ahmad al-Humaidi, Yusif bin ʿIsa and Muhammad Thnian al-Ghanim.

Three hundred and fifty men were invited to cast their votes at Diwan al-Saqir. This small electorate of merchants and the intelligentsia represented the cream of society. The remaining 65.000 or so of the population were marginalised and excluded from the democratic process, so that the Legislative Council could safely be described as an elitist or aristocratic council.[66] Members of the National Bloc won most of the seats and included Mishʾan al-Khudair, Sulaiman al-ʿAdsani, Sayyed Ali Sayyed Sulaiman, Abdullah al-Saqir, ʿAbdulatif al-Ghanim, Yusif al-Marzuq, Sultan al-Kulaib and Yusif al-Saleh al-Hamidi. Other members were National Bloc supporters, most importantly Yusif bin ʿIsa al-Qinaʿi who was elected vice president of the council.[67] The council consisted of 14 members, ten elected from among the people and four elected from the ruling family, with the Crown Prince Shaikh Abdullah al-Salem becoming the Legislative Council's president. This was also the first elected council to appear in the Gulf.[68]

The council introduced many reforms, revoked several fraudulent monopolies and pushed for developments in the fields of health and education. It won the respect of both the ruler and the people, apart from Saleh al-Mulla's group, certain members of the ruling family, and individuals of Iranian origin and Shi'is who were excluded from the elections and

---

[64] Al-Rumaihi, "The 1939 Reformist Movement," 36. Also; Salah al-ʿAqqad, *Political Movements in the Gulf from the Beginning of Modern Eras until the Crisis of 1990–1991* (Cairo: Anglo-Egyptian, 1991), 232.

[65] Al-Adsani, *Mudhakarat*, 28.

[66] Najat al-Jasem, *Political and Economic Development of Kuwait between the Two Wars 1914–1939* (Kuwait: al-Majlis al-Watani Lilthaqafah wa al-Funoon wa al-Aadab, 2002), 165–166. Also, ʿAbdulmehsin Jamal, *Lamahat min Hayat al-Shiʿa fi al-Kuwait* (Kuwait: Dar al-Naba', 2005), 82.

[67] Al-Jasim, *Political and Economic Development*, 165.

[68] ʿAbdullah Al-Nuri, *Muthakkarat min waqt al-Shaikh Ahmad al-Jabir al-Hakim al-ʿAashir lil Kuwait* (Kuwait: That al-Salasil, 1978), 21–46. Also, "Administration Report for the Political Agency, Kuwait, 1939" in the *Annual Report of the Persian Gulf Political Residency for 1938*, IOR: R/1/P. & S./12/3894 (London: British Library).

the legislative council. Members of this disenchanted group intensified their efforts to bring down the council; thus, when the council requested that an ammunition warehouse be placed under the council's control, both al-Mulla's group and the British Political Agent were dismayed. The group seized the opportunity to mobilise the ruler and the British Political Agent against the council which, however, stood its ground and refused to withdraw its request.

The stand-off escalated to the point where it was feared an armed clash might ensue, especially after some members of the ruling family had armed several pro-establishment tribes and instructed them to lay siege to the council members who were hiding inside the main ammunition warehouse at Dasman Palace. Yusif bin ʿIsa al-Qinaʿi mediated between the two parties, especially as the balance of military power was on the side of the ruling family, and succeeded in persuading the council members to surrender. As a result, Bedouins loyal to the emir toured the streets chanting "Rule is for Allah and then al-Subah."[69] Two council members attempted to contact the British Political Agent to settle the problem but he refused to extend any help and even advised the emir to grant himself veto power over the council's decisions to avoid similar problems in the future.[70]

The council convened to discuss what had transpired, and several members reproached al-Qinaʿi for failing to defend the council members before the ruling family. The reason behinds al-Qinaʿi's stance was that he believed the National Bloc had exaggerated its political demands when it suddenly took over all powers from the ruler and the ruling family for the newly elected council. As a part of the religious establishment al-Qinaʿi considered reform of the social domain more important than the political domain, and Islamists represented by al-Qinaʿi gave more weight to social reform over political reform. When these elements contradicted each other, they preferred to protect the social project rather than to support the political project. Al-Qinaʿi did not believe in changing the political system or taking power from the hands of the Emir, since the real problems were found in the social domain and included various social ills such as the spread of alcohol consumption, lack of a good education

[69] Al-Adsani, *Mudhakarat*, 73.

[70] "Administration Report for the Political Agency, Kuwait, 1939" in the *Annual Report of the Persian Gulf Political Residency for 1938*, IOR: R/15/5/206/425 (London: British Library).

for boys and girls, corruption in the judicial system and so on.[71] Further-more, al-Qina'i has a good relationship with the ruler, Ahmad al-Jaber, who supported many of al-Qina'i's social projects, such as al-Ahmadiyyah school which allowed the reformists a free hand in shaping the social domain. For the reasons noted above and because of the good relation-ship between Ahmad al-Jaber and al-Qina'i, the latter was constrained from acting against the former.

The incident also placed the president of the council and Shaikh Abdullah al-Salem al-Subah in an unenviable position. Shaikh Abdullah tried to strike a middle ground between the two sides but had in the end to side with his own ruling family. The emir entrusted Shaikh Abdullah with running the council and issued a decree confiscating all weapons that were in the hands of the people, to ensure that all legislative and executive powers remained with the ruler.[72]

The Second Legislative Council 1939

Fresh elections were called on 27 February 1938 in order to select members for the second Legislative Council. Those eligible to vote rose from 300 to 400, while council seats were increased to 20. According to a British document, attempts were made to buy votes; yet the coun-cil's make-up did not differ by much from its predecessor.[73] All former members were re-elected along with some new faces, while only three of the opponents of the previous council won seats. Shaikh Abdullah al-Salem was again re-elected as president. Although the council was infused with the same ethos as the first one, it was no match for the power of the Emir who was now fully supported by the British Political Agent.[74]

Shaikh Ahmad al-Jaber proposed a new constitution based on the constitution of the Emirate of Transjordan which effectively conferred absolute power on the ruler despite the existence of a legislative council.[75] However, the reformists were very resistant to the changes introduced

[71] Al-Qina'i, *Safahat*, 35–40.

[72] Al-Jasim, *Political and Economic Development*, 179.

[73] Al-'Adsani, *Mudhakarat*, 82–83.

[74] Al-Ibrahim," Development of the Constitutional Movement," 80.

[75] "Administration Report for the Political Agency, Kuwait, 1940" in the *Annual Report of the Persian Gulf Political Residency for 1939*, IOR: R/15/5/206/55 (British Library, London).

by Shaikh Ahmad al-Jaber and the new constitution, an opposition that was accompanied by vitriolic criticism from the Iraqi press and the Qasr al-Zuhur radio station. Appalled by these developments the Shaikh summoned Yusif bin ʿIsa al-Qinaʿi and asked him to keep the opposition in check, but al-Qinaʿi indicated that it was quite impossible to stem the tidal wave emanating from the press. Al-Qinaʿi also succeeded in reining in Shaikh Ahmad al-Jaber on several occasions and managed to prevent him from harming the reformists as, for instance, in the case of ʿAbdulatif Thnian al-Ghanim who had sent a letter to Qasr al-Zuhur radio station inciting the public against the ruling family and was on the verge of being arrested.[76]

Shaikh Ahmad al-Jaber tightened his grip on power by proposing a new constitution, but the council voted against ratifying it. This led to a new political crisis which ended with the dissolution of the council on 7 March 1939, only a few months after it had been voted into power. Shaikh Ahmad al-Jaber was encouraged by the support of the British Political Agent, and by ʿAbdulʿaziz bin Saʿud, who having congratulated Shaikh Ahmad on the dissolution of the council, then offered to send him members of the Mutair and al-ʿAjman tribes to help him to consolidate his power before the virus of democracy spread further in the region.[77]

THE 1940S

The Second World War had far-reaching implications for the region. In Kuwait, people were grappling with the effects of the war on their trade and livelihoods, while the British Political Agent played a central role in consolidating the shaikh's grip on power so as to pre-empt any undesirable political developments that might distract him from international events. Shaikh Ahmad al-Jaber also strengthened his power base by appointing members of the ruling family to high- and mid-level government positions. The tide of reform also lost some of its popular support due to the various political crises noted above. The reformists were too keen to reap the fruits of their reforms too fast and found themselves embroiled in political battles that have a negative impact on their mission.

[76] Al-'Adsani. *Mudhakarat*, 118.

[77] "Administration Report for the Political Agency, Kuwait, 1940" in the *Annual Report of the Persian Gulf Political Residency for 1939*, IOR: R/15/5/206/99 (British Library, London).

The end of the Second World War saw the beginning of a new era in the history of Kuwait. Due to the discovery and export of the first shipments of oil in 1946, Kuwaiti society was catapulted from extreme poverty to unprecedented levels of prosperity. Although the ruling family took the lion's share of the oil revenues, a considerable share was channelled to the general population who responded by increasing their support for the ruling family, seeing them as the source of affluence after years of recession and a devastating world war. Pearl fishing, which had been a main pillar of the Kuwaiti economy, had been crushed by the production of artificial pearls in Japan; thus, the oil seemed heaven-sent, and after years of the ruling family taking money from the people and the merchants, the balance of economic power was reversed. Now the government had become the party that disbursed money and provided the merchants with their main contracts. In effect, the ruling family now secured political power through the economy.[78]

The Rise of the Muslim Brotherhood in the Arab World

Hasan al-Banna had founded the Muslim Brotherhood at the end of the 1920s, as a response to political and intellectual developments in Egypt and the Arab region as a whole. The movement was a natural extension of Islamic and nationalist thinking, as well as being a form of resistance to colonisation and the Westernisation of Egyptian society.[79] Initially, the Muslim Brotherhood's thinking was inspired by the intellectual and organisational trends of several movements, chiefly Sultan ʿAbdulhamid II's notion of Pan-Islamism as a means of unifying Muslims under one anti-colonial banner, in addition to the Nationalist Party of Mustafa Kamil Pasha, Muhammad Farid and ʿAbdulʿaziz Jawish that emerged in Egypt according to the same principles of Pan-Islamism but with a greater focus on Arabism.

Yet the greatest influence on the movement was the reformist trend of Jamal al-Din al-Afghani and his students Muhammad ʿAbduh and Muhammad Rashīd Rida (the latter had been Hasan al-Banna's

---

[78] Al-Ibrahim," Development of the Constitutional Movement,"95.

[79] R. Hrair Dekmejian, *Islam in Revolution: Fundamentalism in the Arab World* (New York: Syracuse University Press, 1995), 8–19.

mentor during his time et al.-*Manar*, the journal established by Rashīd Rida).[80],[81],[82] Tariq al-Bishri explains the genealogy of the reformist trend starting from al-Afghani, the founder of a political Islam that resists colonisation and works to unify Muslims, and also refers to Muhammad ʿAbduh's role in disseminating the idea of reform in the fields of *fiqh* and Qur'anic interpretation, as well as extolling the virtues of education. Rashīd Rida followed ʿAbduh's efforts by linking reform with returning to the principles of the Golden Age of Islam. Hasan al-Banna came at the end of this chain of reformist figures when he proposed a holistic vision of Islam and succeeded in incorporating thinking with activism, *daʿwah* with dynamic organisation, and politics with religion.[83]

Although the Muslim Brotherhood movement was a natural extension of former Islamist and nationalist movements, its emergence marked a turning point in the modern history of Islamist activism. The Muslim Brotherhood freed political issues from their narrow elitist framework and took them into the public sphere. Also, by linking thought with activism through the organisation, their ideas spread throughout Egypt where urban and rural dwellers became part of everyday political and religious debates and worked together to tackle these issues under the umbrella of the Muslim Brotherhood. The charisma and influence of al-Banna and the lively activism of members of the Muslim Brotherhood who penetrated various sectors of society enabled the Muslim Brotherhood successfully to in mobilise the Egyptian "street."[84]

In one of his most important letters, addressed to members of the Muslim Brotherhood, al-Banna defined the movement,

> Dear brothers, you are not a welfare organization, nor a political party, nor a local association with strictly limited aims. Rather you are a *new spirit* making its way into the heart of this nation – reviving it with the Qur'an; a *new light* dawning, dispelling the darkness of materialism through the knowledge of Allah; a *resounding voice* rising high – echoing

[80] Muhammad 'Imara. "50 Sanah mundhu Istishhad Hasan al-Banna: al-Mashruʿ al-'Islami li Nahdat al-'Ummah" *Al-Mujtamaʿ* (9 February 1999), 22.

[81] Tariq al-Bishri, *Al-Malamih al-Aammah Lilfikr al-Siasi al-Islami fi al-Tarikh al-Mu 'asir* (Cairo: Dar al-Shuruq. 1996), 16–26.

[82] Al-Banna, "Between Yesterday and Today," 85–102.

[83] Al-Bishri, *Al-Malamih al-Aammah*, 16–26.

[84] Mitchell, *The Society of the Muslim Brothers*, 295.

> the message of the Apostle (PBUH). ... If someone asks you: "To what are you calling?" say: "We are calling you to Islam, which was brought by Muhammad (PBUH): Government is part of it, freedom is a religious obligation." If someone should say to you: "This is politics!" say: "This is Islam, and we do not recognize such divisions."[85]

This definition focused on the comprehensiveness of the Muslim Brotherhood which, in turn, represented Islam as an all-inclusive system covering all aspects of life, an identity to which both the educated and uneducated could relate. Al-Banna avoided miring his audience in unnecessary details, preferring instead to write brief letters and deliver short eloquent speeches to serve the objective of creating a dynamic movement capable of tackling political and social contingencies without recourse to superfluous intellectual disagreements over trivia. The Muslim Brotherhood was marked by a great degree of pragmatism, despite subscribing to what some might describe as an unrealistic notion of the dominance of Islam and its ability to lead the world at a time when Europe was colonising many Arab and Muslim countries. Al-Banna proposed the Muslim Brotherhood as the saviour of the Muslim *umma* [nation] from the state of deterioration and backwardness it was reeling under. In order to reach this goal, he drew up a clear plan that started by creating the real Muslim person, then the Muslim family, the Muslim society, and then the Muslim *umma* that would lead the world.[86]

Because of his international vision of the Muslim Brotherhood, al-Banna's concern with spreading the movement among the people of Egypt was equalled by his interest in disseminating its message in other Arab countries. Thus, the Hajj season was the perfect opportunity to meet people from all over the world, some of whom were greatly influenced by al-Banna's personality and way of thinking. Al-Banna kept in touch and invited some of them to Egypt to get to know his movement better. He also sent some of his representatives to various Arab countries to spread the Muslim Brotherhood's ideas and establish branches of the organisation.

Mustafa al-Siba'i, founder of the Muslim Brotherhood in Syria, has been a student et al.-Azhar University and became involved in Egypt's vibrant political life, including participating in demonstrations against the

---

[85] Al-Banna, "Between Yesterday and Today," 101–102.

[86] Ibid, 85–102.

British. During his studies et al.-Azhar, alSibaᶜi met al-Banna and became a member of the Muslim Brotherhood. On his return to Syria in 1942, al-Sibaᶜi contacted a number of religious scholars, Islamist organisations, and various Syrian figures and succeeded in persuading them to form a single, strong organisation that would be a branch of the Muslim Brotherhood movement in Syria. Al-Sibaᶜi was elected *al-Muraqib al-ᶜAam* [General Observer], as the head of the movement in 1945.

ᶜAbdulatif Abu-Qura from Jordan admired the Muslim Brotherhood's stance on the Palestinian cause and worked to establish a Jordanian branch of the Muslim Brotherhood in 1945, following a series of meetings with al-Banna and other leaders of the Muslim Brotherhood. In Iraq, a number of young men were influenced by the Muslim Brotherhood publications they received from Egypt, as well as by the Egyptian teachers who were members of the Muslim Brotherhood and who had come to Iraq to work. Chief among those was Husain Kamal al-Din who established the Faculty of Engineering in Baghdad, and Muhammad ᶜAbdulhamid Ahmad who taught in Basra's schools. At the same time, Muhammad Mahmud al-Sawwaf left Iraq to study et al.-Azhar where he was introduced to the Muslim Brotherhood. Upon his return to Iraq, he and the famous religious scholar Amjad al-Zahawi founded the Islamic Fraternity Society in 1948. This was a front for the Muslim Brotherhood, due largely to the difficulty of naming their society after the mother organisation in Egypt because of problems they were facing at that time from the Royal family.

In addition to his effort to spread the movement internationally, al-Banna met King ᶜAbdulᶜaziz bin Saᶜud during Hajj in 1936 and invited him to join the Muslim Brotherhood and apply its principles to the newly-founded state. ᶜAbdulᶜaziz tactfully refused, announcing "We are all Muslim brothers," although the Muslim Brotherhood did succeed in entering Saᶜudi Arabia much later. It also took much longer for the Muslim Brotherhood to find its way into the Gulf countries which were quite detached from the Arab world's major cultural and political centres, such as Cairo, Baghdad and Damascus. Kuwait was the first Gulf country to become acquainted with the Muslim Brotherhood ideas, as is discussed later.

Although the Muslim Brotherhood movement spread to a number of Arab countries, it retained its core identity. All branches adopted the Egyptian hierarchical model, though with some modifications to accommodate differences in opinions, circumstances, and security concerns. All branches were united in their adherence to the ideas of Hasan al-Banna which, in addition to his memoirs, were collected in a single volume entitled *Rasail al-Imam al-Shahid Hasan al-Banna* [The Letters of the Martyred Imam Hasan al-Banna]. These ideas shaped the structure and identity of the Muslim Brotherhood and education topped the list of priorities. Al-Banna believed that the first stage of Islamist revival lay in gradual reform, first of the individual, then, as noted, the family, society and the state leading to a Caliphate that could lead the world with its Islamic values.

Despite the clarity with which al-Banna outlined the various stages of shaping the Muslim individual and Muslim family, later stages were less clearly defined and became even less so as talk turned to the desired Caliphate. The Muslim Brotherhood was a great educator but politically somewhat amateurish, possibly because it was easier to deal with issues on an individual basis but not with wider social and political ones. Moreover, al-Banna had very little experience with politics and his assassination at the very young age of 40 contributed to the lack of maturity in some of his ideas. The security crack-down on the Muslim Brotherhood in Egypt, Syria and Iraq paralysed the Movement's intellectual output in terms of developing a social and political model that could offer a more comprehensive approach, particularly as the Muslim Brotherhood's members were often too busy protecting themselves and their movement from persecution.

Moreover, the shift from public work in the first decade of the movement's life and during the life of its founder (whose death and the loss of its intellectual and organisational compass shook the Muslim Brotherhood to the core), to the secret underground activism required to protect the lives of its members, contributed to this lack of comprehensive vision. In addition, following the death of al-Banna the Muslim Brotherhood suffered considerably, due to the absence of a fully-integrated social project and the new leadership's lack of charisma compared with al-Banna. The movement witnessed yet another setback with the rise in the Arab world of the nationalist/secularist parties of Jamal ʿAbdulnasser, Communism and the Baʿath Party. All these factors restricted the Muslim Brotherhood's work to education and training and hampered the political participation which was often at the whim of the leader in any given Arab country.

The Muslim Brotherhood was not the only movement born in response to Western political domination and cultural colonisation following the collapse of the Ottoman Empire. A similar movement,

Jamaat-e-Islami, was founded in India in 1941 by Abul Aʻla Maududi. Maududi began by challenging critics of Islam then moved on to establish a practical project inspired by Islamic values, similar to the Muslim Brotherhood. The idea was born following calls by the Indian National Congress for the establishment of a secular state that would serve to unify Indians from various sects, chiefly Muslims and Hindus. As his writings show, Maududi rejects the notion of a secular state based on nationhood rather than Islam.[87] As far as he was concerned, the interests of a nation state present a conflict with the universality of Islam where Allah is the source of government. The road to such a state is by building the *ummah* then a state. This *ummah* would spread the message of Islam among people. According to Maududi, an ideal would be governed according to the principle of Shura with Islamic terms of reference in what is known as a "Theodemocracy."[88] In addition to the Muslim Brotherhood and the Jamaat-e-Islami, Hizb al-Tahrir was established in 1953 by Taqi-uddin al-Nabhani whose ideas first spread in Palestine and Lebanon before reaching other parts of the world.

According to the Party's official website

Hizb al-Tahrir is a political party whose ideology is Islam. Its objective is to resume the Islamic way of life by establishing an Islamic State that executes the systems of Islam and carries its call to the world. Hizb al-Tahrir has prepared a party culture that includes a host of Islamic rules about life's matters. The party calls for Islam in its quality as an intellectual leadership from which emanates the systems that deals with all man's problems, political, economic, cultural and social among others. Hizb al-Tahrir is a political party that admits to its membership men and women, and calls all people to Islam and to adopt its concepts and systems. It views people according to the viewpoint of Islam no matter how diverse their nationalities and their schools of thought were.[89]

The Party's goals were not different from those of the Muslim Brotherhood and the Jamaat-e-Islami, albeit the methods were different.

---

[87] Charles J. Adams, "*Maududi and the Islamic State*," in John Esposito (ed.) Voices of Resurgent Islam (Oxford: Oxford University Press, 1983), 100–104.

[88] Abul A'la Maududi, *Islamic Law and Constitution* (Lahore: Islamic Publications, 1969).

[89] Hizb al-Tahrir, "Tarʻif," Official Website of Hizb al-Tahrir. (accessed 5 April 2014).

Several Islamic movements and groups—and later offshoots thereof—emerged in the Muslim world, each with its own distinctive methods despite the similarities in goals and objectives. Some groups were established for the sole purpose of spreading the Islamic faith and have no interest in politics. They focused exclusively on *da'wah* and raising pious Muslims. Other movements such as Takfir wal-Hijra [Excommunication and Exodus] believed that modern Muslim societies were closer to Kufr than they were to the true spirit of Islam and as such described them as "ignorant societies." Jihadi offshoots of these groups believed in the use of force to establish a true Islamic state. Some Islamic groups focused on local issues while others were more international in their concerns. Many theories have been proposed to explain the spread of those Islamic movements especially with the Islamic revival of the 1970s and 1980s and the emergence of Jihadi Islam in the 1990s and the beginning of the twenty-first century. While Islamic movements may have initially be born in response to Western political, military and cultural hegemony (sometimes described by Islamic movements as Secular and other times as Christian), Islamic ideologies became increasingly popular following the failure of secular movements (nationalist, Ba'athist, Marxist, etc.).[90] And contrary to what occurred in the case of Christianity, secularism and Westernisation contributed to the rise of Islamic movements.[91] Secularism also failed to win the hearts of people.[92] Many considered the spread of Islamic ideologies a natural occurrence since Islamic values have always been the prominent ones in Muslim societies and any return to Islamic thought is a return to a point of origin prior to the arrival of secularism. Many Islamic leaders had studied in the West and their programmes reflect Western influence on their methods and way of thinking.[93]

[90] John Esposito, *Voices of Resurgent Islam* (Oxford: Oxford University Press, 1983), 11–14.

[91] Ernest Gellner, *Conditions of Liberty: Civil Society and its Rivals* (London: Penguin Books, 1994).

[92] Aziz al-'Azamah, al-Almaniyya min Manthour Mukhtalif, (Bbeiruit: Centre for Arab Unity Studies, 1992), 221–248.

[93] Dale F.Eickelman and James Piscatori, *Muslim Politics* (Princeton, NJ: Princeton University Press, 1996), 28–36.

CONCLUSION

Cultural and intellectual movements in Kuwait, the product of several internal and external factors, gained increasing popularity over the years as calls for reform reflected changing political landscapes across the whole Arab region. Reformists soon found themselves at loggerheads with the Kuwaiti ruling family, those close to them, and with British interests in the region, while the discovery of oil further consolidated the power of the ruling family and led to disarray among the reformists.

The reformist movement was distinguished by unity of its objectives which revolved around the need to spread knowledge and combat illiteracy. The movement called for furthering the values of *shura* and democracy, establishing elected councils (municipal, educational and legislative), and modernising in a manner that did not conflict with Islamic values. Its most distinctive feature was the absence of any ideological conflicts within its ranks. In Lebanon, for example, the secular reformist movement was opposed to the Islamist reformists, despite both being Pan-nationalist in orientation. The difference in Kuwait was that the secular movement—like the European model—limited nationalism to the Arab world whereas the Islamist movement called for both Arabs and Muslims to unite, a view supported by Rashīd Rida.

Calls for reform had a number of clear goals, focused mainly on education in a society with a very high illiteracy rate. Reformists gradually broadened their agenda to emphasise the values of *shura*, democracy, and free elections, and also advocated modernity, such as granting women bigger roles in society, provided this did not conflict with the values of Islam. Their goals were not controversial and gave no cause for disagreement as happened in the case of Greater Syria where secularist and Islamist reformers clashed, with the secularists following the European model and adopting an Arab nationalist agenda while the latter called for an Arab Islamic identity since they considered the two a unified entity. Due to the conservative nature of Kuwaiti society, which was predominately Muslim though with some Christian and Jewish families, Kuwaiti reformers followed an Arab Islamic path.

Several domestic and foreign factors shifted the political and cultural landscape of Kuwait. The discovery of oil changed the economic and demographic structure, especially after large numbers of immigrants seeking work arrived in Kuwait. The broader Arab world was also deeply influenced by the emergence of liberation movements in other parts of the world and Communism found fertile ground in which to flourish in the Middle East, while the Palestinian issue and the establishment of Israel probably had the biggest impact on people's awareness of the need to struggle against colonialism and Western imperialism. All these factors helped shape Arab consciousness in general and by default that of Kuwait in particular. Foreign and domestic factors contributed to the rise of intellectual and cultural trends in Kuwait, where reform was concomitant with dramatic changes in the Arab region but was very much impeded by the ruling family and British interests. Oil discoveries had greatly strengthened the position of the ruling family which rejected most calls for reform.

While these developments were taking place, the Muslim Brotherhood movement emerged in Egypt and was transported to Kuwait where it was well-received because it represented an extension of the Islamic nationalist intellectual trends for which Rashīd Rida had called. Nonetheless, Gulf societies, which were less complex than those of Egypt, Iraq and the Levant, were not used to political and social organisations, and found the notion of an organised movement quite alien, despite the existence of several nationalist and left-wing movements. Kuwait was not a source of culture or of particular political importance; rather, it was on the receiving end of political and cultural trends from the Egyptian, Levantine and Iraqi educated elites who, attracted by the oil boom, had come to work in Kuwait. These circumstances were to bring about many changes, both domestically and regionally, in the wider Arab world.

CHAPTER 3

Organisational Structure of the Movement in Kuwait

INTRODUCTION

The political project of the reformists petered out because of the detrimental influence of the conflict on society following the political confrontation between the Nationalist Bloc and the ruling family. Islamist reformists such as Yusif bin ʿIsa al-Qinaʿi found themselves in a tricky position. On the one hand, al-Qinaʿi was a crucial element in the reformist project that opposed the actions of the ruling family. On the other hand, he rejected the military action taken by the council when it seized Nayef Palace by force.[1] This disagreement between the reformists weakened the movement to reform the political system in Kuwait. However, other social and intellectual reforms, such as cultural clubs and intellectual discussions in *diwaniyya* continued via different channels. In this politically-restricted and intellectually-open environment, the new foreign ideology of the Muslim Brotherhood found its way into Kuwaiti society through the efforts of a young merchant, ʿAbdulʿaziz al-Ali al-Mutawwaʿ, who was a student of Yusif bin Isa al-Qinaʿi.

---

[1] Disagreements between Yusuf bin Isa and the members of the council started when he disagreed with them over the methods of dealing with the ruling family, and these disagreements grew until the two parties finally parted ways after the seizure of Nayif Palace. See al-ʿAdsani, *Mudhakarat*, 75.

A. A. Alkandari, *The Muslim Brotherhood in Kuwait*, Contemporary Gulf Studies, https://doi.org/10.1007/978-981-99-3050-0_3

The Muslim Brotherhood Ideology Enters Kuwait

The Muslim Brotherhood was the first Islamist organisation to be inspired by modern organisational theories and structures such as Marxism, and is the largest Islamist organisation in the world today. It was established in 1928 in Egypt by Hasan al-Banna, and rapidly gained a huge following, estimated at half a million members and fifty branches in Egypt by 1935.[2] The Muslim Brotherhood established *The Muslim Brotherhood* newspaper in 1933, *al-Nathir* newspaper in 1938 and *al-Shihab* newspaper in 1947, along with other newspapers and journals to propagate the ideology of the Muslim Brotherhood.[3] In Egypt, the popularity of the movement threatened not only the government of Mahmoud al-Nuqrashi, but also the interests of Britain, France and the United States, because of its call to free Egypt from British control and eliminate imperialism and foreign presence in the region. In 1949, the Muslim Brotherhood was accused of assassinating al-Nuqrashi, with mourners at the funeral calling for the "head of al-Banna for the head of al-Nuqrashi."[4] Shortly after, also in 1949, al-Banna was assassinated. He left behind the largest Islamist movement in Egypt, which continued to spread its message to other Arab countries: to Djibouti in 1932, Syria in 1939, Transjordan in 1943, Sudan in 1946 and also Kuwait in 1952.

In 1941, ʿAbdulʿaziz al-Mutawwaʿ[5] met Muhammad ʿAbdulhamid Ahmad, a member of the Muslim Brotherhood from Egypt, in Basra, where he was teaching.[6] This meeting was followed by others between

---

[2] Iman al-Dabbagh, "Jamʿiyyat al-Ukhwah al-Islamiyya fi Iraq: Dirasah 'An Nash'at Harakat al-Ikhwan al-Muslimin fi al-Iraq 1949–1954" (MA Thesis, University of Mousil, 2010), 34–36.

[3] Ibid.

[4] Ibid.

[5] ʿAbdulʿaziz al-Ali al-Mutawwaʿ [1910–1996] descends from the famous family of al-Qinaʾi that was known in business in Kuwait and Iraq. His father, Ali Abdulwahab al-Mutawwaʿ, was also a famous merchant in Kuwait and a religious man as well. ʿAbdulʿazizal-Mutawwaʿ studied at al-Mubarakiyya and was influenced by Shaikh Yusuf bin Isa al-Qinaʾi.

[6] Muhammadʿabdulhamid Ahmad [1911–1992] was an Egyptian teacher and a member of the Founding Body of the Muslim Brotherhood. In 1944, Ahmad was sent by the Egyptian Ministry of Education to Iraq as the Iraqi Education Ministry had requested a number of teachers from Egypt to teach in Iraq. When Hasan al-Banna learned

the two men and eventually led to al-Mutawwaᶜ joining the Muslim Brotherhood. Ahmad sent an introductory letter to Hasan al-Banna about al-Mutawwaᶜ and asked for al-Mutawwaᶜ to be accepted as a member in the movement.[7] In 1941, al-Mutawwaᶜ formally became a member of the Muslim Brotherhood and spent the month of Ramadan visiting Egypt where he met al-Banna and members of the movement for the first time in a spiritual and intellectual environment. Al-Mutawwaᶜs experience of the Muslim Brotherhood in its heyday under the leadership of al-Banna himself inspired and motivated him to carry this ideology back to Kuwait.[8] While they were in Mecca for the Hajj in 1946, al-Banna consented to the establishment of a Muslim Brotherhood branch in Kuwait.[9]

When they returned to Kuwait, ᶜAbdulᶜaziz al-Mutawwaᶜ and his brother Abdullah started to work on building a new network among their friends and people they knew. They also invited ᶜAbdulᶜaziz Jalal, a teacher and a member of the Muslim Brotherhood in Egypt, to visit Kuwait to help them set up the new branch. Additionally, a few members of the Palestinian Muslim Brotherhood (Muhammad al-Najjar, Khalil al-Wazir and Khalid al-Hasan) arrived in Kuwait in the aftermath of the Israeli occupation of Palestine in 1948 and offered their help in establishing the new branch of the Muslim Brotherhood in Kuwait.[10]

The period between 1946 and 1952 witnessed the early beginnings of the Muslim Brotherhood in Kuwait led by a small group along the lines of its Egyptian counterpart. The activities of the al-Mutawwaᶜ brothers

---

about this, he encouraged Ahmad to go to Iraq to help Muhammad al-Sawwaf establish a branch of the Muslim Brotherhood in Iraq. While he was teaching in al-Maytam High School and Sina'at Baghdad School in Baghdad, Ahmad worked on forming the Muslim Brotherhood in different parts of Iraq such as Mosul and Basra. See 'Abduh Dusugi, "Muhammadᶜabdulhamid Ahmad... 'Aamid Tullab al-Ikhwan al-Muslimeen." *Wikipedia of the Muslim Brotherhood*. Last modified 2011 (accessed 21 August 2013). www.ikhwanwiki.com/index.php?title=محمد_عبد_الحميد_أحمد.

[7] Abdulwahid Aman (founder of the Muslim Brotherhood Organisation in 1968), interview by Ali alKandari, Turkey, 21 July 2010.

[8] Ibid.

[9] When he met al-Banna in Mecca, ᶜAbdulᶜaziz was with his younger brother Abdullah al-Mutawwaᶜ.

[10] Sulaiman Al-Hamad (Palestinian member of al-Irshad), interview by Ali al-Kandari, Kuwait. 5 October 2010.

in Kuwait paved the way for the new ideas of the Muslim Brotherhood to spread locally. In late 1949 and early 1950, the small informal nucleus of the Muslim Brotherhood group in Kuwait comprised a few Kuwaitis from notable families, such as Abdullah Budai and his brother Muhammad who, with Muhammad al-ʿAdsani, Abdullah al-Kulaib and others, decided to go public by forming *Jamʿiyyatal-Irshadal-Islami* [the Islamic Guidance Society] in 1952.

THE BEGINNINGS OF THE MUSLIM BROTHERHOOD, *JAMʿIYYAT AL-IRSHAD AL-ISLAMI* IN 1952

The 1940s witnessed the modest beginnings of the Muslim Brotherhood in Kuwait during which time the movement was launched by a handful of people and disseminated through the distribution of Islamic books and pamphlets. This small group soon took its activities to a new level. In 1952, according to Abdullah al-Mutawwaʿ, the members held several meetings in the homes of Abdullah al-Kulaib and ʿAbdulʿaziz al-Mutawwaʿ and decided to establish *Jamʿiyyat al-Irshad al-Islami*.[11] Al-Irshad, as its members called the society, was the formal pseudonym for the Muslim Brotherhood in Kuwait, which resembled the society in Iraq that was known as *Jamʿiyyat al-Ukhuwwah al-Islamiyyah* [the Islamic Fraternity Society]. The oppressive political atmosphere at the time made it extremely risky to name it "the Muslim Brotherhood" officially, probably also because of the negative association of the name with Kuwait's old enemies, the Saʿudi *Al-Ikhwan* (Brotherhood).[12] Abdullah al-Mutawwaʿ recalls how al-Irshad was started,

---

[11] ʿAbdullah al-Mutawwaʿ (founder and President of Jamʿiyyat al-Islah), interview by Rajab Damanhuri, "ʿAbdullah al-Mutawwaʿ in his Memoirs," *Al-Harakah*, 3 September 2006, 5.

[12] Al-Ikhwan in Saʿudi Arabia (1911–1930) was a Bedouin Wahhabi militia which, as a military force, helped ʿAbdulʿaziz Ibn Saʿud to control the Arabian Peninsula during the second and third decades of the twentieth century. Ikhwan was made up of Bedouin tribes, mainly Mutair and Ajman. Ikhwan rebelled against Ibn Saʿud because of his religious laxity when he forbade them to raid into neighbouring states specially Iraq to bring them under their control. After controlling most of the Peninsula, Ibn Saʿud found himself in conflict with the Ikhwan and cracked them down in the Battle of Siblah in 1930. See Hafiz Wahbah, *Jazirat al-Arab fi al-Qarn al-ʿIshrin* (No Publisher: no date), 285–301.

the background of the establishment of al-Irshad can be traced to the vibrant enthusiasm of a number of Muslim youth in creating an Islamist movement similar to other Islamist movements in Egypt, Syria, and Iraq. That explains the emergence of an Islamist coalition in the form of Jamʿiyyat al-Irshad al-Islami.[13]

The founders finalised formal procedures and paperwork for the new Society which emerged during Ramadan 1371 (May 1952) to represent Islamist opinion, specifically that of the Muslim Brotherhood. In its first publication, al-Irshad revealed that,

> The goal of our society is to provide an education that is compatible with our religion and great history, and to support true *aqidah* and pure *tawhid* with good deeds. Also, it aims to raise good Muslims and connect them with other Muslim brothers ... and to protect the *ummah* from moral deviance by educating a generation of solid believers who can build a strong society, and present Islam as an esteemed faith and global system that can address the problems of life and create the ideal society.[14]

In the introduction to *Al-Barnamaj al-Tawjihi* [The Guiding Programme], al-Irshad declared that "this society is a religious one and does not interfere in politics as a group; its goal is wise preaching and guidance based on the values of tolerance."[15] The goals and methodology of al-Irshad as al-Barnamaj al-Tawjihi can be summarised as: apolitical, global, cultural and intellectual, and in touch with local issues with a modified methodology, goals, and curriculum borrowed from the mother organisation of the Muslim Brotherhood in Egypt.

Al-Barnamaj al-Tawjihi also specified the conditions of the membership and the penalties incurred by breaching the membership rules, stating that "members must be Muslim and have good manners, and if a member breaches the rules, he will jeopardize the reputation of the society; the board of directors will advise, warn, or dismiss a member in violation of

---

[13] Damanhuri, "ʿAbdullah Al-Mutawwaʿ in his Memoirs."

[14] Al-Barnamaj al-Tawjihi, 2–6.

[15] Ibid.

the rules."[16] In his book *Ayyam al-Kuwait* [Days of Kuwait], Ahmad al-Sharabasi[17] examines the goals, internal rules, and activities of al-Irshad and summarises the society in a few words,

> Anyone who reads the by-laws of the society [al-Irshad] will discover the diversity of methods and goals, and this is what characterized modern Islamist movements. Preachers in modern Islamist movements believe that Islam is a religion and a state, worship and leadership, Qur'an and sword, mosque and school, temple and barrack, and it is the religion of economics, sociology, education, culture, and sports. Therefore, programs created by and for the movement aim to embody this comprehensive concept of Islam.[18]

A board of directors was established consisting of Shaikh Yusif bin Isa (honorary president), ʿAbdulʿaziz al-Mutawwaʿ (vice president and general observer) where the name refers to the head of the society and the movement and was taken directly from the mother organisation of the Muslim Brotherhood in Egypt,[19] Muhammad al-ʿAdsani[20] (secretary),

---

[16] Ibid.

[17] Ahmad al-Sharabasi [1918–1980] was an Egyptian religious scholar who graduated from al-Azhar in 1945 and worked as a teacher for a long time. His relationship started when he met a Kuwaiti student in Egypt, ʿAbdulʿaziz Hussein, who established *al-Biʿthah* journal in 1946, for which al-Sharabasi wrote regularly until 1954. Al-Sharabasi wrote his book *Ayyam al-Kuwait* [Days of Kuwait] after visiting Kuwait in 1951 where he met Kuwaiti politicians, intellectuals, and other figures and participated in many activities of different clubs and society including al-Irshad. See Ahmad al-Sharabasi, *Ayyam al-Kuwait* (Cairo: Dar alKitāb al-Arabi, 1953).

[18] Ibid., 308–309.

[19] Ali al-Zumai, "The Intellectual and Historical Development," 83.

[20] Muhammad Yusuf al-ʿAdsani [1925–...] is from from the famous al-ʿAdsani family that inhabited Kuwait from the mid-eighteenth century and originated from al-Hasa, in eastern Arabia. In the twentieth century, many members of this family were involved in politics in opposition to the ruling family, including Sulaiman alʿAdsani (member of the Legislative Council 1938), Khalid al-ʿAdsani (member of Legislative Council 1938 and a member of al-Kutlah al-Wataniyya), and the father of Muhammad, Yusuf al-ʿAdsani (who was also a member of Legislative Council 1938). Muhammad himself was elected to Parliament in 1967 but refused the post, returning later to be elected as the President of the Parliament in 1981. Muhammad and other members of the al-ʿAdsani family were known for being opposed to the ruling family, especially in 1938 and 1939, and this caused an armed conflict between the opposition and the government led to some of them, such as Sulaiman al-ʿAdsani, having to escape. See Michael Herb, *Kuwait Politics*

and the rest, like Yusif al-Nisif,[21] held lower positions such as head of the youth branch, while others were ordinary members of society.[22] There were also members from other Arab countries who had to work in Kuwait or came to help build up al-Irshad. For instance, Muhammad Salīm was sent by the Muslim Brotherhood in Egypt to help with promoting the movement and the society it aspired to create. According to al-Nisif, Salīm was the most influential person in al-Irshad because of his outstanding abilities in administration and organisational development as well as his propagation of the Muslim Brotherhood's ideas through Friday sermons.[23]

There were also Palestinian members who had moved from Palestine to Kuwait when the conflict with the Zionist movement escalated. The Palestinians were known for being well educated in comparison with Kuwaitis, which enabled them to work in education and in technical fields. The Palestinian members of al-Irshad used to work in the mornings, and dedicate their afternoons to the society. The society took the Muslim Brotherhood to a higher level in Kuwait and al-Irshad, as their front line, opened the door for them to access different sectors in society such as the ruling family, merchants and workers, and to move freely and officially to spread their ideas, especially among the youth who became the bedrock of the society.

Organisational Activities

When ʿAbdulʿaziz al-Mutawwaʿ and Hasan al-Banna met in Mecca in 1946, they agreed to launch a branch of the Muslim Brotherhood in Kuwait. After that, al-Mutawwaʿ became a member of the Maktab al-Irshad [the Guiding Office—similar to a Board of Directors] of the

---

Database, "Muhammad alʿAdsani" (accessed 21 August 2013). http://www2.gsu.edu/~polmfh/database/DataPage1016.htm.

[21] Yusuf al-Nisif [1930–...] is from the notable family of al-Nisif that belongs to what is known in Kuwait as the traditional merchant class. Yusuf al-Nisif joined al-Irshad in 1953 as a student at Shuaikh High School until its closure in 1958–1959. Because of his leadership skills, in addition to the status of his family, al-Nisif played an important role at the school by mobilising students. When al-Nisif left for England for higher education he left al-Irshad and broke off his relationship with the Muslim Brotherhood.

[22] Most of them were from mercantile and middle-class families.

[23] YusifAl-Nisif (member of al-Irshad), interview by Ali al-Kandari, Kuwait, 10 December 2010.

mother organisation in Egypt, and the founding body of the Muslim Brotherhood, and attended the meetings of these leading bodies of the movement in Egypt along with Muslim Brotherhood leaders from other countries such as Mustafa al-Siba'i (Syria), Muhammad al-Sawwaf (Iraq), Ali Jaballah (Sudan), Muhammad ᶜAbdulrahman Khalifah(Jordan), and others from Palestine, Lebanon and Djibouti.[24] Between 1946 and 1952, al-Mutawwaᶜ worked on building the new branch of the Muslim Brotherhood, helped by members of the movement from other countries (such as Muhammad Salīm from Egypt). When ᶜAbdulᶜaziz al-Mutawwaᶜ had succeeded in establishing the first group in Kuwait's Muslim Brotherhood, he undertook the founding of al-Irshad.

Initially the organisation of the Muslim Brotherhood in Kuwait was fairly simple, although as membership numbers increased, the organisation developed structurally, creating a hierarchal and rather more complex organisation. As in Egypt, the structure of the Muslim Brotherhood in Kuwait was built on a system of *usar* "cells," in which every *usrah* consisted of five to eight members, including the *usrah*'s leader. The group's activities were aimed largely at the public, with a few special preparatory programmes meetings confined to male, largely adolescent Muslim Brotherhood members only.

Organisational Structure of the First Organisation

In terms of organisational structure, the Muslim Brotherhood divided Kuwait City into the three districts in which most Kuwaitis lived: Mirqab, Qiblah, and Sharq.[25] Thus, there was less focus on those who lived outside the walls of Kuwait City in areas such as al-Jahra' or Abu Hulaifah. The movement used the institution of al-Irshad to spread its ideas throughout society and to recruit people to its mission by creating two sections specifically for this purpose: a men's section and a students' section. The men's section was made up of the older members of the Muslim Brotherhood such as Muhammadal-ᶜAdsani, Muhammad and

---

[24] ᶜAbdullah al-ᶜAqil, *Min Aᶜalam al-Harakah al-Islamiyyah al-Muᶜasirah* (Kuwait: al-Manar, 2001), 375–380.

[25] These areas had a high density of Kuwaiti population before the urban reorganisation of Kuwait which moved people from the older areas to the newly built areas outside the old wall of Kuwait City. See Allan Hill, "Aspects of the Urban Development of Kuwait" (PhD diss., Durham University, 1969).

Abdullah Budai and Rashid al-Duaij. Members of the men's section ran al-Irshad as well as general activities within Kuwaiti society. Members of the students' section included Ahmad al-Duaij, Isa al-Mishari, Abdullatif al-Ruwaishid, Faisal al-Masʿud and Yusif al-Nisif, as well as a few Arab teachers.

The students' section was most active among students at Shuwaikh High School.[26] According to Faisal al-Saniʿ,[27] the activities of the Muslim Brotherhood were quite prominent at Shuwaikh High School which had become the centre of political and ideological activities since the disso-lution of the Legislative Parliament in 1938. Al-Saniʿ provides a good description of the political and ideological activities at Shuwaikh High School:

> There were many political groups at the high school such as Arab Nationalists, Ba'athists, Communists, Hizb al-Tahrir, however, the Muslim Brotherhood had the best organization and mobilization which increased its influence among students. Both students and some Arab teachers worked on spreading the Muslim Brotherhood's ideology and mobilizing students into their organization. The structure of the organization was based on what they called *usar* system which was a key characteristic, in addition to their enthusiasm, of the success of their efforts to rally students more than Arab Nationalists, Ba'athists, Communists, and other groups.[28]

According to Yusif al-Nisif, the open environment at Shuwaikh High School apparently supported the Muslim Brotherhood's activism by enabling its members to spread their ideologies and move freely and without restriction among the students. The main activities that the Muslim Brotherhood students used to attract their colleagues intellec-tually were sport and Scouts. The students' section of al-Irshad was the best haven for youth because of the new, interesting and entertaining activities for students, along with religious activities that made parents feel more confident about the Muslim Brotherhood and al-Irshad. In the small society of Kuwait, around 300 students used to attend al-Irshad's

---

[26] It was the first and the only high school in Kuwait at that time. See ʿAbdullah al-Nuri, *Qisat al-Taʿlim fi al-Kuwait fi Nisf Qarn* (Kuwait: That al-Salasil, no date).

[27] Al-Sani' was a student at Shuwaikh High School. See Falah Al-Mdairis, "Marhalat Ta'sis al-Ikhwan al-Muslimeen wa Buruzha fi al-Kuwait," *Al-Qabas Newspaper*, 4 June 2006.

[28] Ibid.

programmes which, given the small size of Kuwaiti society at that time, represented a sizeable number.[29]

There were several reasons for the rapid success of al-Irshad. First, the conservative nature of Kuwaiti society offered fertile ground for Islamic ideology to flourish. Ordinary people welcomed al-Irshad by participating in its different activities and allowing their sons to be part of this new movement. Secondly, as Aman asserts, al-Irshad was part of the regional Islamist revival that had started with Muhammad Rashīd Rida and continued with the Muslim Brotherhood in Egypt, Iraq and Syria. In addition, Islamist revival had had an early influence on Kuwaiti intellectuals and religious scholars such as Yusif bin Isa al-Qinaʿi, Abdullah Khalaf al-Duhaiyyan and ʿAbdulʿaziz al-Rushaid, as well as on visiting Arab scholars like Muhammad al-Shanqiti and later Ahamad al-Sharabasi. Islamist revival dominated the intellectual discourse in Kuwait which prepared the environment for an Islamist movement.

Thirdly, Al-Irshad did not present any threat to the regime of al-Sabah ruling family. On the contrary, the path that Yusif bin Isa al-Qinaʿi followed by focusing on the social more than on the political domain buttressed the ruling family's position, and as a result, they welcomed the new Islamic society of al-Irshad, knowing that Yusif bin Isa al-Qinaʿi was its honorary president. Fourth, the experience of Muslim Brotherhood members from more sophisticated Arab countries played a crucial role in creating and running the society professionally, which impressed the less-sophisticated society of Kuwait. Although there were many ideological groups in the society, they did not embark on direct confrontation, which gave every group space to work peacefully among the general population and students in particular. This peaceful environment encouraged al-Irshad to put all its energies into spreading its ideology among people and intermingling with them. Al-Irshad was the first society of its kind in Kuwait because of its well-organised and various activities, which appealed to the various sectors of society.[30]

---

[29] Al-Nisif, interview.

[30] Al-Nisif, interview.

The Decline

This dynamic activity on the part of al-Irshad did not last long. At the end of 1953, only two years after its establishment, the first spark of conflict was ignited among the founders and was transmitted to the members. This conflict split al-Irshad into two groups: one led by ᶜAbdulᶜaziz Salem (whose real name was Najib Juwaifil)[31] and Muhammad alᶜAdsani, and the other by Muhammad Salīm and ᶜAbdulᶜaziz al-Mutawwaᶜ. According to Yusif al-Rifaᶜi, the conflict started when Juwaifil's militant background and al-ᶜAdsani's family history of opposition to the government clashed with the quietist approach of Salīm and al-Mutawwaᶜs towards the ruling family.

This disagreement escalated when two members of the ruling family, Abdullah al-Jabir al-Subah (the brother of the former Emir at that time and the head of the Education Administration) and Fahad al-Salem al-Subah (the brother of the current Emir at that time) asked to become honorary members of al-Irshad. The request was welcomed by al-Mutawwaᶜ and Salīm; however, on the basis of al-Banna's teachings that the movement should stay away from the control of notables and any existing political bodies, al-ᶜAdsani and Juwaifil were less positive and disliked the idea of any links with the ruling family.[32] Juwaifil also attracted a sizeable group of young members to al-Irshad, and, away from

---

[31] Najib Juwaifil (...–1987) was an Egyptian member of the Muslim Brotherhood and a member of the secret apparatus. Juwaifil participated in the 1948 war against Israel with the military wing of the Muslim Brotherhood. During the conflict between the head of the Muslim Brotherhood, Hasan al-Hudhaibi and the secret apparatus, Juwaifil supported the leader of the secret apparatus ᶜAbdulrahman al-Sindi against alHudhaibi. However, when Nasser attacked and pursued the Muslim Brotherhood leaders, Juwaifil escaped from Egypt, moving from one country to another, including Syria, Jordan, Algeria, Sudan and Kuwait, causing problems among the local Muslim Brotherhood branches in every country he visited. Many Muslim Brotherhood leaders, such as Mustafa al-Sibaʿi (the General Observer of the Muslim Brotherhood in Syria) and Ahmad Raʾif (a Muslim Brotherhood historian), link Juwaifil to the Egyptian *Mukhabarat* and to Nasser personally. Juwaifil lived away from his home until his death. When his wife died in 2005, *Al-Ahram* the pro-government newspaper, announcing her death, wrote an obituary describing her as the wife of the Minister Plenipotentiary, Najib Juwaifil! See 'Abduh Dusugi, "Muhammad Najib Juwaifil: al-Lughz al-Muthir," *Wikipedia of the Muslim Brotherhood*. Last modified 2011 (accessed 22 August 2013). www.ikhwanwiki.com/index.php?title=نجيب_جويفل. See also al-Nisif, interview.

[32] Al-Banna, *Al-Rasa'il*, 113.

the eyes of al-Mutawwaᶜ, created a special unit similar to the secret apparatus of the mother organisation in Egypt, which created a crisis of trust between the two leaders.[33] Juwaifil and al-ᶜAdsani organised several clandestine activities with this group and designed a militant jihadi curriculum that was more radical than Muhammad Salīm's programme. However, the activities of this group never extended past the training camp, due probably to the hasty departure of Juwaifil from Kuwait in mid-1955.[34]

The other issue that escalated the conflict was Jamal Abdulnasser's attack on the Muslim Brotherhood in Egypt, after which ᶜAbdulᶜaziz al-Mutawwaᶜ remained silent while alᶜAdsani insisted on a public display of opposition against Nasser. Ahmad al-Ruwaishid states that al-ᶜAdsani accused al-Mutawwaᶜ of refraining from voicing any opposition in order to protect his business interests in Egypt.[35] Al-Mutawwaᶜ responded by stressing the importance of respecting Egypt's domestic affairs and avoiding transferring the conflict between Nasser and the Muslim Brotherhood to Kuwait since it would negatively affect the movement in Kuwait.[36] Another reason of this conflict as al-Ruwaishid asserts is the refusal by al-ᶜAdsani of centralising the leadership and management of al-Irshad in the hands of al-Mutawwa', demanding a more democratic structure,[37] and criticised the long absence of al-Mutawwaᶜ whose business travels had caused al-Irshad's progress in Kuwait to slow down and had affected the organisation's ability to make important decisions.

As a result of this disagreement, al-Irshad split into two camps, each of which worked separately from the other, and although al-Irshad continued with business as usual, many members started to leave the society because of the tense environment. Troubles escalated

---

[33] Yusifal-Rifaᶜi (member of al-Irshad), interview by Ali al-Kandari, Kuwait, 8 August 2010.

[34] There was an attempt to destroy the shop of a Kuwaiti merchant who had dealings with Jewish merchants, but for unknown reasons, the operation was cancelled. Yusif al-Rifaᶜi, interview.

[35] Initially ᶜAbdulᶜaziz al-Mutawwaᶜ established his business in Kuwait but then moved it to Basra. However, because of troubles while he was in Basra, he was forced to move all of his business to Egypt. At the time of Nasser's attack on Muslim Brotherhood, more than half of al-Mutawwaᶜs wealth was in Egypt. Ahmad al-Mutawwaᶜ (son of ᶜAbdulᶜazizal-Mutawwaᶜ), interview by Ali al-Kandari, Kuwait, 25 August 2010.

[36] Ibid.

[37] Ahmad al-Ruwaishid (member of al-Irshad), interview by Ali al-Kandari, Kuwait, 3 August 2010.

when Muhammad Salīm left Kuwait because of the conflict, and when ᶜAbdulᶜaziz al-Mutawwaᶜ decided to resign from his position as the General Observer of al-Irshad. In a letter that was published in *Al-Biᶜtha* journal on 1 October 1953 he wrote,

> In the Name of God, the Most Graceful and the Most Merciful. To the children of my Nation and to the members of Jamᶜiyyat al-Irshad al-Islami. Dear Brothers: you have honoured me with your trust and overwhelmed me with your favour by choosing me as a member of the Municipal Council and as the General Observer of Jamᶜiyyat al-Irshad. Therefore, I vowed to God and promised you to do well and do my best and to live for my country and in my country so my primary residence would be in Kuwait.
>
> However, my intent to serve Kuwait more broadly in Egypt and other Arab countries has made residence in Kuwait difficult. Setting up a business office in Cairo and the growing business in Arab countries has been a source of great embarrassment in my relationship with my brothers, colleagues, and supervisors.
>
> Therefore, I hope that my brothers will forgive me and accept my refusal of re-election [as a General Observer] and would like to thank them for their noble feelings and generous sentiments.
>
> Every charitable activity for the sake of the nation is considered holy worship, and every institution that champions the cause of national achievement is a mosque that prayers should be held in. If I cannot work in the front rows, I will work in the back rows, or any place where I can work and fulfil my duty toward my nation. I will work in the back lines believing that my brothers who are working in the front are more capable than me in taking responsibility, and residing in Kuwait.
>
> I would like to thank all of you again for your precious trust, and I vow to God to fight with every reformist who seeks the best for our small country, Kuwait, and for the greater Arab nation. May God lead you to the best of our nation's future.
>
> (ᶜAbdulᶜaziz al-Ali al-Mutawwaᶜ)[38]

As his son Ahmad mentions, in an attempt to keep the organisation united, ᶜAbdulᶜaziz al-Mutawwaᶜ blamed the problems of al-Irshad on his absence, without mentioning the other accusations. A number of his followers refused to accept his resignation, and in a signed petition in

---

[38] ᶜAbdulᶜaziz al-Mutawwaᶜ, "Ila Abna' Watani," *al-Biᶜtha Journal* (Kuwait: Center for Research and Studies on Kuwait, October 1953), 514.

which they elaborated on his excellent leadership abilities and faithfulness to the organisation requested him to withdraw it.[39] However, all attempts to stop him from resigning from al-Irshad failed, despite efforts from such Muslim Brotherhood figures as Mustafa al-Siba'i (General Observer of the Muslim Brotherhood in Syria), Muhammad Mahmoud al-Sawwaf (General Observer of the Muslim Brotherhood in Iraq), and Kamil al-Sharif (a leading figure of the Muslim Brotherhood in Jordan).[40]

After al-Mutawwa's resignation, the Board of Directors met to elect a new General Observer from the two candidates: Muhammad al-'Adsani and 'Abdulrazzaq al-Saleh who was close to 'Abdul'aziz al-Mutawwa'. The Board duly elected al-Saleh as the second General Observer of al-Irshad in the hope that he would rise to the challenges of the struggling society. Al-'Adsani remained in his position for some time in order to focus on his youth group before leaving al-Irshad. Inevitably this group did not survive since many of its members were high school students and had to leave Kuwait to study abroad, while Juwaifil's sudden departure had left al-'Adsani without any support.

Meanwhile, in the aftermath of al-Manshiyya incident, Nasser started to attack the Muslim Brotherhood in Egypt and abroad, accusing them of being opportunistic and violent.[41] This animosity spread from Egypt to other parts of the Arab world, including Kuwait, since Nasser's voice carried significant weight throughout the region. This obsession with Nasser in the Arab world and his regime's strong media campaigns negatively changed the image of the Muslim Brotherhood in Kuwait. Al-Nisif describes the beginnings of this change, noting that when al-Irshad members dealt with ordinary people in the street, they used to say quite bluntly that "we know that you [the Muslim Brotherhood] are good, but your problems with Nasser have changed everything... if there is a prophet after Muhammad that would be Nasser."[42] While the presence and the popularity of the Muslim Brotherhood were declining, Nationalists, Communists and other non-Islamist groups were flourishing.

---

[39] A copy of the letter is in possession of Ahmad 'Abdul'aziz al-Mutawwa'. See Appendix A.

[40] Ahmad 'Abdul'aziz al-Mutawwa', interview.

[41] Dusugi, "Muhammad Najib Juwaifil."

[42] Al-Nisif, interview.

Before the conflict started between Nasser and the Muslim Brotherhood, reformists in the Arab world had not distinguished between Islam, reformism, and modernity in the way that Rashīd Rida did.[43] Among Syrian and Lebanese reformists, where the Christian influence was important, there were huge disagreements on many issues concerning the shape and the identity of the future state and the role of Christians, although this disagreement existed only among Syrian and Lebanese reformists because most of the people and reformists in the rest of the Arab world were Muslims. Therefore, until the confrontation between Nasser, who imported communist ideology, and the Muslim Brotherhood with their Islamist-based ideology, Rida's Islamic model had dominated reformist and nationalist discourse in Egypt and the rest of the Arab countries, except for Syria and Lebanon. Kuwait was not far away from this ideological change, with the Nationalists renouncing Islamic ideology and becoming more secular as they moved more towards leftist and nationalist ideologies where they began to flourish. All the secular groups had a part in attacking the Muslim Brotherhood and al-Irshad in Kuwait, and made this part of their discourse on the fight against opportunism, backwardness and darkness.

While this severe attack on al-Irshad did not altogether end its activities, attendance at lectures and general support gradually diminished. *Al-Irshad* journal was published less regularly and became totally divorced from local concerns due to a shortage of Kuwaiti writers and particularly to the effects of internal conflict. The magazine was eventually transformed from a publication that represented al-Irshad to one that stood for a new school which was established by al-Irshad to continue the work of the Society for Eliminating Illiteracy and was then expanded to cover all levels of education: elementary, middle and high school.

This school was established in 1958 by ʿAbdulwahid Aman[44] who had moved from Basra to Kuwait in 1957. Al-Irshad school was the only successful project during the period of al-Irshad's decline (1954–1959). With numbers increasing to 1,000 students, Aman, the manager, was encouraged to move to a bigger building donated by the government, and Jasim al-Marzuq, the Minister of Education, agreed to the

---

[43] Albert Hourani, *A History of the Arab People* (Cambridge: Belknap Press of Harvard University Press, 2002).

[44] Aman is discussed later in more detail.

al-Irshad students enrolling in public schools.[45] Al-Irshad's student group continued to operate, especially in Shuwaikh High School. For instance, the school decided in 1957 to divide the students into groups of 100–150 who would elect the leaders of each group; five of al-Irshad members were elected as leaders of five groups.[46] However, when the leaders of al-Irshad's student group graduated, such activities ceased, and with them leaving Shuwaikh High School the presence of the Muslim Brotherhood in such schools diminished.

Politically, al-Irshad became dormant except for a few activities organised by other groups in Kuwait, such as the events held in support of the Algerian Revolution and of Egypt during the Suez Crisis in 1956 that were arranged by the nationalist coalition of Kuwaiti Clubs. Al-Irshad also participated in an event held in February 1959 by the Nationalist Cultural Club to celebrate the unity between Egypt and Syria, although the event took a surprising turn when Jasim al-Qatami, a prominent Nationalist leader, harshly criticised the tribal system of government in Kuwait in front of important members of the ruling family, including Abdullah al-Jabir. As a result, the government decided to close down all clubs in Kuwait, including al-Irshad. According to Hasan al-Madhun, al-Irshad re-opened shortly after due to the good relationship with the ruling family; however, it was not recognised by the public or by its members most of whom failed to return after the closure. Realising that the environment was too hostile for a reopening, the members themselves closed al-Irshad again, effectively putting an end to this institution that had enjoyed a brief but influential impact.[47]

THE DISPERSAL OF THE MUSLIM BROTHERHOOD

The period from the mid-1950s to the Six-Day War in 1967 was dominated by nationalist ideologies, especially the secularist branches of nationalism. The Islamist movement was quite fragmented and was further weakened by the withdrawal of its historic leaders like ʿAbdulʿaziz al-Mutawwaʿ and Muhammad al-ʿAdsani, as well as non-Kuwaiti figures

---

[45] Aman, interview.

[46] The members who became leaders of groups included ʿAbdullatif al-Ruwaishid, Salim Turki, Yusif al-Nisif, and ʿIsa al-Mishari. Al-Nisif, interview.

[47] Al-Madhun, interview.

such as Muhammad Salīm and Najib Juwaifil; this resulted in the absence of any truly intellectual and organisational leadership for the Muslim Brotherhood. Many Muslim Brotherhood members had joined the Nationalist movement or had simply been side tracked by life's concerns. Given the difficult circumstances faced by the Muslim Brotherhood, such as the conflict with the Nationalists, internal divisions within the Muslim Brotherhood and the decision to close down al-Irshad, the Muslim Brotherhood found itself struggling through some very difficult times between the mid-1950s and 1960s.

However, several Kuwaiti, Palestinian and Egyptian members remained in touch on a personal rather than an organisational level. Kuwaitis would gather at the *diwaniyya* of Muhammad Budai, and would meet non-Kuwaitis at the *diwaniyya* of Abdullah al-ʿAqil who had come from Zubair. Such gatherings usually included former members of the al-Irshad as well as Islamists who sought intellectual refuge from the rising tide of Arab Nationalism and Leftist ideologies. Islam and spiritual issues were debated, and Islamist figures from abroad were often hosted.

The activities of the *diwaniyya* of the Budai brothers in practice became a gathering of former members of al-Irshad such as Muhammad and Abdullah Budai, Salim Turki and Humud al-Rumi, in addition to Yusif al-Nisif who was entrusted with the task of selecting books to be read by the group. Al-ʿAqil's *diwaniyya* focused on issues related to the Muslim Brotherhood in other places like Iraq, Egypt and the Levant. Several other Arab Muslim Brotherhood gatherings, such as those of the Palestinians and the Egyptians, were quite large. Since the security fears of the Egyptian led them to isolate themselves, especially as Nasser had made a point of chasing them down all over the world, they had very little contact with members of the Muslim Brotherhood from other countries. Such gatherings kept the Islamist trends alive in Kuwait,[48] and also formed the birthplace of al-Manar library, *Jamʿiyyat al-Islah al-Ijtimaʿi* [the Social Reform Society] and the calls for participating in parliamentary elections and other activities that preceded the rebirth of the Muslim Brotherhood organisation in 1968.

---

[48] Al-Zumai, "Intellectual and Historical Development," 172–173.

THE ARRIVAL OF ʿABDULWAHID AMAN TO KUWAIT IN 1957 AND ATTEMPTS TO REVIVE THE ISLAMIST MOVEMENT

The Iraqi President ʿAbdulkarim Qasim, who was allied with the Communists in the early years of his presidency let the Communists loose against his and their opponents, especially the Nationalists and the Muslim Brotherhood. A group of young Communists in Basra attacked the two main Muslim Brotherhood institutions, Jamʿiyyat al-Islah al-Ijtimaʿi and al-Manar Islamic bookshop, but were repelled by members of the Muslim Brotherhood. However, news that the Communists were planning to eliminate young leaders of the Muslim Brotherhood in Zubair, namely Abdullah al-ʿAqil, ʿUmar al-Dayel and ʿAbdulʿaziz al-Rabiʿah, forced the Muslim Brotherhood to ask those three to leave Zubair and head to Kuwait. All three duly joined the weak Islamist movement in Kuwait, in an attempt to prop it up and breathe some life into it.[49] ʿAbdulwahid Aman was another member of the Iraqi Muslim Brotherhood who travelled to Kuwait from Basra for purely economic reasons; he became the most influential figure in the history of the Muslim Brotherhood in Kuwait and succeeded in relaunching the movement in 1968.

Aman was born and raised in Basra in Iraq where it was the norm for many families to have homes in both Kuwait and Basra for trade purposes and because several Kuwaiti families had come originally from Basra. Aman's neighbours were the al-Qanaʿat family, and his house was within walking distance of one of the houses owned by Ali al-Mutawwaʿ, the father of ʿAbdulʿaziz and Abdullah al-Mutawwaʿ. At that time, Iraq was much more advanced and progressive than Kuwait. Aman's father owned a house in Kuwait where he worked and another in Basra where his family lived. While growing up Aman was greatly influenced by several Muslim Brotherhood authors and joined the Muslim Brotherhood in Basra following a meeting with Muhammad ʿAbdulhamīd Ahmed, envoy of Hasan al-Banna to Iraq.

While studying accounting at the University of Baghdad in the late 1940s, where the intellectual environment was fraught with conflict between various ideologies, Aman's personality and thinking were very much shaped by this challenging scholarly milieu. The Muslim Brotherhood in Baghdad was influenced by various nationalist and other left-wing ideologies which tended to be highly organised, and very secretive. As in

---

[49] Al-ʿAqil, Interview.

Turkey, Egypt and the Levant, these organisations were widespread in Iraq at that time. The fierce conflict between various intellectual groups and ideologies had a direct impact on reshaping the Iraqi Muslim Brotherhood organisation into a more complex, conservative and clandestine movement. This new trend was in sharp contract with the open nature of the original Muslim Brotherhood founded by Hasan al-Banna in Egypt, although the hostile policies of Presidents Nasser and Sadat towards the Muslim Brotherhood in Egypt eventually made it less open. The highly-organised nature of the Muslim Brotherhood was quite evident in Baghdad and to a lesser degree in other parts of Iraq.

Having obtained both a degree and new modes of thinking, Aman returning to Basra with the clear aim of disseminating the results of his newly-acquired knowledge. However, the death of his father meant that Aman, as the eldest son, found himself suddenly responsible for all his siblings in addition to his work with the Muslim Brotherhood.[50] ʿAbdulʿaziz al-Mutawwaʿ who had first met Aman during a work visit to Basra now offered him a highly-paid job in Kuwait, which Aman felt compelled to accept to support his family. Aman moved to Kuwait in 1957 at a time when the Muslim Brotherhood there was divided and weak. His work in ʿAbdulʿaziz al-Mutawwaʿs office brought him closer to ʿAbdulʿaziz's brother Abdullah. Abdullah then convinced Aman to leave ʿAbdulʿaziz and work for him instead; he also invited Aman to be active in al-Irshad to prop up the moribund movement. Aman accepted both offers and began work in earnest.

Disagreements between ʿAbdulʿaziz al-Mutawwaʿ and Muhammad al-ʿAdsani had greatly weakened the leadership of al-Irshad and, as noted, had eventually forced both of them, and many other members, to abandon the cause altogether. Nevertheless, despite the gradual petering out of all its activities, al-Irshad managed to survive by the skin of its teeth under the leadership of ʿAbdulrazzaq al-Saleh, who galvanised efforts to establish al-Irshad school to eliminate illiteracy. Aman volunteered as an accountant at the school, working during the evening shift in addition to his job at Abdullah's office in the morning.

During Aman's tenure, the school expanded to include students from the primary to the secondary levels and was transformed from a school for adult illiterates to a formal educational establishment which adopted

---

[50] Aman, interview.

the 1955 government curriculum, a new system that comprised two years of preschool, four years of primary school, four years of middle school and four years secondary school.[51] There were soon 1,000 students, most of them of various other Arab nationalities. The school was located near the existing government headquarters before it moved to one of the Board of Education buildings, the Khalid bin al-Walīd School. The increasing enrolments led to another move, this time to al-Muthanna School, which remained open even after the al-Irshad school had closed down in 1959. The building eventually became the headquarters of the Kuwait Finance House, after which students were transferred to other government schools.

Abdullah al-ʿAqil who came from Zubair, with its Najdi origins that were very similar to Kuwaiti culture, moved to Kuwait soon after Aman had arrived from Basra. In Zubair, Abdullah al-ʿAqil, ʿUmar al-Dayel, ʿAbdulʿaziz al-Rabiʿah, in addition to ʿAbdulhadi and Yaqub al-Bahsain had worked on spreading the ideas of the Muslim Brotherhood in their society. They founded three libraries in Zubair (al-Manar, al-Hidaya and the Muslim Brotherhood library) in order to spread Islamist ideas in society. Al-ʿAqil went on to study in Cairo at al-Azhar, where he formed strong bonds with the Muslim Brotherhood movement there and eventually joined them. He returned to Zubair after graduating and focused all his efforts on spreading the Muslim Brotherhood ideas through Jamʿiyyat al-Islah in Zubair and at al-Manar Library.

When Abdullah al-ʿAqil, ʿUmar al-Dayel and ʿAbdulʿaziz al-Rabiʿah left Zubair, following communist death threats, they settled in Kuwait with help from Fahd al-Nafisi. Al-ʿAqil joined Aman in reviving the Muslim Brotherhood in Kuwait, starting with the setting up of a library fashioned after al-Manar library in Basra. The Kuwait branch of al-Manar library was launched in 1960 with the support of a number of Islamists under the supervision of al-ʿAqil and Aman. As the only source of books about Islam and the Brotherhood at a time when Nationalist and Leftists dominated social and political domains, al-Manar was very popular among young people with an interest in Islamist movements.[52]

---

[51] *Official Website of the Ministry of Education in Kuwait*, "Marahil al-Taʿlimfi Dawlat al-Kuwait." Last modified 2012 (accessed 2 September 2013). www.moe.edu.kw/SitePa ges/kw_his.aspx.

[52] Al-ʿAqil, interview.

Despite these attempts to revive the Islamist spirit through al-Irshad, its school and the new library, efforts to attract old and new members to the movement failed miserably, due to the internal conflicts within the Muslim Brotherhood, combined with Nasser's propaganda machine which resorted to fear-mongering to scare people away from the Muslim Brotherhood by portraying it as backward, oppressive and treacherous.[53] Such media pressure was compounded by security pressures in Egypt and Iraq. The Muslim Brotherhood in Kuwait shared the plight of the movement in other countries, and although Islamists in Kuwait in general and the Muslim Brotherhood in particular were never targeted by Kuwait's Ministry of Interior, they did suffer from media and social isolation.

As the influence of the Islamists began gradually to dwindle during the 1950s, secularist nationalist parties and Islamist movements made fierce attempts to gain control of the social domain, as was clearly evident in the calls to liberate women from the shackles of tradition, custom and Islamist teachings. From the mid-1950s to the mid-1960s social change was remarkably rapid, as society left the old customs and traditions behind and adopted a more Westernised lifestyle. The loss of the social domain over which they had maintained total control for centuries shocked the Islamist movements, which perceived this modernising process as a great threat to the social space it had historically dominated as well as further evidence that colonial powers were winning the battles for the hearts and minds of local communities. Their response was to launch an attempt to reclaim the social domain through a new project which was the establishment of the *Jamʿiyyat al-Islah al-Ijtimaʿi*, the Social Reform Society.[54]

Generally speaking, the attempts of Aman and al-ʿAqil to revive the Muslim Brotherhood and Islamic thinking took different ways. Although they did not succeed in rebuilding the Muslim Brotherhood organisation in the beginning, their work focused on general Islamic activities such as launching the al-Manar Islamic bookshop, running al-Irshad school and helping to establish Jamʿiyyat al-Islah al-Ijtimaʿi. These attempts were informed by their experience in Iraq, but this by itself was not sufficient to create an established Islamist movement, even though they did succeed in spreading Islamic thinking among young people interested in Islamist activities, such as some Boy Scouts and students at al-Irshad school.

---

[53] Al-Zumai,"Intellectual and Historical Development," 173–174.

[54] More details about the Social Reform Society are found in Chapter 4.

The end of the 1950s and 1960s in Kuwait was a period of great decline for Islamist movements in favour of the secularist nationalist movement. Islamists had failed in their efforts to present their ideas and principles to the general public and opted instead to withdraw from public life. The writings of Sayyid Qutb were particularly influential. Notions popularised by Qutb, such as "*jahiliyyah*" (age of ignorance of divine guidance), "emotional isolation" and "fighting tyrants," as well as stories of the suffering of Muslim Brotherhood members in Nasser's prisons (including the symbolic and romanticised account of Qutb's imprisonment and subsequent execution), constituted the intellectual background for a whole generation of Kuwaitis, along with the teachings of Hasan al-Banna which called for spreading the message of Islam and establishing a true Islamic state. Aman states that Qutb's writings were much admired by many young Kuwaitis to the extent that they withdrew from a society they thought had abandoned tradition and morality. They blamed the Nationalists who controlled the media and influenced political life, for these forms of depravity, and found in Qutb's ideas consolation and a refuge from social rejection.

As William Shepard explains, Qutb's ideas developed during the ordeal in prison. Qutb's glossary and terms such as *taghout* [the despot] in reference to the repressive ruler (at the time Jamal ʿAbdulnasser), and *Jahiliyya* which Qutb used to refer to those who did apply the teachings of Islam. Qutb called upon the pious few to detach themselves from Jahili societies, not physically, but emotionally and work towards reinstating the rule of Islam through the notion of Allah's Sovereignty (*hakimiyyah*), the idea that Allah is the source of all laws.[55] These ideas were proposed at a time when members of the Muslim Brotherhood were being persecuted by Nasser. Those influenced by Qutb's ideas perceived society as irreligious based on the notion of *Jahiliyya*. But the leader of the Muslim Brotherhood opposed to this idea. The Supreme Guide Hasan al-Hudaybi published a book entitled "Duʿat la Qudhat [Preachers, Not Judges]" in which he emphasised the difference between faith and actions by remarking that a true believer may commit sins but that does not make him a Kafir or a disbeliever since he is usually aware that he has sinned. Al-Hudaybi opined that "the notion of *hakimiyyah* is a new term that ought

[55] William E. Shepard, "Sayyid Qutb's Dooctrine of Jahiliyya," *International Journal of Middle East Studies*, 35, No. 4 (November 2003), 521–545.

not to be used to judge any Muslim, especially since many misunderstood what Qutb meant by the term."[56]

Al-Hudaybi did not directly criticise Qutb despite correcting his understanding of some Qur'anic verses as the one dealing with Allah's government. He also elaborated on many articles of faith pertaining to religious disaffiliation, takfir and other issues Islamists commented on during their time in prison. Al-Hudaybi called for re-reading Qutb's ideas in the light of the Muslim Brotherhood's interpretations. The Muslim Brotherhood leadership succeeded in keeping the movement together and defined the parameters of their thinking in Egypt. Qutb's dichotomies (*taghout* vs. *hakimiyya*—Muslim Society vs. Jahili Society) did not have any noticeable influence on the Kuwaiti Muslim Brotherhood who enjoyed excellent relations with the ruling family. Nor did the latter opposed Islam as source of legislation, in addition to the fact that hereditary rule had had long been accepted in Islam.

The 1967 war with Israel which, under Nasser's leadership, was lost by the Arabs, shook the foundations of Arab Nationalism and ended Nasser's support for nationalist parties and movements and his state-funded propaganda machine directed against the Gulf State leaders (who were described as "the enemies of God").[57] Arab public opinion entered a period of introspection to examine the causes of the 1967 defeat, as well as the Arab nationalist philosophies and methods. It was the perfect opportunity for the Islamist movement to rise from the ashes and renew the call for adopting Islam as a solution to all political, social and economic problems. Others called for following in the footsteps of the Islam's golden generation (the Prophet and the four Caliphs), which many middle- and lower-class Kuwaitis found very appealing. The collapse of nationalist ideologies in the Arab world undoubtedly caused a shift to right-wing schools of thought, such as Islamism. Society welcomed this shift while the Islamists seized the opportunity to mobilise once again, following a period of stagnation and pressure from governments that had viewed them with great suspicion, due mainly to Nasserist propaganda that branded them as agents of the West. In Kuwait, young Muslim

[56] Hasan al-Hudaibi, Duʿat la Qudat, *Wikipedia of the Muslim Brotherhood*. Last modified 2011 (accessed 5 April 2014).

[57] Riadh al-Rayyis, "Arab Nationalism and the Gulf" (PhD diss., University of Exeter, 1986), 123.

Brotherhood leaders were united under one banner to set the stage for a new and more organised phase of the Muslim Brotherhood.

THE NEW ORGANISATION IN 1968

The 1967 defeat, which put a nail in the coffin of Nasserite and Pan-Arabist ideology, was heaven-sent for the Islamists who had long suffered from the effects of antagonistic public opinion. Islamists, especially the Muslim Brotherhood, had been equally persecuted by several Arab security apparatuses, but the new political atmosphere that arose after the 1967 defeat provided them with an ideal opportunity to move more freely and hit back at secular nationalist ideologies. Islamists blamed secularism for the trouncing that had been inflicted on Muslim societies. Aphorisms which propounded the merits of Islamic faith and rule duly spread far and wide and found their way into the hearts and minds of an Arab Muslim society still reeling under the pain of defeat. Arab societies began to embrace Islamic thought which, coupled with the lifting of pressure on the Muslim Brotherhood in Egypt, set the scene for a new era in many Arab countries.

Leaders of various Islamic activist groups in Kuwait agreed it was time to unify their scattered efforts under one Muslim Brotherhood umbrella. Following an initiative by ʿAbdulwahid Aman, assisted by Salim Turki who was on good terms with various Islamic groups adhering to the ideology of the Muslim Brotherhood, consultations were held between several young movements; former al-Irshad members with their extensive experience in organised movements also took part in the consultations. Young groups that had previously been under the leadership of ʿIsa al-Shahin and others, now unified under one Muslim Brotherhood umbrella. The new leadership of Aman, Abdullah al-Mutawwaʿ and Mishari al-Bedah organised a meeting to introduce all the members to each other, although integration proved quite easy since most Islamists had already met previously through the Jamʿiyyat al-Islah and al-Muhanna Mosque in Hawalli. The goal was clear: to establish a new organisation of the Muslim Brotherhood movement in Kuwait under one leadership.

The first meeting was held in September 1968 at the residence of ʿAbdulwahid Aman in the Kaifan area. Participants agreed on a list of ideas and objectives, and scheduled a meeting with a bigger group of young activists who wished to join the newly-formed organisation. The second meeting was held a week later in the presence of around 30 members well known for their commitment to Islamic thought and who formed the nucleus of the new Muslim Brotherhood organisation. ʿAbdulwahid Aman was chosen as leader of the group with Salim Turki as his deputy. The organisational structure of the Kuwaiti Muslim Brotherhood was based on its Egyptian[58] and Iraqi counterparts but with more influence from the latter due to Aman's historical links with the Iraqi version of the Muslim Brotherhood.[59]

A thorough reading of the Muslim Brotherhood by-laws reveals that most of the power resides with *al-Muraqib al-ʿAam* (General Observer) who is defined as the president of the Muslim Brotherhood in Egypt and head of the *Maktab al-Irshad* (Guidance Bureau) and Shura Council and has the right to attend all meetings held by various committees of the Muslim Brotherhood.[60] Al-Muraqib also directly supervises the work of all the Muslim Brotherhood's branches. In 1949, on the eve of the assassination of its founder, Imam Hasan al-Banna, the number of members of the Muslim Brotherhood in Egypt alone was estimated at one million.[61] The organisational cell *"usra"* [family] is the smallest unit in the Muslim Brotherhood and lies at the bottom of the pyramidal organisation structure with an average of five to eight members supervised by a *naqib* [captain].[62] The naqib is responsible for providing intellectual and educational training to young cadres. He prepares a report about each member and nominates those whom he thinks are ready to move up the organisational ladder. ʿAbdulhalim Mahmud offers insights into the structure and intellectual and educational methods of the Muslim Brotherhood in Egypt in his book *Education Methods of the Muslim Brotherhood*, in which

---

[58] Muhammad Zaki, *Al-Ikhwan al-Muslimun* (Cairo: Wahbah, 1954), 99.

[59] Aman, interview.

[60] See Section 1, Chapter 1, Article 2 on the Official Website of the Muslim Brotherhood, "General and International Codes of the Muslim Brotherhood." Last modified 30 December 2009 (accessed 22 July 2012) www.ikhwanonline.com/new/Article.aspx?ArtID=58497&SecID=211.

[61] In 1945, al-Banna announced that the number of Muslim Brotherhood members has reached 500 thousand members. Mahmud ʿAbdulhalim, *al-ʿIkhwan al-Muslimun: Ahdathsanaʿat al-Tarikh* (Alexandria: Dar alDaʿwah, no date), 384.

[62] The *naqib* or *nuqabaʿ* system was taken from the organizational system used by the Prophet Mohammad to organise his Companions and followers in different parts of Arabia. In one of the Prophet's sayings to his followers in Medina "chose ten of you to be Nuqabaʿ," i.e. as representatives for them. See Ahmad bin Hanbal, *Musnad Imam Ahmad* (Riyadh: Dar Ihya' al-Turath al-Arabi, 1993), 462.

a whole chapter is dedicated to the notion of the *usra* and its importance as a stepping stone.[63]

The organisational ethos of the Muslim Brotherhood rests on the belief that organised work is the most effective tool for transferring Islamic reformist thought from the confines of books and ideas to the solid ground of reality. Muslim Brotherhood thinkers firmly believe that the main problem resides in the absence of good leadership to guide people away from foreign influence and onto the path of independence, and to build a modern Islamic state where the Muslim Brotherhood will arrive to fill the gap in the political order. Hasan al-Banna, founder of the movement, who was aware that his project would come into direct conflict with government interests, colonial powers and other local political forces, stressed the importance of being steadfast in the face of oppression and persecution and warned the Muslim Brotherhood members that the cost of reform would be very high. Despite the difficulties faced by the Muslim Brotherhood, it adhered to non-violent methods which advocated starting with the reforming of individuals, followed by families, society and finally the state. Such a huge project necessitated the establishing of a movement like the Muslim Brotherhood.

According to Muhammad Ahmad al-Rashid, training members, especially leaders, to carry out the tasks entrusted to them was essential for the success of the Muslim Brotherhood project.[64] The Muslim Brotherhood also regards their project as a "holy mission" to restore Islamic values in Muslim societies. Thus, protecting the organisation, as the carrier of the project, in order to ensure the survival of the reformist project, became a fundamental objective. Al-Banna pointed out that what distinguished the Muslim Brotherhood from other movements and groups was its non-partisan nature and its comprehensive vision; the Muslim Brotherhood, he argued, was a movement with an all-inclusive and wide-ranging programme covering all aspects of life. It aimed to unite people under one slogan and one objective; however, before addressing the masses, such a slogan and objective were to be directed in the first instance to members of the Muslim Brotherhood themselves who were required to

[63] ʿAli Mahmud, *Wasaʾl al-Tarbiyah ʾInd al-Ikhwan al-Muslimin* (Egypt: Dar al-Wafaʾ, 1989).

[64] Muhammad Ahmad al-Rashid, interview.

cast aside their own personal interests and work towards achieving the Muslim Brotherhood's goals.

This explains why the Muslim Brotherhood engages in an arduous process of training and re-educating its members to avoid the pitfalls and problems faced by other parties and groups who often end up fighting over power and influence. Such forms of education also ensure physical and mental resilience in the face of challenges. The history of the Muslim Brotherhood is testimony to the success of this strategy especially when, for example, the regimes of Nasser, Sadat and Mubarak cracked down on the movement's members. Nor has the Muslim Brotherhood witnessed any major dissents which have threatened the organisation's structure. The high degree of discipline and respect for leadership guarantees the resilience of the organisation.[65]

The Iraqi Experience and Influence

Although the Muslim Brotherhood branch in Kuwait derived its principles and inspiration from Egypt, the greatest influence, as noted, came from the Iraqi branch of the Muslim Brotherhood due to the historical links between the new leadership of the Muslim Brotherhood in Kuwait and the Iraqi branch. The Iraqi Muslim Brotherhood was not as open as its Egyptian counterpart despite the fact that, under the leadership of Muhammad Mahmoud al-Sawwaf who was known for his mild mannerisms and spontaneity, the Muslim Brotherhood had initially been very accessible. The Muslim Brotherhood's front in Iraq was *Jam'iyyat al-Ukhuwwah al-Islamiyyah* [Islamic Fraternity Society]. Al-Sawwaf's style was reminiscent of al-Banna's, in terms of its focus on *da'wah* in Iraq. Various branches of the Muslim Brotherhood were set up in Iraqi cities and attracted many people. Following the revoking of licences of all parties to operate in Iraq during the period of Hashemite rule, the Muslim Brotherhood remained active through the *al-Ukhuwwah* society from 1943 until 1954. This period was notable for the Muslim Brotherhood's great freedom to attract new members and spread the group's ideas. However, the last few years of Hashemite rule were marked by political upheavals, with most Nationalist, Communist and Leftist parties declaring

---

[65] Al-Rashid, interview.

their fierce opposition to the British-controlled ruling family. The 1956 war against Egypt also left an indelible mark.

The Muslim Brotherhood came together to debate these political developments and elected Muhammad al-Sawwaf as the General Observer with Kamal al-Qaisi as his deputy. These were to be the last elected leaders; since from then on, most Muslim Brotherhood leaders were appointed rather than elected. The 1958 coup, which was led by Abdulkarim Qasim and which saw him seek the support of Communists to establish and stabilise his rule, threw the country into turmoil. The Communists effectively terrorised their opponents to the extent of committing atrocities such as the massacre of Kirkuk, and also persecuted the leaders of Nationalist and Ba'thist parties and the Muslim Brotherhood. Al-Sawwaf survived an assassination attempt and was arrested and sentenced to death, but several government leaders interfered on his behalf to plead with Qasim to spare him. He was released from jail and fled to Sa'udi Arabia via Syria in 1960.

The new political order placed great limitations on the activities of the Muslim Brotherhood. Following the departure of al-Sawwaf and his deputy al-Qaisi, the movement decided to select a new leadership that could tackle these political challenges. Abdulkarim Zaidan[66] was chosen as leader, a position to which he agreed, subject to several conditions such as choosing by himself three of the foundational committee members to act as advisers. His most important condition was that he should not be bound by *shura* (Consultation), and he presented the organisation with a study that outlined the non-compulsory nature of entrusting the leader with *shura*. The Muslim Brotherhood agreed to Zaidan's conditions, seeing in him the perfect man to lead them through this critical phase. Around fifty members from various Iraqi cities were there for his inauguration. In addressing the issues of the moment, the new leadership adopted a different approach. Political, media and security pressure on the Muslim Brotherhood forced it to go underground, after which

---

[66] Abdulkarim Zaidan (1917–…) is a religious scholar and a member of the Muslim Brotherhood in Iraq. In 1960, Zaidan became the General Observer of the Muslim Brotherhood in Iraq until 1990s where the organisation went underground under the rule of communists and Ba'thists. *Wikipedia of the Muslim Brotherhood*, "'Abdulkarim Zaidan." Last modified 5 January 2014 (accessed 5 January 2014). www.ikhwanwiki.com/index.php?title=عبدالكريم_زيدان.

Zaidan remained virtually unknown, even to the Iraqi government intelligence services, to the extent that he was actually nominated for the post of Minister of Religious Affairs during the Baʿth rule; however, his name as Muslim Brotherhood leader was leaked by some dissenting members, thus preventing his appointment from materialising.

Zaidan was a man of very few words, and his deputy, Saleh Saʿdun, was equally reticent.[67] Saʿdun supervised all the Muslim Brotherhood departments and reported to Zaidan whose identity remained a secret. The circumspect and very guarded personalities of the two men stamped the movement with a secretive character which soon became the norm as the Muslim Brotherhood gradually put an end to most of their public activities. The security situation in Iraq at the time also forced other parties to go underground and shroud their activities in mystery.

The Muslim Brotherhood then decided to face up to the Communists and other secular political forces by establishing their own political party to represent Islamist trends. *Al-Hizb al-Iraqi al-Islami* [the Iraqi Islamic Party] was established in 1960 and from then on served as a political front for the Muslim Brotherhood after *al-Ukhuwwah* Society had been closed down. The party was very active in challenging Communists and refused to cooperate with Baʿthists and Nationalists because *al-Hizb al-Islami* considered that these last two were not much different from Communists in their rejection of Islam. The party also clashed with Qasim and the Communists on a number of occasions, including the sending of a memo to the government containing scathing criticisms of its performance. Several party leaders were arrested, but mediation efforts secured their release. A decree was issued dissolving the party less than one year after its establishment.[68]

The Iraqi Muslim Brotherhood continued to work in secret, finding inspiration in the writings of Sayyid Qutb that were the polar opposite to the secular thought of Communists and Baʿthists. An Iraqi Muslim Brotherhood member who met Qutb in Egypt was told by the latter that the organisation closest to his line of thinking was the Iraqi one.[69] The Iraqi Muslim brotherhood was highly centralised with most of the powers vested in Zaidan who saw it as his right, as an elected General Observer,

---

[67] Al-Dabbagh. "Jamʿiyyatal-Ukhwah al-Islamiyya," 57–58.

[68] Ibid., 134–142.

[69] Ibid., 151.

to do whatever he saw fit, even if the majority or the Shura Council disagreed with him. From his strong background in Islamic scholarship and *shariʿa*, Zaidan wrote a memo in which he defended the powers he enjoyed from a logical and religious perspective. From a religious perspective, Zaidan quoted the verse "So by mercy from Allah, [O Muhammad], you were lenient with them. And if you had been rude [in speech] and harsh in heart, they would have disbanded from about you. So pardon them and ask forgiveness for them and consult them in the matter. And when you have decided, then rely upon Allah. Indeed, Allah loves those who rely [upon Him]" (3:159),[70] which he understood to mean that Allah had instructed Prophet Muhammad to consult his Companions but then decide for himself how to proceed. Logically, Zaidan argued, the leader was held liable for all his actions and thus should not be forced to follow the opinion of others if he was not convinced it was the right path to follow. Being responsible for one's decisions and actions meant being able to choose freely and not be subject to the choices of others especially since at the end, he was the one who would be held fully responsible for his actions.[71] Zaidan cited a few examples from history to support his theory, such as the story about Caliph Abu Baker when he insisted on dispatching troops formed by the Prophet under the leadership of Osama bin Zaid although his Companions were of the view that they should not be dispatched but kept instead in Medina to protect it from the threat of apostates. Zaidan also mentioned another incident when Abu Baker insisted on fighting apostates who refused to pay *zakat* despite the objections of his Companions who advised granting them more time. In both cases, the leader followed his own opinion despite the objections of others.[72]

As previously noted, the literature of the Iraqi Muslim Brotherhood focused on the importance of secret work. A case in point is an unpublished memo from the leadership of the Iraqi Muslim Brotherhood branch listing the rules and regulations and philosophy of the movement in Iraq. The memo referred to various types of secrecy such as the secrecy of activities, organisation and identities. Secrecy of activities meant carrying out the task of daʿwah in great secret, and the best way to do that

[70] Quran.com.

[71] ʿAbdulkarīm Zaidan, *Usul al-Daʿwah* (No Publisher, 1976), 211–213.

[72] Ibid.

was through direct contact with individuals and bases. Activities usually involved a small number of people who would meet socially, go together on trips and so on. The movement recommended members hide their membership even from their closest relatives. The identity of members, especially leadership figures, was also kept secret, and aliases were used in correspondence. The Muslim Brotherhood considered secrecy an essential component of *da'wah* dictated by political contingencies.[73]

As a result of the militant threat to the organisation, the Muslim Brotherhood in Iraq established a secret armed branch to protect the organisation; it also participated in planning a number of coups but always pulled out at the last minute, either because the plan was exposed or because they were not ready for the fallout. Armed activities were kept secret until fierce disagreements broke out between veteran Muslim Brotherhood members and Zaidan, who was criticised for his centralised administration. The veteran members were also critical of what they perceived as his weakness and inability to face up to the government. Some members left the Muslim Brotherhood and so a few names were leaked, including Zaidan's identity. The Ba'thist government, which staged a coup in 1968 to overthrow Qasim and the Communists, also learned of the existence of the armed branch of the Muslim Brotherhood at the end of the 1960s and early 1970s. The Ba'th Party purged the political scene of all political opponents, and having got rid of the Communists, turned its attention to the Muslim Brotherhood. After the names were leaked, the government put the Muslim Brotherhood members under surveillance, and several members who lashed were assassinated by the government.[74] In 1971, Zaidan announced the dissolution of the Muslim Brotherhood to protect its other members.[75] Some respected the decision, but others who rebelled against it were later traced and expelled by the government.[76]

---

[73] Al-Dabbagh, "Jam'iyyat al-Ukhwah al-Islamiyya," 172–173.

[74] Shaikh 'Abdul'aziz al-Badri was killed after his criticism of the Ba'th, along with 42 Islamists who were executed after military trial. Al-Dabbagh, "Jam'iyyat al-Ukhwah al-Islamiyya," 675.

[75] Zaidan once said to a member of the Muslim Brotherhood, "what is more important: protecting them [the members of the Muslim Brotherhood] from gibbets and massacres and keeping them for a day that will come where they will play an important role – or shall I burn them in fire now?" See al-Dabbagh, "Jam'iyyat alUkhwah al-Islamiyya," 578.

[76] Ibid.

The Muslim Brotherhood in Iraq suffered from many internal problems, the most dangerous of which were the lack of trust in their leadership, and disagreements over how the organisation should be managed. The divergent intellectual, educational and organisational resources from which the various members drew their inspiration had a clear impact on the direction these members adopted. Some were inspired by the Egyptian teachers who came to work in Iraq while others were influenced by the Sufis and their belief in working openly. Another group subscribed to Zaidan's advocacy of secrecy. The final blow came with the leaking of names to the Ba'th government which cracked down on the Muslim Brotherhood until most members had been assassinated or were forced to flee the country.

In Kuwait, the burgeoning Muslim Brotherhood organisation was heavily influenced by the experience that the Iraqi Muslim Brotherhood had witnessed. The teachings of Hasan al-Banna were the bedrock of all Muslim Brotherhood branches, yet different circumstances left their imprint on each branch. Also, the great gap in numbers between the Kuwaiti branch of the Muslim Brotherhood, whose members did not exceed thirty when it was formed, and the Egyptian movement with its hundreds of thousands of members, made the Kuwaiti branch seem very humble and simple in comparison with its Egyptian and Iraqi counterparts. The members who met at Aman's house opted to establish the Executive Office and the Supervisor of the Organisation, which paralleled the Guidance Bureau and the General Observer respectively. It was a very simple organisation, with Abdullah al-Mutawwa' and Mishari al-Bedah in leadership roles while Aman managed the youth department in addition to being the Supervisor of the Organisation.[77] Over time the organisation of the Muslim Brotherhood grew and soon included a women's branch and a social work department. Yet, due to its small size and to certain security concerns, the movement never ventured beyond basic activities such as *da'wah* and social gatherings. The relatively young age of both the members and the organisation meant that the movement lacked depth of vision and knowledge of the intricacies of the Kuwaiti political and economic order which, not unnaturally, differed from those of Egypt and Iraq.

---

[77] Aman, interview.

Aman states that the Kuwaiti branch of the organisation had been founded on the principles of educating the young in order to overcome the shortcomings of its predecessor, al-Irshad, and the reasons that had led to its demise. It aimed to revive the Muslim Brotherhood organisation in Kuwait and unite its members under one sturdy umbrella, and to combat the secular trends of nationalists. This new generation of young men and women would be entrusted with the task of establishing the desired Islamic society, in their homes and social circles and finally society as a whole, to tackle all forms of corruption. This was not a new goal for the organisation, but it sought to implement these objectives in a manner more suited to Kuwaiti society and the abilities of the new movement. Political reform as a theme was absent from the new movement's literature, as, to a lesser extent, was economic reform, although the writings of ᶜIsa ᶜAbduh and Muhammad Baqir al-Sadr, which were published by al-Manar bookshop, did refer to these issues. Thus, the Muslim Brotherhood emerged in Kuwait as an "educator" rather than as a "politician."

In addition to the Muslim Brotherhood branch in Iraq, Zubair, an old cultural and Islamic centre, had a great influence on Kuwait due to the close proximity between the two. AlᶜAqil explains that many residents of Zubair and Kuwait share a common origin from the tribes of Najd, making Zubair closer to Kuwait in terms of culture, customs and traditions than Iraq.[78] Zubair was more culturally and scientifically advanced than Kuwait and exerted a great influence on the young state. Home to the first school in the region, al-Dweihis School, established in 1781 to teach Hanbali school of jurisprudence,[79] and al-Fudailia School for girls[80] which was established at the end of the nineteenth century, Zubair was the source of many Islamic reformist ideas which spread to Kuwait with the influx of magazines, religious teachers and scholars from Zubair to Kuwait.[81] Many Kuwaiti students studied in Zubair such as Shaikh Abdullah al-Duhian in 1892 and Shaikh ᶜAbdulᶜaziz al-Rushaid

---

[78] Al-ᶜAqil, interview.

[79] ᶜAbdulᶜaziz al-Nasir, *al-Zubair* (Saudi Arabia: Wahj al-Hayat Communications, 2010), 261–275.

[80] Ibid., 253–254.

[81] Among the teachers who had come to Kuwait to work as a teachers or judges were Ali Al-Shariki who lived in Kuwait from 1810 to 1813 and worked as judge and Abdul-Malik Al-Mubaid who taught at al-Mubarkiyya school upon the request of Yusuf Bin Issa in 1912 before moving to Al-Ahmadia.

in 1903. Many Najdi families moved to Kuwait and Saudi Arabia after the collapse of the Najdi rule and the Iraqi of Zubair in 1920, but the biggest wave of immigration occurred after the discovery of oil in the Gulf region.[82] Immigrants brought with them new ideas such as the thought of the Muslim Brotherhood which had spread in Iraqi and Zubair before Kuwait. Mohammed Abdul-Hamid who was studying in Basra introduced the ideology of the Muslim Brotherhood into Zubair. Young men and Sheiks influenced by him established a number of religious and cultural organisations similar to those founded by the Muslim Brotherhood in Baghdad and Basra. The Muslim Brotherhood library was established in 1946 followed by al-Hidayya and al-Manar libraries.[83] The Muslim Brotherhood established a branch of the Islamic Brotherhood Society in Zubair in 1950. The Society was dissolved by the Iraqi authorities in 1954, and so the Muslim Brotherhood founded the Social Reform Society as a replacement. The influx of Brotherhood members from Zubair to Kuwait in the 1950s and 1960s galvanised the Kuwaiti branch of the Brotherhood at a time when the movement was being persecuted elsewhere. The new arrivals founded a number of cultural and religious organisations similar to the ones in Zubair such as al-Manar library, al-Islah and other foundations that the Muslim Brotherhood still operates in Kuwait until the present day.

The Foundations of the Kuwaiti Muslim Brotherhood Movement

The Kuwaiti Muslim Brotherhood movement benefited greatly from the Iraqi experience, and its organisation was based on the principles adopted by the Iraqi model. The movement was established with a limited number of families (*usra*) who were mostly urbanite members due to the ease with which they embraced Muslim Brotherhood thinking, most of them having witnessed the Muslim Brotherhood's first experience in Kuwait. The new leadership also consisted of urbanite elements, so it seemed natural to embark on the process of *da'wah* among this group. The message of the new organisation was being spread among young elements but in a more secretive manner than before. Members would contact young men on an

[82] Al-ʿAqil, interview.

[83] Umar al-Dayil, *Safahat min Tarikh al-Daʿwah al-Islamiyya fi al-Zubair* (unpublished-undated handwritten pamphlet), 8.

individual rather than a collective basis. There was much more emphasis on religious and moral issues without reference to political and intellectual concerns, so as to avoid disagreements with the individual being approached.[84]

Sports and recreational programmes were among the best methods of attracting people to the organisation, which did not identify itself as Muslim Brotherhood to members outside the movement. Once the members of the Muslim Brotherhood had ascertained that an individual was committed to the principles of Islam on which the movement was founded, they would invite him to join the group; the process of meeting the individual to invite him to become a member usually took around two years. The Kuwaiti branch also borrowed extensively from their Iraqi counterparts in terms of *da'wah* and organisation. On the level of *da'wah*, the Muslim Brotherhood took great care to establish a comprehensive educational system with equal emphasis on the spiritual, physical and intellectual aspects of education.

Young people were the prime target for the organisation. Excursions, camps and gatherings were organised along the lines of the Iraqi model although that dated back to a model designed by Hasan al-Banna himself. Gatherings of almost fifty people would be organised in someone's home or on the seaside or even at the mosque, and were considered a crucial means of focusing on the spiritual growth of the movement's young members. The programme would usually start after evening prayers or after breaking their fast, and the group would then recite verses from the Qur'an and pray throughout the night before going to sleep after dawn prayers. During excursions, the group would spend time at someone's weekend home or chalet, with the programme focusing on refining leadership, managerial and intellectual skills. Sports contests and games would be held in addition to lectures by established members, while camping programmes aimed at instilling Islamic values in addition to physical training and were similar to those of the international scout movement with its emphasis on mental, physical and spiritual development.

Muhammad Ahmad al-Rahsid explains the organisational structure which was based on a nucleus of less than ten members headed by a *naqib* who was directly linked to the *raqib*, a person of higher status and, in turn, linked with the upper leadership. This hierarchy was inspired by the

[84] Aman, interview.

Iraqi model which devised the post of *raqib* although it did not exist in the Egyptian model.[85] The *naqib*'s role was more important than that of the *raqib* because he was the one who prepared new members spiritually and intellectually. The daily contact by the *naqib* with individuals placed him in the position of guide and mentor. He/she was also entrusted with the task of following through with individuals from the moment he/she were first introduced to the *naqib* until they became full members. The *usra* was the cradle from which individuals drew their intellectual, organisational and spiritual inspiration. The movement was thus constantly in motion, spreading the message of the Muslim Brotherhood and attracting new members. The Muslim Brotherhood leaderships in Egypt, Iraq and Kuwait took great care in preparing *naqibs* for their roles and singled out them for specific directives where *naqibs* would be required to obey all orders from above and put the organisation first, ahead of their own interests, to ensure that the main goals of the movement were realised.[86]

The Establishment of the Movement on the Philosophy of the Iraqi School in 1968

ʿAbdulwahid Aman played a major role in shaping the structure and outlook of the Kuwaiti movement, bestowing upon it the characteristics of its Iraqi counterpart. From a quick comparison between the Iraqi and Egyptian movements and their impact on the Muslim Brotherhood in Kuwait, it is immediately evident that despite the importance of the Supreme Guide in the Egyptian model, there were other members who took part in the decision-making process, in addition to a comprehensive body that followed through with the leadership to ensure that all decisions were implemented. This body consisted of the deputy Supreme Guide, the secretary general and the deputy general. The charisma and leadership abilities of Hasan al-Banna made him the centre of decision-making, while the security grip of Nasser's regime highlighted the role of Hasan al-Hudaybi, the second Supreme Guide of the Muslim Brotherhood, in managing the crises and challenges faced by the movement. But the central role of Supreme Guide began to wane in favour of the Guidance Bureau. Such new forms of management allowed other

---

[85] Al-Rashid, interview.

[86] Ibid.

members to participate in the decision-making process and transformed the spirit of the movement from being leader-based into one that was more institutionalised.

In the case of the Iraqi branch of the Muslim Brotherhood, the movement lacked any clear structure under al-Sawwaf due to his spontaneous and relaxed personality. When Zaidan assumed power, the Muslim Brotherhood entered a new era marked by challenges from other organisations and from the government itself. The movement took on new forms and gradually became more centralised as Zaidan moved in on most of the powers. For security reasons, as noted above, his deputy Saʿdun was entrusted with all the tasks.

The organisational structure demonstrated the centralised nature of power within the Muslim Brotherhood under the leadership of Zaidan and Saʿdun. The structure of the Kuwaiti branch was influenced by the Iraqi more than the Egyptian organisation. Aman enjoyed far-reaching powers similar to the Iraqi model. *Shura* was also marked out for the Supreme Guide without obligation, as set forth by Zaidan in Iraq. These rules were distributed in a memo among the members to reassure them of the legitimacy of the leadership's actions. Yet, it was not a smooth operation; Abdullah al-Nafisi, one of the Muslim Brotherhood's veterans, stipulated *shura* as a precondition for his agreeing to join the movement.[87] Though he joined the organisation later, he left for other reasons. The majority of members approved of Aman's decision, not out of conviction, but rather because they trusted him as a person and a leader.

Even though most of the powers were vested in Aman, the centralised mode on which the Kuwaiti branch was founded did not reflect on the form of its organisational structure; the *Shura* Council elected members of the leadership, including the highest officials. Authorities were generally vested in the upper echelons of the Muslim Brotherhood who, in turn, supervised the work of other departments. Aman paid close attention to the structural and organisational aspects of the new movement by

[87] Abdullah Al-Nafisi (1945–...) a politician and a political scientist graduated from AUB and Cambridge where he received his PhD. Al-Nafisi was influenced by the Muslim Brotherhood literature and was invited to join the Muslim Brotherhood but he refused for the reason mentioned above. Later on, al-Nafisi got influenced by Leftist ideology for 10 years, however, he returned to Kuwait and joined the Muslim Brotherhood after denouncing Leftist ideas. He represented the Muslim Brotherhood in the Parliament in 1985. However, al-Nafisi left the Muslim Brotherhood and started criticising the movement in many of his writings. Al-Nafisi, interview.

ensuring that the powers and authorities of various departments were kept separate. He managed the movement in a hierarchical manner whereby each member referred to his direct supervisor if he needed to contact someone in another department. This naturally resulted in most powers becoming centralised in Aman's hand which meant the movement looked up to the leadership in all matters, even those pertaining to their own relationships with each other. Although the organisation's codes did not entrust all the authorities to the leader personally but rather to the leadership office, reality on the ground, members' backgrounds and the fact they were influenced by the Iraqi branch all signified that the Supervisor was the one with all the power.

As pointed out above, the new Kuwaiti Muslim Brotherhood organisation followed the Iraqi model. In addition to centralised authority, the identities of both leaders and members of the Muslim Brotherhood were kept secret from new members and the general public, as in the Iraqi case. This did not prevent some members of the organisation and the public from recognising certain individuals as members of the Muslim Brotherhood from their discourse, manner of dress and beards. The Kuwaiti government was also aware of the names of the leaders because of the strong ties between Abdullah al-Mutawwaᶜ and members of the ruling family. Al-Mutawwaᶜ played a major role in creating trust between the government and the Muslim Brotherhood and also in alleviating anxiety that the movement was trying to undermine the ruling family or else had ties with foreign elements. These good relations between the Muslim Brotherhood and the government in Kuwait raises questions as to why the movement chose to keep its activities under wraps without there being any real threat to Islamist movements from the government or the other political and social movements. In Iraq, it was quite understandable for the Muslim Brotherhood to go underground, but in Kuwait no such justification existed. The only explanation was that the events in Egypt and Iraq had greatly impacted the structure and mode of work of the Muslim Brotherhood in Kuwait.

The main impetus behind all these principles of operation (centralised authority, nonobligatory nature of *shura* and secrecy of work) was the need to build a strong organisation. Muhammad Ahmed al-Rashid, the Muslim Brotherhood thinker who belonged to the Iraqi movement, referred to this as the "*al-Qaᶜida al-Sulbah*'" [the solid base], which is defined as the nucleus of the Muslim Brotherhood and the base on which the movement is founded.[88] This solid base must reflect the unique political, cultural and social forces that sympathise with, or are antagonistic to, the Muslim Brotherhood. Aman worked hard to achieve these goals by working closely with his first group to prepare a generation of Muslim Brotherhood members who were loyal to the leadership and possessed a thorough understanding of the whole philosophy behind the movement. Muslim Brotherhood members endured hardships to attract others to their movement and invested a lot of time and effort physically and intellectually to prepare members for the solid base. The special qualities required in the solid base meant that the leadership needed to take great care in selecting members.

The Mechanism of Mobilisation

Various independent religious scholars and shaikhs played a positive role in spreading the message of Islam among members of the public and young people, which contributed to the time being right for society to embrace the Muslim Brotherhood. Shaikhs such as Hasan Tannun[89] from Sudan and Shaikh Hasan Ayyub, an Azhar graduate from Egypt,[90] spread Islamic culture among the masses and were widely-respected and revered for their depth of knowledge and for the authority imparted by well-rounded and well-informed religious scholars back then. Hasan Ayyub's lessons at al-Othman mosque in the al-Nuqra area emphasised the importance of charity work, an interest shared by Abdullah al-Ruwwaih, and the two collaborated to establish the al-Othman Zakat Committee at al-Othman mosque in 1973; this was the first *zakat* committee of its kind in

---

[88] Al-Rashid, interview.

[89] Hasan Tannun (1916–1992) was a Sudanese religious scholar who moved to Kuwait in the late 1960s for work, becoming an influential shaikh especially among the youth. See ʿAbdullah Al-ʿAqil, *Wikipedia of the Muslim Brotherhood*, "Al-Waʾz al-Muwaffaq.. Hasan Tannun." Last modified 2011 (accessed 22 August 2013).

[90] Hasan Ayyub (1918–2008) was a member of the Muslim Brotherhood in Egypt who faced hard times in prison under Nasser. In the late 1960s, he moved secretly to Kuwait where he worked as a preacher. *Official Website of Hasan Ayyub*, "Biography of Hasan ʾAyyub." Last modified 22 August 2013 (accessed 22 August 2013). www.hasanayoub. com/.

Kuwait.[91] Tannun and Ayyub had originally arrived in Kuwait in the mid-1960s, at the request of some Islamist activists, to give religious lessons as well as to spread Islamic culture and thought among members of Kuwaiti society.[92] A series of lessons and articles entitled "The Message of the Mosque" by Ayyub was intended to attract people to the mosque, an aim in which he was very successful.

In addition to these two, Shaikh ʿUmar al-Ashqar and Shaikh ʿAbdulrahman ʿAbdulkhaliq, both educated in Jordan and then at the Islamic University in Saʿudi Arabia, came to Kuwait. Their studies in Saʿudi Arabia had proved short-lived after they were accused of destroying mannequins that had been imported to display women's clothing in some shops in Medina. Al-Ashqar later recalled that the mannequins had caused quite a stir in the city, especially among the Islamists. Al-Ashqar and ʿAbdulkhaliq, both with connections to Salafi groups, including the Juhayman al-ʿUtaibi[93] group, had conferred with them on how best to put a stop to this sin. They agreed to lecture people on the importance of ensuring that these idols did not spread, and advised shop owners against using them. After an initial period of lecturing and dispensing advice, al-Ashqar and ʿAbdulkhaliq were shocked to learn that, despite the Salafi groups not advocating such a course of action, the shops where the mannequins had been displayed had been destroyed. It soon emerged that Juhayman's group had been behind the destruction,[94] and a decision was taken to deport Al-Ashqar and ʿAbdulkhaliq for spearheading the campaign against the mannequins. The two of them moved to Kuwait in summer 1965 to resume their activities though without belonging to

---

[91] Official Website of Zakat al-Othman, "Know Us" (accessed 22 August 2013). http://othzk.com/page-1.html.

[92] ʿAbdullatīf al-ʿAtiqi, "Inhiyar al-Fikr al-Yassri," *Al-Qabas Newspaper*, 7 October 2010.

[93] Juhayman al-ʿUtaibi (1936–1980) was a Wahhabi religious activist opposed al-Saʿud because of their deviation from Islam, as he believed. After a series of events, Juhayman and a few hundreds of his followers seized the Grand Mosque in Mecca on 20 November 1979 and declared his brother-in-law, Mohammad alQhatani as the Mahdi Muntathar who "will apply Islam and justice in the world." After few weeks, Saʿudi Special Forces, assisted by French Special Forces, took back the Grand Mosque and captured Juhayman and his group and executed them all. See Thomas Hegghamer and Stephane Lacroix, "Rejectionist Islamism in Saʿudi Arabia: The Story of Juhayman al-Utaybi Revisited," *International Journal of Middle Eastern Studies*, No. 39 (2007), 103–122.

[94] Al-Ashqar, interview.

any particular group. Along with Hasan Ayyub and Hasan Tannun, they played a major role in spreading Islamic thought.

The lessons given by al-Ashqar and ʿAbdulkhaliq were very well attended and revolved around Islamic *fiqh*, *ʿaqidah*, and *shariʿa*. The Salafi influence was evident in their lessons, especially in issues related to *ʿaqidah*. They continued to teach at Kuwaiti mosques for a number of years and accumulated a large following among Kuwaiti and foreign students, due to the practical nature of their lessons which differed from the lectures of Ayyub and Tannun. The four of them delivered a series of lectures at the al-Islah society, and were on very good terms with its members.

Al-Islah was the front for the Islamists in Kuwait. As mentioned above, it was established in response to an invitation from Abdullah al-Mutawwaʿ for all Islamists to come together. The Society was run by a group of independent Islamists, and the Muslim Brotherhood had no direct bearing on its management, since the movement had not been set up until 1968, when its sole focus was on forming the solid base of the Muslim Brotherhood rather than on anything else. The relative youth of the Muslim Brotherhood members prevented them from assuming leadership roles in the al-Islah society as did the secretive nature of the organisation's work.

After the Muslim Brotherhood was formed in Kuwait in 1968, organised work began in earnest. Aman explains how the Muslim Brotherhood's members were arranged into five *usras* according to age and location. Work was focused initially on spreading *daʿwah* among the young through personal contacts and without revealing the identity of the members and their affiliations. Once the young recruit's credentials were ascertained, he would be asked to join the organisation. This was representative of the manner in which the Muslim Brotherhood operated in many countries, including Kuwait. The new organisation focused mainly on bringing together young men and introducing them to Islamic values. With time, methods of attracting new members became more varied and included inviting them to mosques, schools and neighbourhood meetings. The Muslim Brotherhood also established centres and youth clubs, such as the al-Kasb Club at Najib al-Rifaʿi's house, Abu Bakr Club at Abdulmuhsin al-Othman's house and a centre at Mohamed al-Ruwaiyyih's house in al-Shamia area.[95] The organisation introduced these

---

[95] Aman, interview.

young men to Islamic values and Muslim Brotherhood thinking through methods designed by Hasan al-Banna and developed by the Iraqi organisation. Methods included private lessons, fasting, night prayers, special programmes, camping trips and excursions, in addition to lessons at the mosque.

From the outset, members, who were selected on the basis of their faith, intellectual abilities and physical prowess, were taught the importance of respect and loyalty to the organisation. Muhammad Ahmad al-Rashid explains how the idea of terms and conditions was developed by the Iraqi organisation which also developed the notion of stages through which a member had to pass until he was deemed fit to become *naqib*. The details of these conditions were set forth in the "*al-Shurut*" [provisos or conditions] letters; al-Rashid had played a big role in drawing up these letters when he lived in Iraq, and they were later modified to suit the nature of activities in Kuwait. They were taught, among other letters of guidance, to *naqibs* and candidates for being *naqib* and remained the basis for work for a very long time, even after the solid base had been founded. There were two levels initially, which had progressed to four before a member was made *naqib* in order to ensure that he/she was ready for the tasks that lay ahead. The idea of levels originated with al-Banna who explained that there were types of "advocates of ideas" who liked or supported or implemented these ideas, although such divisions generally lacked any further details as to how best to choose a Muslim Brotherhood member and promote him/her. The Iraqi movement developed these levels with clear criteria, and they were later adopted by the Kuwaiti branch.

The *da'wah* that the Muslim Brotherhood decided to work on started at mosques. At the time, praying five times a day at the mosque was not very common, but the movement succeeded in attracting a number of young men to the mosque. Young Muslim Brotherhood members spread the idea in person at the schools they were attending. It was a slow process at first due to the secrecy and the newness of the whole experiment. Support from former members of al-Irshad and the founders of al-Islah gave the young men good cover to enable them to move freely. Their efforts were also supported by giving them full use of the old headquarters of al-Islah in Umm Sedda and the new building in al-Rawdah in which to hold their various activities. Other venues included mosques, with the help of mosque imams, such as the al-Muhanna Mosque in Hawalli.

The division of members' work was based on their geographic location but that did not prevent them from holding joint activities in order to concentrate the work within the boundaries of the areas near the capital, from which most members hailed, in addition to al-Salimiyya area where most of the ʿAwazim tribe was concentrated. The absence of the Muslim Brotherhood from more distant areas prompted the leadership to attempt to penetrate places such as al-Jahra' in the north, al-Farwania in the west and al-Ahmadi and al-Fintas in the south. They took their inspiration from al-Banna, who used to visit far-flung villages in Egypt. The *usra* would visit a certain area on a Friday and attend Friday prayer at one of its famous mosques to deliver the sermon and get to know the young men of the area. They would visit the area a number of times to stay in touch with the young men they had attracted to the Muslim Brotherhood through lessons in the Qur'an and other activities. They succeeded in penetrating these remoter areas and recruited many young men, especially from the tribes of ʿAnza, Shammar, al-Dufair, Mutair, al-Reshaida, alʿAjman, Otaiba, and al-ʿAwazim, as well as a number of urbanites. Ali Zumai', a Muslim Brotherhood member, at that time recalls that *daʿwah* focused on the sons of influential families within the tribes. The movement had better luck among the tribes of Farwnia than it had with al-Jahra' and al-Ahmadi.

The solid base of the Muslim Brotherhood was formed in less than a decade with various *usra*s spread throughout Kuwait, especially among middle-class urbanites and poorer classes. Compared with al-Irshad, the Muslim Brotherhood was not very successful in appealing to the sons of influential urbanite families, but had a positive impact on the educated class that was similar to that of the nationalist parties because this was a dynamic section of society. The Muslim Brotherhood did not aim to work among Shiʿa because of doctrinal differences with them and because they were more likely to subscribe to a Shiʿi religious movement or to secularist nationalist ideologies.[96]

---

[96] The Iranian revolution later changed the nature of the relationship between the Shiites and the nationalist movement.

Muhammad Ahmed al-Rashid and the Intellectual Formation of the Movement

Aman was greatly concerned with unifying the ideological and intellectual resources of the organisation of members to avoid the pitfall of ideological disagreements over cultural and political issues like those that occurred in Syria and Iraq and among the members of the al-Irshad whose diverse intellectual and organisational backgrounds had led to many arguments. Aman drew his inspiration from the diaries and memoirs of the Iraqi Muslim Brotherhood.

ʿAbdulmenʿim Saleh al-Ali, who went by the alias Mohamed Ahmed al-Rashid, was the author of the most important "letters of guidance" of Iraq's Muslim Brotherhood. They were later used in a number of other countries and are considered second in importance to the letters of al-Banna. Al-Rashid had to flee from the Baʿth regime and was invited by Aman to seek asylum in Kuwait and to design the organisational and intellectual frames of reference for the Kuwaiti Muslim Brotherhood. The two men had already met in Baghdad, and their firm friendship prompted al-Rashid to accept Aman's invitation and offer; he arrived in Kuwait in the early 1970s.[97]

Al-Rashid's writings were unique in their field of Islamic thought and in the religious and historical sources he drew upon. He coined the terms "fiqh of *daʿwah*" and "fiqh of movement." His teachings outlined the principles the movement should adopt. These were not simply religious teachings or detailed plans but rather detailed principles. His style, similar to that of Sayyid Qutb, was animated and very inspiring, mixing Islamic tradition with modern-day realities and creating links between the two. This nexus between abstract values and reality on the ground meant that members' faith in the movement was well grounded on both an intellectual and a practical level. The Muslim Brotherhood was not viewed merely as a tool but rather as an idea and a weapon for achieving the desired goal. In fact, membership in the Muslim Brotherhood was considered by many as an article of faith.

The first of the organisational letters had appeared in Iraq as the conflict between various political parties intensified, and were greatly influenced by leftist ideas that were widespread at the time. A letter entitled "The Cause and the Islamist movement" published in 1960 outlined

---

[97] Al-Rashid, interview.

the differences between the goals and objectives of the Islamist movement, and left-wing movements like the Nationalists and Communists. The purpose was to deter Muslim Brotherhood members from becoming mesmerised by these other ideologies. It also sketched out the organisational framework of the movement in the light of the difficult security conditions prevailing, and the wave of internal dissent that was unsettling the organisation.[98]

The letters of '*al-Shurut*' [provisos] directed at middle-tier leadership included a detailed overview of the conditions for accepting new members by requiring them to take a series of educational and physical tests to ensure they were genuine, rather than elements planted by intelligence services or other parties. The "*Al-Naqib* Reminder" letter was concerned with the most important element in the movement, the *naqib*. The letter and an internal publication entitled "*Al-Naqib* Journal" were directed at *naqibs* and contained directives and recommendations as to how recruit and train members. *Naqibs* were trained in the art of organising meetings and activities, editing pamphlets and documents, etc., in addition to managing *usra*. The letter of "*Siyasat*" [Policies] outlined the principles of political work, to prepare members for dealing with various political movements and parties and for assuming power in Iraq.[99]

These letters were marked by their simple and direct discourse. They were greatly influenced by the difficult circumstances in Iraq which complicated the lives of the members of the Muslim Brotherhood. Although they had a lot in common, the letters written in Kuwait were different from those produced in Iraq. Al-Rashid's life in Iraq had been quite volatile compared with the quiet and easy life he led in Kuwait where he wrote the letters of "*al-Muntalaq*" [the Start],[100] "*al-ʿAwaʾiq*" [the Obstacles],[101] "*al-Masaar*" [the Path][102] and "*Sinaʿat al-Hayat*"

[98] Ibid.

[99] Al-Rashid, interview.

[100] Muhammad Ahmad al-Rashid, *al-Muntalaq* [the Start] (Dubai: Dar al-Mutalaq, 1994).

[101] Muhammad Ahmad al-Rashid, *al-ʿAwaʾiq* [the Obstacles] (Dubai: Dar al-Muntalaq, 1994).

[102] Muhammad Ahmad al-Rashid, *al-Masar* [the Path] (Cairo: Dar al-Nashr Liljamiʿat, 2010).

[the Making of Life][103] plus '*Rasa'il al-'Ain*' [the letters of Eye] serial. All these letters formed the basis of Islamic thinking and organisational ideology for the Muslim Brotherhood in Kuwait and other branches in the Arab world.

Al-Muntalaq summarised the mobilisation lessons of the movement that al-Rashid brought with him to Kuwait and established the foundations of movement for the Muslim Brotherhood there. This form of thinking would not be suitable for a political or secular party because many of its ideas were drawn from Islam as a religion. *Al-Muntalaq* set forth clear directives to members who had faith in what they were doing, and was not a document to introduce the Muslim Brotherhood to the public. Al-Rashid drew parallels with the Muslim nation's glorious past and the Muslim Brotherhood by emphasising the spirit of pride and loyalty in the hearts and minds of members. He also drew attention to the comprehensive nature of Islam and the importance of collective work in facing the challenges of colonisation.

Al-Rashid combined religious leadership with administrative management as a precondition for leading the movement. Emphasising the need for training a generation of members on the "*al-Qa'ida al-Sulbah*" [the solid base] principle was one of the most important lessons which he had learnt from the Iraqi experience. The idea was to draw upon the same intellectual sources to avoid what had happened in Iraq where members' diverse sources of knowledge had caused major disagreements over methods and strategies. The same had happened with the al-Irshad in Kuwait. Al-Rashid argued that the foundational generation must be chosen carefully and be welltrained in unifying goals and objectives. One of the main principles instilled in the foundational generation was a notion to which Sayyed Qutb had alluded: the sense of isolation or alienation from one's society, *al-'Uzlah al-Sh'uriyyah*.[104] However, in contrast to Qutb's notion, the Muslim Brotherhood in Kuwait did not believe that Kuwaiti society had strayed completely from religion, having shunned some aspects like women's attire, alcohol, interests on loans, etc. this for

---

[103] Muhammad Ahmad al-Rashid, *Sina'at al-Hayat* [the Making of Life] (Damascus: Dar al-Fikr, 2005).

[104] *al-'Uzlah al-Shu'uriyyah* emerged as a consequence of the hard times that Muslim Brotherhood members had faced under Nasser when they were tortured and killed. Also, Nasser's media drive against the Muslim Brotherhood helped feelings of isolation from the society to grow among Islamists, some of whom saw this society as a *Jahiliyya*.

al-Rashid signified society's neglect of the principles of Islam. It was thus essential for members to preserve, and remain steadfast within, an environment that was hostile to Islamist movements. Moreover, the Muslim Brotherhood in Kuwait did not adopt the revolutionary ideas of Qutb due to its conviction that the Kuwaiti context was not the same as the Egyptian one. Yet, some members of the Muslim Brotherhood, such as Ismail al-Shatti, adopted Qutb's revolutionary ideas for a while before abandoning them later.

Al-ʿAwaʾiq was a continuation of the principles contained in *al-Muntalaq* for shedding light on the organisational, social and intellectual problems that might face the movement and how best to tackle them from an intellectual and religious perspective. Al-Rashid began by emphasising the importance of commitment to the movement as a strategy for overcoming these obstacles. He listed obedience to the leadership as another important component based on the organisational principle that "no group could survive without obedience." Faith in leadership, the ideology, and group work were the best ways to combat all manner of troubles. However, stressing the building of ties between the members of the Muslim Brotherhood and the organisation was greatly exaggerated, to the extent that members became caught up with the group in all aspects of their lives (work, marriages, home, excursions, etc.). In an obvious enforcement of Qutb's idea of *al-ʿUzlah al-Shʿuriyyah*, the movement created an environment and a Muslim Brotherhood society in which the individual lived out all the ideals of the group but was totally divorced from his wider social context.[105]

The second letter written by al-Rashid following his arrival in Kuwait spoke about the obstacles and problems that might face the movement. It was a pre-emptive set of instructions to avoid previous problems that had impacted the Muslim Brotherhood in the past. The best strategy to avoid recurrence of these setbacks was to design an approach that would instil in the young recruits the principles of obedience and commitment to the group. Al-Rashid devised organisational rules that served as titles for a number of articles, such as "*al-Jundiyyah Tariq al-Qiyadah*" [Soldiery is the Path to Leadership], to entrench the values of loyalty and obedience. These organisational rules were of special relevance to the solid base on which the movement was founded in a hostile environment.

---

[105] Al-Rashid, interview.

Soldiery meant total obedience, fortitude and endurance. Moreover, the only path to leadership was for the member to be a solider for a while, during which time his faith and skills were tested. Soldiery also entailed the notion of promotion in rank, since members rose in rank according to the time they had served and their abilities. On this basis, members were expected to consult the leadership on all matters, including sacrifice, because "sacrificing one's life without permission is a waste."[106]

The rule that keeping secrets from other members led to problems was meant to discourage members from complaining secretly to each other by finding venues in which they could solve these problems and nip hem in the bud. By way of example, al-Rashid cited what had happened in Iraq when members began to complain about Zaidan's methods, and referred to this kind of talk among members as "*najwa*" (a collusive exchange between two people). This was a term borrowed from the Qur'an and had a great impact on those of great faith. He created a link between the term in the Qur'an and the organisational rule in a bid to integrate religion with rules of exchange. In another letter, al-Rashid emphasised a member's sense of confidence in himself, his thinking and his membership in the Muslim Brotherhood. The notion is reminiscent of that of "God's chosen people" in Judaism and Christianity and also dovetailed with Qutb's term "*al-Isti'la al-Imani*" [Superiority through Faith].

Al-Masar focused mainly on the movement's external and internal politics with special emphasis on its educational policies. External politics referred to dealings with the government, and other parties and movements. Al-Rashid had a very dim view of other political parties and movements especially the Nationalists, and in his view, the government was exploitative and pro-colonialist. His own experiences in Iraq had greatly influenced his view of the "Other." The internal politics of the Muslim Brotherhood was inspired by the Communist experience in the Soviet Union and their strategy of building the organisation gradually and secretly by laying down roots during the stage of "silent establishment" in order to "create the base" and "build the elite."[107] The solid base must not engage in any conflict or reveal itself, and the movement had to be given time to come together in complete secrecy.

---

[106] Muhammad al-Rashid, *Al-Masar*, 62.

[107] Muhammad al-Rashid, *Al-Masar*, 111.

Al-Rashid also argued that the Muslim Brotherhood must not enter the political arena until it was sufficiently strong and powerful to establish an Islamic state. This discourse of monopolising power had been part of the Iraqi political scene at a time which was fraught with coups d'état and the liquidation of all rivals. Achieving these goals in Iraq necessitated the adoption of very strict rules for selecting members and forming the solid base. Once the first stage had been completed, the movement could afford to ease some of the rules for taking on new members and benefiting from their wide expertise. This last notion was based on a socialist ideal of making the most of members' abilities according to their field of expertise.[108] Al-Rashid also focused on the women's branch of the movement, which would train women to help out their husbands by providing them with a good home environment. He also referred to the need to recruit members from among villagers and tribes.

Al-Masar was directed at the middle- and upper-leadership as opposed to the previous letters which focused on policies, establishment and obstacles and were directed at new members to introduce them to the *da'wah*. It outlined the instructions and methods of managing the organisation and recommended approaching intelligent and influential individuals who would form the solid base. *Al-Masar* also prepared the upper and middle leadership for the shift from secret work to public activities. Al-Rashid noted that the period between the two stages was very critical and meant adapting to the tough conditions of making that transition. Going public meant abandoning pure education and *tarbiyah* in order to interact with the rest of society, with all its leanings and trends that needless to say differed from those of the Muslim Brotherhood. The foundational generation had been raised on the principles of *da'wah* and the conflict between good and evil and that it was a matter of life or death was drastically different from the values espoused by the rest of society. Some members of the Muslim Brotherhood would object to going public and would rather stop at *tarbiya*, so *al-Masar* put forward the idea of opening gradually through a transitional period so that the leadership could comprehend its magnitude and successfully tackle the challenges and obstacles that the organisation would face during the transition.

---

[108] Fathi Yakan, *Official Website of Fathi Yakan*, "Fiqhiyyat Tanzimiyya: About Shura" (accessed 23 August 2013). www.daawa.net/display/arabic/efuqh/efuqhdetail. aspx?eid=144.

The letter "*Sina'at al-Hayat*" [the Making of Life] letter that al-Rashid wrote in the 1990s was different from all his previous work. For the first time, he was proposing a renewal of the Muslim Brotherhood's organisational strategies following the greater degree of openness that the Muslim Brotherhood was experiencing in several Arab countries. The letter explained for the first time how the Muslim Brotherhood should act after assuming power as the Sina'at al-Hayat, which echoed al-Banna's "professorship of the world." Both notions rested on an Islamic approach to various aspects of life (the economy, literature, art, think tanks, etc.) that were made possible only by educating and preparing a generation capable of carrying out these tasks. It would also need to win the trust of the public and plan for the future. Al-Rashid called upon more public works and for the first time referred to the global nature of the movement and its battle against other international organisations, such as the Zionist movement and the World Council of Churches.[109]

This novel approach by al-Rashid took the movement a step further towards theorising statehood and civilisation and not just the way the organisation should be run. He argued that change could only start on a micro-level through preparing leaders capable of assuming positions of power at the level of the state or bigger. He was still clearly preoccupied with the notion of monopolising power, although to a lesser extent than previously. As in his previous letters, he focused on *tarbiya* and the importance of portraying Islam in the best possible light by reviving Islamic art, establishing an Islamic economic system and Islamic planning centres. All this would reflect the true spirit of Islam and its inherent beauty for all to see and compare with their current way of life.

The Challenges Faced by the Muslim Brotherhood

From the beginning, the Kuwaiti Brotherhood sought to establish a strong organisation and avoid the mistakes of Islamist movements in other Arab countries. The focus was on instilling values of loyalty, obedience and full commitment in the members. *Shura* was adopted on a non-compulsory basis, with powers concentrated in the hands of one leader to ensure that affairs ran smoothly. The movement also aimed to establish a strong intellectual and organisational approach that would pull the

---

[109] Al-Rashid, interview.

members together through the writings of Muhammed Ahmed al-Rashid and, afterwards, the movement's curriculum committee. Yet none of this could prevent the occurrence of some internal conflicts. The absence of the culture of civil society institutions and the stringent stipulations of the movement with regards to secrecy led to several problems.

The first of these was a general feeling of unease among members of the lower ranks for being excluded from the decision-making process, especially in relation to issues that impacted directly on them. During the first preliminary meetings in 1968, Abdullah al-Nafisi objected to the non-binding nature of *Shura*, with this issue eventually leading him to decide against joining the movement. As mentioned above, with regard to *Shura*, Aman had relied on studies that had been prepared by Zaidan and that he himself had published in his book *The Principles of Da'wah*. Fathi Yakan, the General Observer of the Muslim Brotherhood in Lebanon, shared Zaidan's views of the matter.[110] Initially, the young age of the members meant they had great faith in their leader, so the issue of *Shura* was not problematic. However, as time went by and as members acquired more experience and became more exposed to the experiences of Islamist movements in other countries, they demanded the matter be opened to fresh debates.

Soon after this, Nasser had died, and as the Muslim Brotherhood members in Egypt were released from jail, they began to travel far and wide all over the Arab world, creating links between various Muslim Brotherhood branches intended to preserve the identity of the organisation under one umbrella. One of the most important principles of global Muslim Brotherhood was the binding nature of *Shura*. The question was therefore resolved in Kuwait since the organisation there became increasingly linked with the global Muslim Brotherhood in which Kuwait had a representative in the early 1980s.[111]

The second problem that the Muslim Brotherhood had to face for a long time was related to the global nature of the movement. Abdullah al-'Aqil, whose Muslim Brotherhood background had been acquired during his years of study in Cairo, believed in the universality of Islam and the globalisation of the Muslim Brotherhood *da'wah*. As such, the Kuwaiti

---

[110] Aman, interview.

[111] Ibid.

Muslim Brotherhood should include members from various Arab nationalities, especially the Palestinians almost half a million of whom were living in Kuwait at the time.[112] The term *"al-Tanzim al-Muwahhad"* [the Unified Organisation] was proposed for referring to a movement that brought together members of various nationalities. Al-ʿAqil recruited new members regardless of their nationalities in a separate organisation which he named the *al-Tanzim al-Muwahhad* in the late 1970s.[113]

Aman, on the other hand, disagreed with al-ʿAqil about the realistic prospects for such a unified organisation in the light of the social and security concerns unique to each Arab context; at this time, the Yemeni or Syrian Muslim Brotherhood member, prior to the Hama massacre, was leading a relatively free life, while the Iraqi and Egyptian Muslim Brotherhood members were being persecuted both at home and abroad. Moreover, social conditions and the economic and social gap between Kuwaitis and foreign workers had negatively impacted on the relationship between the two sides. The Kuwaiti movement emphasised the existence of such social differences, but members of *al-Tanzim al-Muwahhad* rejected these claims as racist.[114]

Due to al-ʿAqil's good relationship with the Muslim Brotherhood in Egypt, he succeeded in persuading them that the Unified Organisation was the true representative of Kuwait in the Global Muslim Brotherhood. However, the Kuwaiti branch sent a delegation to Egypt to present their point of view to The Global Muslim Brotherhood which was forced to send a representative to find a solution to the problem. The representative's arrival was followed shortly after by the arrival of *al-Murshed* himself (who at that time was ʿUmar al-Telmisani). This was because of the importance to the Global Muslim Brotherhood of the Kuwaiti branch, based mainly on its publishing of the journal *al-Mujtamaʿ* [the Society] which was the Muslim Brotherhood's only platform for publishing their views. A compromise was reached whereby an office was established to bring together the Kuwaiti Muslim Brotherhood, *al-Tanzim al-Muwahhad*, and the Palestinian Muslim Brotherhood

---

[112] Hassan A. El-Najjar, *The Gulf War: Overreaction & Excessiveness* (USA: Amazon Press, 2001) (accessed 24 August 2013). http://www.gulfwar1991.com/Gulf%20War%20Complete/Chapter%2010,%20Palestinians%20in%20Kuwait,%20Terror%20and%20Ethnic%20Cleansing,%20by%20Hassan%20A.%20El-Najjar.htm.

[113] Al-ʿAqil, interview.

[114] Ibid.

in Kuwait which had refused to participate in the Unified Organisation due to the special nature of the Palestinian question. Time proved the Kuwaiti movement right, since each community was more concerned with its own set of issues while earning their living drained all the energy of foreign Arab workers. Eventually, the Kuwaiti branch became the only legitimate representative of the Muslim Brotherhood in Kuwait in the office of the Global Muslim Brotherhood in the late 1980s.[115]

The biggest problem facing the Muslim Brotherhood was the emergence of the Salafi movement which began to compete with the Muslim Brotherhood over control of the social domain. The Wahhabi branch of Salafia thinking was a familiar presence in Kuwaiti society which had elements originating in Najd, the birthplace of the Wahhabi movement. The Wahhabi ideology did not spread very much because Kuwait's shaikhs were more influenced by al-Hasa and the reformist trends mentioned above. Also, the Kuwaiti society had historically adopted a negative stance towards Wahabism because of the several wars between Kuwait and the movement. Therefore, the social domain remained dominated by the reformists, secularists and Islamists. The emergence of the Salafis had a bigger impact on the Muslim Brotherhood than the secular nationalists had done since Salafis share aspects of their own mission (mosques, *fatwa*, charity, *da'wah*, etc.) with the Muslim Brotherhood. The Salafi trend began with the teachings of ʿAbdulkhaliq and al-Ashqar who transmitted the Salafi-Wahhabi mode of thought from the Islamic University in Medina in Saʿudi Arabia. Although neither was affiliated with any particular movement or party, the Salafi influence was evident in their teachings, and this encouraged many young men to examine it further. Among these men were Musaʿid al-ʿAbduljadir and Abdullah al-Sabt who had a small group that differed from that of the Muslim Brotherhood.

There were no major disagreements between the Muslim Brotherhood and the Salafis between 1965 (when al-Ashqar and ʿAbdulkhaliq arrived) and the early 1970s, simply because the Salafi movement did not have any particular leaders (al-Ashqar and ʿAbdulkhaliq never identified themselves as Salafis). Most of the shaikhs and Islamist leaders were either from the Muslim Brotherhood or were influenced by them. But the arrival of al-Rashid in 1974 changed everything. He began writing articles in *al-Mujtamaʿ* journal in addition to delivering lectures at al-Islah, while

---

[115] Aman, interview.

his teachings included references to many Sufists such as Ibrahim bin Adham and al-Harith al-Muhasabi. Quoting ascetics and Sufists did not appeal to ꜥAbdulkhaliq who, with his Wahhabi background, had fought fiercely against Sufism in the Arabian Peninsula. Indeed, Wahhabism had emerged as a response to the Wahhabist belief that Sufism tarnished the purity of Islam. In reaction to al-Rashid, ꜥAbulkhaliq also wrote articles in *al-Mujtamaꜥ* attacking al-Rashid's Sufist references. ꜥAbdulkhaliq also delivered a lecture at al-Islah warning against the dangers of Sufism. This open form of criticism was the exception rather than the norm among Islamist movements whose members preferred to discuss these matters in the framework of a small circle of people rather than publicly.

Al-Rashid's response reflected Newton's third law "for every action there is an equal and opposite." He wrote another series of articles in *al-Mujtamaꜥ* defending the Sufist figures to whom he had alluded in his previous writings. For almost a month and a half, the two men argued openly on the pages of *al-Mujtamaꜥ*, thereby creating a great deal of confusion among the small Islamist movements, especially the Muslim Brotherhood. Eventually the leadership decided to try and resolve the matter amicably. A meeting was summoned by Aman, and was held in his presence, with al-Ashqar as arbiter between the two parties. Following several hours of heated debate, al-Ashqar finally acknowledged that the Sufist figures that al-Rashid had mentioned were among Islam's most prominent symbols of piety and that drawing upon such legacy was very favourable.[116]

ꜥAbdulkhaliq did not take too well to this change of mind, especially from his long-time friend who had been with him in Jordan, Medina and Kuwait, and gradually withdrew from al-Islah. He attracted a group of young men who found in him a mentor and a leader, and for the first time, the Salafi movement emerged as a real entity with a well-educated leader.[117]

This point in the mid-1970s marked the beginning of a ferocious conflict between the Muslim Brotherhood and the Salafis which reached epic proportions in the mid-1980s as a result of Salafi attempts to dominate the social domain, especially among religious Sunnis. Kuwaiti Salafis

[116] The debate between al-Rashid and ꜥAbdulkhaliq were on the pages of *al-Mujtamaꜥ*, editions number 193, 194, 195, 196, 197, and 198.

[117] Al-ꜥAbduljadir, interview.

opened the door to the Wahhabi creed and facilitated its penetration of Kuwaiti society, by inviting Sa'udi shaikhs to visit Kuwait, and publishing books and tapes by Salafi figures as Muhammed bin 'Abdulwahhab, the movement's founder, and other modern figures such as 'Abdul'aziz bin Baz and Muhammed bin Othaimeen from Sa'udi Arabia and Nassereddin al-Albani from Jordan. The Salafis considered themselves the heirs to the Wahhabi movement in Kuwait and were very popular among Najdi and tribal Kuwaitis who were a natural extension of the Wahhabi movement. The movement had originated in Najd and was later joined by a number of tribes who were known as "the brothers of the believers in Allah" or "the Brothers," although they were different from the Muslim Brotherhood. As well as appealing to those two sectors of society, the Salafi movement competed with the Muslim Brotherhood for control over mosques and various other religious platforms (see Chapter 4 for a detailed account of these struggles).

These internal problems affected the Muslim Brotherhood in Kuwait although without leading to the collapse of the movement as happened in several other countries. This may have been due to the success of the founders in building a strong organisation on a solid base; similarly, the great trust placed in the leadership nipped any criticisms in the bud. Because the organisation had been able to establish the solid core it had aspired to from the start, its members were highly disciplined and committed to their leadership, despite its centralised nature, while their administrative and intellectual skills, following years of training, were of the highest calibre. Undoubtedly, drawing from the same resources helped to create a harmonious atmosphere among members and the long time they had spent together had fostered strong ties between them.

Shifting to a More Open Era

At the end of the 1970s, almost ten years after the establishment of the new organisation, members began to debate whether it was time to increase their public profile by entering a phase of more openness. Most of these new ideas were proposed by members who had studied abroad, especially in the West, while many members had matured from inexperienced young men to fully-integrated members of society with a different outlook on virtually everything. And since Kuwait enjoyed a relatively good margin of freedom, there seemed no reason to remain underground. However, several members were apprehensive about this proposed openness and questioned its nature and its methods. Many had been encouraged to join the organisation because of its secretive nature and it was therefore paramount for them to protect the movement from government agents, infiltrators and moles.[118]

The debate between opponents and proponents of more openness lasted for quite some time, but eventually, the decision was taken to engage in partial openness by participating in professional associations and *diwaniyyas*. Involvement in the former succeeded, but the movement did not gain success with the latter, as is discussed in later chapters. The Muslim Brotherhood also engaged in a restructuring process in order to include a branch for women that was linked directly with the movement's leader, but the most prominent change was the establishment of a social work department which recruited members who had had long experience in training young men and who were now called upon to spread the Muslim Brotherhood's message among society as a whole. Social work was highly specialised with each sector undertaking a specific mission (teachers, politicians, unionists, etc.). The Muslim Brotherhood also debated the issue of nominating some of their members for the Kuwaiti Parliament, and it was decided to go ahead and field candidates, despite objections by some senior figures that the movement was not yet ready for political life.

However, the movement's ultimate mission remained the education and *tarbiya* of young men and women, which made it quite difficult for the Muslim Brotherhood to make the transition to a new stage under the same leadership of educators. A fear of politics and a preference for education and training led many Muslim Brotherhood members to remain attached to the old system. Despite the change of leadership in 1988, when ʿAbdulwahid Aman handed over the reins to Jasim Muhalhal al-Yasin, one of the members of the solid base that had been formed by Aman, the general pace of the movement remained more or less the same until the Iraqi occupation of Kuwait which changed the history of the region and by default, the Muslim Brotherhood.[119]

---

[118] Aman, interview.

[119] Al-ʿAtiqi, interview.

The Muslim Brotherhood
and the Iraqi Invasion of Kuwait

On 2 August 1991, Iraqi troops launched an army offensive and occupied Kuwait, whereupon Iraq's leader, President Saddam Hussein, proclaimed that Kuwait was now "Governorate 19" of the Iraqi Republic. The Kuwaiti Emir, Shaikh Jaber al-Subah and his Crown Prince Shaikh Sa'ad al-Subah, took up residence in Ta'if in Sa'udi Arabia. The shock of this attack hit the Kuwaiti people very hard; many were abroad on holiday and had no means of contacting their families back home, while fear drove many others to flee the country. The Muslim Brotherhood's first reaction was to call for an emergency meeting, at which members of the leadership who were in Kuwait at the time resolved to stay in the country and offer support to the Kuwaiti people. The movement was geographically restructured to facilitate the delivery of services and aid, and also played a major role in offering religious and moral support to anxious Kuwaitis. In collaboration with certain Kuwaitis, the Kuwaiti Muslim Brotherhood then established "*al-Murabitun*" [The Steadfast] movement whose objectives were to:

1. Liberate Kuwait and reinstate its legitimate rulers;
2. Encourage people to stay in Kuwait;
3. Offer support to those still left in Kuwait;
4. Plan Kuwait's future according to the teachings of Allah.[120]

Al-Murabitun's work was divided between two sections: a military wing, known as the "Kuwaiti Popular Resistance," with a group of Kuwaiti army officers headed by Major General Khalid Budai, and a civilian wing, "the Social Solidarity Committee." Due to the dangerous security situation and the possibility of arrest, the two wings were kept completely separate through a hierarchical cluster structure. The popular resistance was led by non-Brotherhood army officers, while the solidarity committee was managed by the Muslim Brotherhood who had extensive experience in that sphere. The literature of the Muslim Brotherhood,

---

[120] Al-Ghazali, *Kuwait's Forth Wall 3*, 225–228.

especially the works written by Qutb during his periods of imprisonment in Nasser's Egypt, had prepared the movement for these tough conditions.[121]

Kuwait embraced the Muslim Brotherhood during the occupation because of its highly competent organisation and spread throughout the whole society. The movement had branches all over Kuwait and was very successful at running the country's affairs with the help of various sectors of the community. The first branch of the Solidarity Committee was established in Bayan and Mishrif, areas in which many Muslim Brotherhood leaders and members lived, and many Kuwaitis volunteered in the Solidarity Committee which was directly managed by the organisation. The committee's name was intentional as it avoided giving any political or military undertones to its agenda, which was concerned solely with charity and offering social services. Initially, the mosques were the springboard for all the committee's activities and resistance movements, since it was natural for people to gather there five times a day without arousing suspicion. The work of the Solidarity Committee was divided into various domains:

1. The Service Sector

Following the invasion, most of the foreign labour force, which had previously held the majority of jobs in Kuwait, fled the country The Solidarity Committee invited Kuwaitis to operate the necessary basic services and called on people with various skills to help keep major facilities operational. For the first time, Kuwaitis had to rely on themselves to do various jobs. Some of the facilities and services operated by Kuwaitis were:

a. Cooperatives and Bakeries
Cooperatives represented the main source of foodstuffs and other daily needs such as gas. Kuwaitis kept the cooperatives running for a while until the Iraqi authorities issued orders banning voluntary work. This prompted the Solidarity Committee to reject the orders and resort to trickery to avoid being caught. On 22 January 1991, the Iraqi authorities began to supply goods but only to holders of Iraqi ration cards so as to force Kuwaitis to apply for them. The

---

[121] Ibid.

cooperatives responded, before the decision came into effect, by supplying sufficient rations to last people for several months. Also, a number of volunteers were trained to manage bakeries owned by the Kuwaiti Flour Company. The Iraqi authorities tried to fabricate crises such as bread shortages to put an end to civil strife, but bakers frequently hid bread from the Iraqi army to be distributes later among Kuwaitis.[122]

b. Waste Collection

Locals collaborated with the Solidarity Committee to collect waste from residential areas. Special cars were used for this purpose until confiscated by the Iraqi authorities; the Solidarity Committee then allocated special locations in various areas for the collecting and burning of waste.

c. Managing the Red Crescent Society

The Solidarity Committee, in collaboration with members of the Red Crescent Society,[123] reopened the Society's facilities and relaunched their services to offer assistance at centres for people with specials needs and the elderly. The Committee also played a major role in providing medical supplies for hospitals and health centres, in addition to their contribution to the treatment of the injured and passing on secret information.

2. Humanitarian Efforts

As a means of divesting the occupation of any legitimacy, one of Kuwait's most important civil disobedience strategies was refusal to work. In an attempt to impose a sense of normalcy on the country, the Iraqi authorities had called upon Kuwaiti citizens to return to work. Boycotting the new government in this way meant that Kuwaitis lost their main source of income, forcing them to seek alternatives. The situation was much easier for Kuwaitis abroad as they could rely on aid from other Gulf countries and the government of Kuwait in Ta'if. Therefore, one of the Solidarity Committee's main tasks was to ensure that Kuwaiti families who stayed

---

[122] Jamal al-Kandari, interview.

[123] Red Crescent Society is the Islamic equivalent of the Red Cross with which it works internationally in delivering medical and humanitarian aid.

at home were receiving enough money to sustain them. Many Kuwaiti merchants and members of the ruling family contributed to providing families with money and basic foodstuffs. A list sent by the Committee to the Crown Prince Shaikh Sa'ad in Ta'if revealed that more than 50 million Iraqi dinars were distributed among Kuwaitis living in thirty residential areas in Kuwait.[124]

The Solidarity Committee also played a humanitarian role in keeping channels of communication open with the Iraqi authorities regarding Kuwaiti prisoners of war who were being held for various reasons. Visits were organised to enable families to go to see family members in Iraqi prisons in Ba'quba, Ramadi, al-Rashīd and Mosul. The Committee also provided the families of POW's with financial assistance and food, and were also successful in securing the release of a number of POW's before they were transferred to Iraq.

3. Raising Awareness and Providing Social Services

With the departure of many Arab imams and muezzins after the invasion, a number of locals volunteered to perform the calls to prayer and deliver sermons. The Solidarity Committee organised a variety of social and religious activities at mosques to provide locals with some form of useful entertainment and a meeting place where they could exchange news and information away from the prying eyes of the Iraqi army.

Following the Occupation, a number of *fiqh* questions were raised pertaining to dealings with the Occupation authorities, the legitimacy of resistance, using the property of Kuwaitis living abroad at the time, burying the dead, prisoners of war and other issues. The Solidarity Committee formed a religious committee (including Ajil al-Nashmi, ʿUmaral-Ashqar, Muhammad Abdulghaffar al-Sharif, Jasim al-Yasin and others) to issue *fatwas* as appropriate.[125]

The most difficult questions were those related to whether Allah would sanction killing members of the Iraqi army (since killing another Muslim is a great sin), and whether it was acceptable for Kuwaitis to leave the country if they had a legitimate reason to do so.

---

[124] Al-Ghazali, *Kuwait's Forth Wall 3*, 225–228.

[125] Ajil al-Nashmi, interview.

Fatwas sanctioning resistance and killing the enemy were based on the Qur'anic verse,

> Indeed, the penalty for those who wage war against Allah and His Messenger and strive upon earth [to cause] corruption is none but that they be killed or crucified or that their hands and feet be cut off from opposite sides or that they be exiled from the land. That is for them a disgrace in this world; and for them in the Hereafter is a great punishment. (5:33)

The *fatwa* warned against carrying out military operations near residential areas in order to avoid endangering the lives of locals. Another fatwa was issued allowing those who needed to leave the country to do, so while emphasising the importance of staying put for those who had no reason to leave. Due to the suspension of the court system, cases of various types were adjudicated by the committee.

Al-Murabitun issued a magazine to boost morale and encourage people remain steadfast in the face of adversity, although the publishers were forced to issue it from London to avoid persecution. Despite the Iraqi authorities' attempts to ban it, the magazine was distributed at mosques, and in markets and other public places. The Solidarity Committee also put out a DEED (Daily Event Digest) which offered a detailed account of people's daily lives under occupation.

The Post-invasion Era

The work of *al-Murabitun* during the invasion of Kuwait meant that the Muslim Brotherhood made huge strides in social integration. All the former barriers (courtesy of obsolete theories that described society as ignorant and alienating) between the movement and society were effectively removed, thus giving the Muslim Brotherhood far wider exposure as people got to know them and their work much better. The organisation itself also experienced a greater degree of openness by the sheer force of circumstances rather than through any previous planning. Seizing the opportunity to raise the ceiling of their ambitions, the Muslim Brotherhood announced the establishment of a political wing, to be known as The Islamic Constitutional Movement, ICM. A number of social and youth committees were also established as part of their plans to impose a new social reality through opening up into society.

While the post-invasion era was marked by more openness in social and political work, the organisational part remained less conspicuous because of their pervasive fear of any backlash and in the light of the persecution that had been faced by the Muslim Brotherhood in Egypt, Syria and some Gulf countries. The Muslim Brotherhood also preferred to establish a number of fronts under their own supervision and without announcing themselves as an organisation, regarding this as a transitional step towards a complete declaration of the movement.

The new phase did not fundamentally affect the structure of the Muslim Brotherhood. It retained its old divisions into educational, social, political and women's sections, although all of them were expanded and acquired more formal fronts to attract a bigger number of followers. The Muslim Brotherhood did not consider it necessary to restructure the movement, especially in the light of the huge success they had enjoyed with *al-Murabitun* and the Social Solidarity Committee.

The real change occurred in the relationship between the Kuwaiti Muslim Brotherhood and other branches in Jordan and the Sudan who had supported Saddam Hussein's occupation of Kuwait. The Kuwaiti branch expressed its great dismay at the failure of the Global Muslim Brotherhood to adopt a decisive position vis-à-vis the Iraqi occupation of the country. Prior to the Iraqi invasion, local Muslim Brotherhood movements had generally accepted the guidance and directives of the Global Office, but decisions pertaining to certain local issues were left to the discretion of the Muslim Brotherhood in any given country. However, the lack of any clear condemnation of the Iraqi invasion by Egypt, the Global Office and the Sudanese and Jordanian branches angered the Kuwaiti Brotherhood which decided to freeze its membership in the Global Office. They also launched a fierce attack against the Jordanian and Sudanese branches and a number of Islamic figures who had supported the Iraqi invasion, and the Global Office was equally criticised for having failed to support Kuwait in its plight.

After the Kuwaiti government in Ta'if had called upon the United States and Western countries to intervene to end the Iraqi occupation the Global Office and many Muslim Brotherhood branches undoubtedly found themselves in quite an embarrassing position. This was because Islamists, and especially the Muslim Brotherhood, had always criticised the colonial and imperial ambitions of Western countries. It was therefore very hard to accept the idea of foreign intervention against a fellow Arab country like Iraq even if the purpose was to liberate Kuwait. The Global

Office had proposed an Arab solution to the crisis and the replacing of Western military power with armies from Muslim countries, but this idea was rejected by the Kuwaitis who did not think it was particularly viable.

CONCLUSION

Compared with its neighbours, Kuwait is a young and very small country; this placed it in a position to be influenced by, rather than to influence, others in the fields of politics, economics and ideas, a fact that had a considerable effect on the Kuwaiti Muslim Brotherhood. During the 50 years that followed its establishment, the movement went through many changes. Like the mother organisation in Egypt, it was quite open during its formative stages, but soon fell victim to internal struggles that were actually an extension of the same problems that were confronting the Egyptian Muslim Brotherhood. Political events in the Arab world also affected the Kuwaiti Muslim Brotherhood and prompted the members to resort to secrecy following the persecution of their counterparts in Egypt and Iraq, and especially as their new leadership had actually come from Iraq. The movement then sought to rebuild the organisation through a solid core that could spread the Muslim Brotherhood's message all over Kuwait under the veil of secrecy. Despite the benefits gained by the organisation from the invasion of Kuwait, which had won them considerable popularity and public trust, most of their attempts to work openly ended in failure, since the members were afraid of being infiltrated by the government and other parties. The older members had also become used to doing things in the traditional way and were not willing to change.

The Muslim Brotherhood's success in establishing a strong organisation led them to aspire to control the social domain by expanding their social base and changing some of the stereotypes propagated by Nasser and the nationalists in the consciousness of Kuwaitis. Some of these stereotypes were tackled by appealing to a younger generation of men who went on to spread the Muslim Brotherhood's message among other young men through *Al-Islah*, which represented the voice of Islamists in Kuwait. The Muslim Brotherhood also succeeded in becoming influential in various social and professional associations, and its social activities played a similar role in changing these stereotypes, before it began to consider entering the political domain.

CHAPTER 4

Social Activism

INTRODUCTION

The emergence of the Muslim Brotherhood in Kuwait was not an anomaly, given the history of Islamic reformist movements which had been active for decades in Kuwait. The Kuwaiti Muslim Brotherhood was an extension of the Islamic reformist project that began with Jamal al-Din al-Afghani, Muhammad ʿAbduh and Rashīd Rida. Its pronounced aims were to reform society by overcoming the state of intellectual and educational inertia, and to open up to other cultures to keep pace with progress in other parts of the world. It also aimed to improve the status of women whose lives were governed by very strict and traditional modes of thinking. Islamists considered women as part and parcel of any attempt to advance society without that advance jeopardising core Islamic values. The Islamist project was quite hostile to Western ideas which viewed the notion of an Islamic civilisation as an oxymoron. It was equally opposed to secularism and its attempts to introduce new systems of social values. Thus, Islamist movements, including the Muslim Brotherhood, developed in the context of heated debates about intellectual and moral frames of reference. Events in the region had a direct impact on intellectual and political life in Kuwait which was too small to be influential but big enough to be influenced by events in neighbouring countries. The reformist Islamic project and later on the Muslim Brotherhood succeeded in dominating the social domain, as reformists like Shaikh Yusif bin ʿIsa

A. A. Alkandari, *The Muslim Brotherhood in Kuwait*, Contemporary Gulf Studies, https://doi.org/10.1007/978-981-99-3050-0_4

and Shaikh ʿAbdulʿaziz al-Rushaid spread their vision of Islamist reform at the expense of the traditional Islamists.

In this context, the "social domain" refers to all matters related to people's spiritual and social lives. The "religious establishment" was represented by religious scholars, jurists, teachers, Sufis and others, who were concerned with spreading the teachings of Islam. The history of Islam has been rife with examples of the domination of the religious establishment over the social domain. For example, jurists laid down the principles of jurisprudence on the basis of their own understanding of the Qurʾan and Sunnah which, with the consideration of the passing of time and differences between contexts, were the main pillars of the religious establishment and spread throughout the Muslim world. After the death of the Prophet, a substantial jurisprudential tradition was amassed, and jurists remained the only source of jurisprudence and the legal codes that regulated all aspects of a Muslim's life. Since judges were chosen from among well-known jurists, the judiciary was thus put under the control of the religious establishment as well. Mystics and ascetics, represented mainly by the Sufis, played a major role in spreading Muslim values and moral codes among populations. Mosques occupied a prominent position as beacons of spiritual and cultural identities, especially as many Muslims performed all five daily prayers at mosques; naturally, these were under the control of the religious establishment. No authority (legal, military, ruling, etc.) dared to transgress into the social domain, which would have rejected them since they lacked the knowledge base and/or the qualifications to take over the social domain. On the contrary, it was often the case that jurists were active in politics. In general, any ruling elite needed the legitimacy bestowed upon them by religious scholars and jurists in return for the latter holding free rein over the social domain.[1]

In Kuwait, the religious establishment played the same role; however, a new generation of Islamists challenged the traditional conservative Islamists who were accustomed to controlling the religious establishment. The reformist Islamists found themselves engaged in a prolonged competition with the traditional conservatives, and eventually, the reformists

---

[1] Stéphane Lacroix discusses the notion of the "domain" with reference to Saudi Arabian society. His book categorises Saʿudi society into political and social domains, with the social domain including the cultural and religious domains. Stéphane Lacroix, *Awakening Islam: The Politics of Religious Dissent in Contemporary Saʿudi Arabia*, trans. George Holoch (Cambridge MA: Harvard University Press, 2011).

won control over the social domain. However, another competitor, the seculars, then arrived on the scene with a secular project that threatened the authority of the religious establishment over the social domain. The Islamists then found themselves engaged in a lengthy and severe fight with the secularists over the social domain. Meanwhile, the Islamists were also competing with each other over the social domain. In this "internal" struggle, the Muslim Brotherhood succeeded for a while in dominating the Islamic social domain until the emergence of the Salafi movement which, in its turn, vied with the Muslim Brotherhood over control of the religious establishment and social domain.

The Muslim Brotherhood: A Continuation of Religious Establishment and Heirs to the Islamist Project

The Islamist reformist project in Kuwait was represented by religious figures such as Shaikh Yusif bin ʿIsa al-Qinaʿi and Shaikh ʿAbdulʿaziz al-Rushaid and was initially met with fierce resistance from traditional conservative religious forces that had hitherto held full sway over the social domain. By the 1930s, the reformist movement, including both Islamist and nationalist groups, succeeded with time in imposing its will on the social domain while the ruling family retained full authority over the political domain. The ideas of the Islamist reformist movement influenced the Muslim Brotherhood through the friendship between al-Qinaʿi and ʿAbdulʿaziz al-Mutawwaʿ. Both the Muslim Brotherhood and the reformist movement took their inspiration from the same source: the school of Rashīd Rida. While the Islamic figures of the reformist movement, such as al-Qinaʿi, were preoccupied with the affairs of daily life, especially jurisprudence, the newly-emerged Muslim Brotherhood had the task of spreading the message of Islam (*daʿwah*). The Muslim Brotherhood began by forming the first group of young Muslim Brotherhood members at the end of the 1940s and established al-Irshad as the official front for their activities. *Daʿwah* extended to all aspects of social, cultural, religious and intellectual life and served to further the influence of the Muslim Brotherhood over the social domain.

The Muslim Brotherhood and Social Movement Theory

Social Movement theory provides useful tools for demonstrating the functions of Islamist movements, especially the Muslim Brotherhood. The movement employed a variety of approaches mostly within domains controlled by Islamist movements such as mosques, schools and charity organisations to mobilise the Kuwaiti street. The Muslim Brotherhood added new tools inspired by the mother organisation in Egypt (a pyramid organisational structure, *usra* system, etc.). Munson observes that the Muslim Brotherhood used a mix of these tools, noting that the structure of the Muslim Brotherhood and the family system were crucial elements in the struggle against the secularist cultural invasion. The Kuwaiti Muslim Brotherhood succeeded in establishing a set of cultural discourses unique to them through these tools and channels. Their efforts transformed Kuwaiti society, which became increasingly more pious and religiously committed. Both Bayat and Munson argue that existing literature on social movement theory cannot fully explain the Islamist activism in Muslim communities, not because Muslim communities are too unique to fit into any framework, but because those theories tend to be more "Westocentric" rather than global.[2] Most of these theories, except for Resource Mobilization Theory (RMT), assume that social movements emerge in a relatively liberal and democratic political system, while this is not the case in many parts of the world including the Muslim world. While authoritarianism is rooted in political systems from Morocco to Indonesia, Islamist movements are very active on different levels and forms. A new theory is, therefore, needed to explain this massive activism under such authoritarian political systems. Bayat develops a new way of understanding Islamist activism under what he refers to as the theory of "imagined solidarity." Bayat asserts that Islamist activism is fluid and based on a general consensus on major issues such as justice and equality. However, when it comes to the details, actors differ from each other in their perceptions of these issues because of their different experiences and ways of life. Because of these differences, Bayat argues that there is

---

[2] Asef Bayat, "Islamism and Social Movement Theory," *Third World Quarterly*, 26, No. 6 (2005), 891–908, Ziad Munson, "Islamic Mobilization: Social Movement Theory and the Egyptian Muslim Brotherhood," *The Sociological Quarterly*, 42, No. 4 (2001), 487–510.

an "imagined solidarity" among people in general and Islamist activists specifically towards general issues such as the Palestinian/Israeli conflict. Therefore, the mechanism of mobilisation could take any form, from a spontaneous collective action to organised resource mobilisation tactics and strategies. This cohesive opinion on particular issues unites different social sectors as witnessed during the Islamic revolution in Iran where all social sectors united behind Khomeini against the Shah. Bayat's "imagined solidarity" fits the Kuwaiti context during the 1980s and 1990s when the public embraced Islamist ideas presented by the Islamists especially the Muslim Brotherhood. An important indication of the application of the "imagined solidarity" was the rising popularity of Hijab among girls in Kuwait University. Less than 10 girls were wearing the Hijab in the early 1970s compared to hundreds in the mid-1980s and thousands ten years later.

Munson provides a different scope for studying Islamist activism in his study of the emergence of the Muslim Brotherhood in Egypt from the 1930s to 1950s. The Muslim Brotherhood started out of the sight of the government for internal and external factors such as the Second World War. However, in the aftermath of the Second World War, the Egyptian government during King Farouq's reign cruelly repressed the Muslim Brotherhood leaders. This repression, in contrast to the assumptions of New Social Movement Theory, Collective Behaviour and the other theories, did not stop the activity and mobilisation process of this movement either nationally or internationally. Munson argues that the secret of this success lies in the integration between the message of the Muslim Brotherhood and its organisational structure. The interaction between the message and the structure is represented in the movement's resonance with ordinary people's beliefs and needs to be placed under an Islamist theoretical frame and a pragmatic programme. Simple beliefs such as expelling Zionists from Palestine, countering the cultural Westernisation project in Egypt and the Muslim world and reforming or removing the British-controlled government of King Farouq were interpreted in an Islamic way. This Islamic labelling of such issues was projected upon Islamist projects geared to addressing each problem. For instance, the project to counter-attack the cultural project of Westernising Egypt was carried out by launching *da'wah* [preaching of Islam] as a medium to propagate the Muslim Brotherhood message among people. Munson reveals an interesting confidential report by the US State Department by State Department informants from 1954 in Egypt

The most interesting part of our conversation dealt with the manner in which the Ikhwan [The Muslim Brotherhood] carries on its propaganda work in the rural areas. Either in a written document or by word of mouth the Ikhwan's line on current issues is sent to all rural centers where it is explained to four or five fairly literate leaders capable of explaining the issues to others and defending it if necessary. These leaders, in turn, each contact approximately one hundred fellow Ikhwanis and pass on the information. Subsequently it is spread in a less organized fashion among the people by both Ikhwanis and non-Ikhwanis. He [the member of the Muslim Brotherhood] claimed that this mechanism for spreading information is very effective because travellers to rural areas were always in good supply. Therefore, the transmission of information presents no problem.[3]

From this document, it is evident that *daʿwah* represents the product of the interaction between the message and the structure in what Munson calls "the federate structure of the Muslim Brotherhood." Nonetheless, Munson does not rely only on the interconnection between message and structure, but he also explains how the Muslim Brotherhood seizes opportunities according to the political opportunity structure such as the case when the Muslim Brotherhood filled the vacuum after the weakening of the Wafd Party in the mid-1940s until its collapse in 1952. Although the Muslim Brotherhood did not present itself as a political party, it filled a political vacuum and prepared the masses for an inevitable coup d'état by the Free Officers in 1952.

Both Bayat and Munson offer interesting insights into Islamist social movement theory. However, these need to be tested in relation to other movements across the region and developed in order to provide the basics for an Islamist Social Movement Theory. Bayat stresses going beyond simple analysis of the text using an anthropological approach to a more intricate examination of the circumstances surrounding the text: its production, transmission and reception. This leads to the study of the daily dynamics of the social movement to trace the development of strategies, tactics and even ideas, which result in understanding the way an Islamist social movement's goal progresses from the social to the political. The Muslim Brotherhood in Kuwait has a rich experience different from the Egyptian or Iraqi branches of the movement. Different factors

---

[3] US Department of State (USDS). 1949. Confidential Central Files, Egypt, 1954, No. 564, Washington, DC.

influenced the development of the movement in Kuwait such as the relationship with the ruling family, the Islamic Revolution in Iran in 1979 and the Iraqi occupation of Kuwait in 1990–1991. Studying the context within which the Muslim Brotherhood in Kuwait has developed helps also with setting basics for Islamist social movement theory.

Munson argues that the Muslim Brotherhood in Egypt is an Islamist political party that emerged in a repressive political environment. In the Kuwaiti context, this view does not apply to the experience of the Muslim Brotherhood because the movement never witnessed real repression by the ruling family. Although the Muslim Brotherhood in Kuwait possesses its own political views and actions, the movement should not be considered as only a political party. Between the 1960s and the mid-1980s, most of the political literature of the Muslim Brotherhood in Kuwait and Islamists in general discussed international and regional political affairs, specifically the Arab-Israeli conflict and the Western sociopolitical threat against Islam and Muslim societies. In this literature, countering Western hegemony is a manifestation of the real incentive that drives the Muslim Brotherhood as a movement to protect the identity of the Muslim world from the religio-cultural threat. The Muslim Brotherhood in Kuwait is a social movement that aims to reassert the influence of the religious establishment over the social domain through various channels, including politics.

Intellectual and Educational Activities of Al-Irshad, 1952–1958

The intellectual issues on which al-Irshad focused its attention were society and international politics. Domestically, social issues dominated the discourse of al-Irshad, and included the promotion of education, health and hygiene, and the celebration of religious and social events such as Mawlid and Hijri New Year. Internationally, al-Irshad addressed the issues of imperialism, Zionism in Palestine and Islamist movements in other countries. Intellectual activities took different shapes: organising lectures, publishing *al-Irshad* journal and educating an unschooled population, thereby increasing the rate of literacy.

For the members of al-Irshad, Muhammad Salīm designed a special preparatory programme that was intellectually and spiritually rigorous.

During the early 1950s, al-Irshad's main activity was organising its twice-weekly lectures, generally held on Saturdays and Tuesdays.

Muhammad Salīm was in charge of organising the lectures and they were introduced by Muhammad Budai. Many lecturers contributed to these weekly events, including Ahmad al-Khamis, Yusifal-Rifaʿi, ʾAli al-Jassar and Ahmad al-Duʿaij from Kuwait; Ahmad al-Sharabasi[4] and ʾAli ʿAbdulmunʾim ʿAbdulhamid (a teacher at Kuwait's Religious Academy) from Egypt; and Sulaiman al-Hamad from Palestine (a Mathematics and English teacher in Kuwait), whose lectures focused on the Palestinian cause. Al-Irshad also invited guests from other countries such as Muhammad al-Sawwaf (the General Observer of the Muslim Brotherhood in Iraq), Muhammad Bashir al-Ibrahimi (the chief of the Society of Muslim Ulama in Algeria) and his colleague in Alfudail al-Wartilani. The weekly lectures attracted many people, and audience numbers increased from week to week reaching as many as 500 people. In addition to the weekly lectures, the members of al-Irshad used to give speeches and sermons after regular prayers at various mosques in Kuwait, from the north in al-Jahrah to the south in al-Fahahil, and on the Island of Failakah, as well in the city of Kuwait itself.

In addition, the publishing of *al-Irshad* journal by al-Irshad was crucial in spreading the Islamist ideology in Kuwait. The first edition of *al-Irshad* journal was in August 1953, and according to its founder, ʿAbdulʿaziz al-Mutawwaʿ, was to be the mouthpiece of al-Irshad and its ideological vehicle. Al-Irshad's Committee for Press and Publication was in charge of publishing the journal and other occasional supplements. The themes and topics of the journal varied, covering subjects such as imperialism, Islam in the face of capitalism and Marxism, women in Islam, Islamic economy and other intellectual and social issues.

Al-Irshad cooperated with *Nadi al-Muʿallimin* [Teachers Club], which was controlled by the Nationalists, by establishing the Society's Committee for Eliminating Illiteracy, with the aim of increasing literacy

---

[4] Ahmad al-Sharabasi (1918–1980), an Egyptian religious scholar, graduated from al-Azhar and became a famous preacher in Cairo. He was initially close to the Muslim Brotherhood until he disagreed with them; however, he was arrested several times with other Muslim Brotherhood members during the time of Nuqrashi. Al-Sharabasi went to Kuwait in the early 1950s as a preacher and a teacher. He also wrote regularly for al-Biʿthah Journal, which was published in Egypt by Kuwaiti students. After his experiences in Kuwait, al-Sharabāṣi wrote an account of his visit in a book called *Days in Kuwait*. ʿAshraf ʿAntabli, *Wikipedia of the Muslim Brotherhood*, "Ahmad al-Sharabasi: Hayat wa Jihad." www.ikhwanwiki.com/index.php?title=أحمدظالشرباصى Last modified 2011 (accessed 8 September 2013).

rates in Kuwait. Muhammad al-ʿAdsani, Abdullah Budai and Mubarak Turki volunteered to teach reading and writing in the afternoons to illiterate people, most of whom were poor. There were two classes, one in the building of al-Irshad and the other at the Religious Academy of Kuwait, and both were managed by the Society Committee for Eliminating Illiteracy.

For the members of al-Irshad, Salīm designed a special programme to prepare future preachers of Islam from among the members. Salīm explained the programme and its goals in *al-Barnamaj al-Tawjihi* (Guiding Programme), which in effect became the manifesto of al-Irshad.[5] In the introduction to the prgramme, Salīm set out the main goal of al-Barnamaj al-Tawjihi saying that "[it] comes to fulfil the great goal of al-Irshad by preparing the members of al-Irshad by polishing their personal characters and improving their intellectual and spiritual skills to be able carrying the message of Islam to the world."[6] Al-Barnamaj al-Tawjihi consisted of various chapters. For example, *"Tarikh al-Daʿwah"* [History of *Daʿwah*] reviewed the history of the call of Islam in the world, such as Islam in China and the Soviet Union, with a focus on modern Islamic thinkers and the movements of Jamal al-Din al-Afghani, MuhammadʿAbduh, Rashīd Rida, and Sanusī movement; "The Reality of the Muslim World" discussed the political, social, and economic situation of the Muslim world; *"Tarikh al-ʿUthamaʾ"* [History of Great People] examined major figures in Islam such as the first and the second Caliphs Abu Bakir and ʿUmar binal-Khattab, and other figures like Salaḥ al-Dīn. The chapter on "social manners" explained the importance matters like the etiquette of eating and dressing; *"Akhlaq al-Daʿwah"* [Morals of *Daʿwah*] addressed the morals of the *daʿiyah* (the preacher or carrier of the message) such as philanthropic propensity, work ethics, sincerity and honesty, unity and solidarity, understanding the problems of society, etc.; and *"al-Wajib al-Shahri"* [The Monthly Duty] focused on spiritual preparation, such as reading a chapter of the Qurʾan everyday, completing prayers on time and other daily and recurring obligations. In addition, Salīm wrote several supplementary pamphlets specifically for the members, informing them of special tasks and teachings, such as how to deal with each other and the relationship between the *usar* (organisational cells).[7]

[5] *Al-Barnamaj al-Tawjihi* (Beirut: ʿIbad al-Rahman, No Date).

[6] Ibid.

[7] Ibid.

Youth and Students Activities

From the beginning, al-Irshad paid special attention to students to whom it devoted a separate section—one of the organisations' three sections, the others being the financial section and the secretariat. From its first edition, *al-Irshad* journal also dedicated a special page to students. Al-Irshad succeeded in attracting youth via sports and scouting activities and inculcated religious teachings through these activities. The Student Section housed the Sports Unit and the Scout Unit. The Sports Unit formed teams in many different sports, including football, volleyball, basketball, boxing, etc., which used to train in the fields of the Religious Academy of Kuwait and competed with teams from other clubs. Al-Irshad also communicated with Kuwaiti students who were studying in Egypt and introduced them to the Muslim Brotherhood in Egypt, such as the occasion when al-Mutawwaʿ invited Kuwaiti students and Albahi al-Khuli (a prominent Muslim Brotherhood leader in Egypt) as a representative of Hasan al-Hudaibi to a lunch at a restaurant in Giza.[8]

Al-Irshad's Scout Unit was a copy of the mother organisation in Egypt and aimed to prepare boys and young men to fulfil the Scout promise which was altered to match the Muslim Brotherhood ideals.[9] The war against Israel slanted the Scouts of the Muslim Brotherhood towards prepare the youth for *jihad* against Zionism; this led to military-like Scouting activities although they did not use any kind of weaponry. Al-Irshad's Scouts were comparable to a military academy where military traditions and values were taught; however, these were presented from an Islamic perspective and given the religious term, Jihad. The scouts of al-Irshad used to have an annual camp in the desert for two weeks that included the members of Muslim Brotherhood or those who they sought to make into members of the movement. Scouts also participated in the Scout camps of other Muslim Brotherhood branches, such as the one held in Lebanon in 1953 and one that took place in Syria in 1954.[10]

---

[8] Al-Nisif, interview.

[9] MahmudʿAbdulhalim, *al-Ikhwan al-Muslimun*, 347–350.

[10] Al-Nisif, interview.

Al-Irshad and Providing Social and Charitable Services

Prior to the oil boom, Kuwait had lived in difficult conditions, lacking basic services such as health services and even clean water. Therefore, al-Irshad worked to provide some social services and also presented people's needs to the government by way of *al-Irshad* journal and through personal relations with government officials. Although al-Irshad did not position itself as a social services organisation, it worked, as needed, to solve people's everyday problems. For instance, according to *al-Irshad* journal under the title "Fruits and Vegetables of Iraq," al-Irshad took up people's request to improve health services and provide clean water, fruit and vegetables: "recently, many diseases spread in Kuwait, especially eyes diseases, Tuberculosis, and physiological weakness due to the lack of fruits and vegetables that contains needed vitamins to prevent these diseases, and al-Irshad has contributed resources to solving this problem."[11]

Giving to charity is an essential part of the Islamic faith and has become a landmark in Islamic culture. The third compulsory pillar of Islam is *zakat*, where every Muslim who is financially able must donate 2.5% of surplus earnings at the end of the lunar year to help others. Voluntary charity, *sadaqah*, is another form of charitable giving that is encouraged in Islam. *Zakat* and *sadaqah* can be invested in various ways such as through *awqaf* [Islamic religious endowments], as well as giving money directly to needy people.

Al-Irshad created a section for charities that worked in Kuwait and abroad. Inside Kuwait, a group of al-Irshad members worked on gathering money from people in the streets and bazaars and giving it to needy people. They also launched the "winter clothes project" and distributed winter clothing to poor people. The activities of the charity section were more frequent because, from the late 1940s onwards, people in Kuwait benefited from the oil revenues. The most notable charitable activity was supporting expelled Palestinians in Palestine and Jordan. The Vice-President of al-Irshad, Abdullah al-Mutawwaᶜ, headed a special committee consisting of senior members of al-Irshad, such as MuhammadalᶜAdsani, Abdullah al-Kulaib, ᶜAbdulrazzaq al-Saleh, Muhammad Budai and Ghanim alShahin, all of whom dedicated their work to supporting Palestinians. Sulaiman al-Hamad mentions that he

---

[11] "Nashat al-Jamᶜiyyah," *Al-Irshad Journal*, Vol. 1 (August 1953) Jamᶜiyyat al-Irshad: Kuwait, 55–57.

and the committee used to gather money and transport it in person to Palestine; the funds were mainly for refugees (camps, food, medications, etc.).[12]

As already noted, although al-Irshad suffered a period of neglect because of internal conflict and external pressure from the Nationalists, the Muslim Brotherhood succeeded in wielding some influence on the social domain through a number of social media. The al-Irshad School continued its work even after the al-Irshad Society had closed its doors. The Muslim Brotherhood also made up for the lack of properly-trained jurists and religious scholars by affording a platform to religious scholars from inside as well as outside Kuwait. Shaikh Yusif bin ʿIsa al-Qinaʿi was honorary president of al-Irshad, thus bestowing legitimacy and social value upon it. The relative youth of the Muslim Brotherhood movement meant they had little time to train scholars and jurists who could deal with social issues, a shortcoming they tackled later on.

And despite the weakness of the Muslim Brotherhood and of Islamist movements in general from the mid-1950s to the mid-1960s, Kuwaiti and non-Kuwaiti Muslim Brotherhood members exerted some sporadic efforts to keep the movement alive; Aman and al-ʿAqil established al-Manar Bookshop, while the Muslim Brotherhood scouting movement maintained some of its activities, thanks to ʿIsa Shahin and Salim Turki. More importantly, the Muslim Brotherhood collaborated with Islamists from other movements to establish The Society for Social Reform, al-Islah, as a reaction to the rise in secularism which sought to turn the public against all Islamists and any form of religious behaviour. Secularist ideas had spread quite rapidly aided by the economic and political circumstances of the time.

THE IMPACT OF OIL ON CHANGING KUWAITI SOCIETY

Economic development has the greatest impact on a society's political, social and cultural structure, and in the case of Kuwait, society's shift from rags to riches was both rapid and unexpected. For centuries, Kuwaiti society had been accustomed to a culturally and socially static way of life, marked by hardship and a very basic existence, but with little or no complaint from a highly religious society that believed firmly in fate,

---

[12] Sulaiman al-Hamad, interview.

qismah. Quite suddenly, within a brief period of time, a new generation of Kuwaitis was looking forward to making a clear break with the past and enjoying a better future. This break with the past was greatly assisted by the economic revolution that arose out of the discovery of oil and was accompanied by great intellectual and cultural changes, including the introduction of nationalist and left-wing ideologies that opposed the old systems of government like liberal capitalism and theocracies and their concomitant organisations and entities. Because of its traditional and tribal nature, the political regime in Kuwait did not represent either of these systems, but this did not prevent criticism from being levelled against a number of political figures who epitomised the tenets of these two ideologies.

Both urban and Bedouin elements of Kuwaiti society felt the heat of change. Urban society, known as the village-city society, had historically existed within the borders of the capital and had engaged in trade and pearl diving for a living. Bedouins, on the other hand, were associated with land activities such as trade with nearby regions, especially Najd, in addition to raising livestock. They were often mobile, constantly on the move in search of grazing grounds and fresh sources of water. Kuwaiti society, thus, comprised two distinct modes of living: the village-city and the desert, otherwise known as "society within the walls and outside the walls." Notwithstanding those differences, Kuwait society was not completely divided along the middle, since social ties and trade between the two groups were very common, with differences being mostly of a cultural and political nature.

The discovery of oil transformed the Kuwaiti economy which had hitherto relied on sea-related and land activities such as ship-building, fishing, pearl diving, transporting goods, trading in dates and other somewhat old-fashioned modes. Oil necessitated a shift to more complex economic activities, such as imports and exports, construction work and local and foreign investments. Oil-related activities naturally prospered with the arrival of American and British oil companies that had been granted concessions to drill in Kuwait, and the demand for an experienced labour force increased. Western engineers and experts settled in the district of al-Ahmadi, close to the major oil fields in the south. The economic boom soon attracted labour force from Arab countries such as Palestine and Egypt, and Asian countries like Iran, Pakistan and India. With the increase in income per capita, Kuwaitis abandoned what they considered menial jobs and relied increasingly on the Arab and Asian labour force.

Although there are no official figures on the size of the economic activity at that time, it is estimated that the oil sector represented more than 60% of Kuwait's GDP in the 1960s.[13] An important development that transformed Kuwait from an Emirate governed by an al-Subah, with the support of merchants and traders, into a rentier state under the total political and economic control of the ruling family who tried to forge a reality where success and progress were closely associated with the ruling family. Although various ideologies competed with the ruling family in forging this new identity, they stood very little chance of succeeding in the face of the promise of a previously unimaginable luxurious lifestyle that only the ruling family and their control of the oil could provide.

Kuwait's simple and hard-working society was transformed into a greedy consumerist one while people from various backgrounds and cultures gradually meshed with the local community. Travelling was suddenly an affordable pastime, and studying abroad became the norm. Kuwaitis were exposed to new cultures, leading to a conflict between modernity and tradition, between a generation of parents who had had to struggle to make a living and their children, born into money, who wanted to enjoy the same lifestyle as some more advanced Arab and Western countries. The old city wall of Kuwait was demolished allowing those inside the wall to abandon their old decrepit neighbourhoods such as al-Qibla, al-Sharq and al-Mirqab and move to the more affluent, modern, cleaner and architecturally pleasant areas located outside the wall. Bedouins also chose to leave their tents and settle in these modern areas.[14] The transfer into more modern living spaces brought the Bedouins and city dwellers culturally closer but did not lead to full integration; most city dwellers from al-Sharq ended up living in the areas parallel to the coast line (from al-Dasmah to al-Salmiyya). A huge number of Kuwaitis of Najdi origin moved to areas like Abdullah al-Salim, al-Shamiyyah, al-Nuzha and al-Faiha. Some tribes gathered in certain areas; al-Reshaida and Mutair were concentrated mainly in al-Farwaniyyah and the surrounding areas, while al-ʿAjman tribe chose the southern areas of Kuwait close to al-Ahmadi where they had originally lived. This demographic distribution persists till today, although the increase in

---

[13] OECD, *Towards New Arrangements for State Ownership in the Middle East and North Africa* (OECD Publishing, 2012), 59.

[14] Allan G. Hill, "Aspects of the Urban Development of Kuwait," Unpublished PhD Thesis, Durham University, 1969, 153–156.

numbers and the establishment of new residential areas allowed for more integration.

Modern state institutions also benefited greatly from oil money, especially educational establishments. Following the establishment of the Department of Education in 1936 and after appointing teachers from Palestine and Egypt, education was further expanded for both boys and girls. Al-Shuwaikh Secondary School for boys was established in 1953 followed by al-Murqab Secondary School for girls in 1955. Both prepared students to transfer from the primary and middle levels which were the main focus of Qur'anic schools and the more advanced schools of al-'Ahmadiyya and al-Mubarakiyyah Schools for boys, and al-Noor School for girls. With the end of the British mandate in 1961, the Department of Education became the Ministry of Education in 1962. Shuwaikh Secondary School evolved into the country's first university, with the establishment of Kuwait University in 1966. A quick review of figures reveals the rapid pace of educational reform in Kuwait; the number of students rose from 4520 boys and 1772 girls in 1950 to 21,764 and 12,661 in 1958, an annual increase of almost 20%.[15]

Financial institutions witnessed similar leaps; the Department of Finance was established in 1935, the Department of Work in 1945, the Departments of Passport and Investigations in 1948 and 1949 respectively, and many other departments which later became ministries following Kuwait's independence. Undoubtedly, the most tangible progress was made in the field of construction; multi-storey buildings began to appear in addition to new residential areas into which Kuwaitis moved after abandoning their mud homes and tents. Oil revenues were fundamental in improving health services in Kuwait, which led to significant population growth: from 168,793 in 1965 to 307,755 in 1975. Such an increase in less than a decade transformed the structure of society into a community of young people where almost 40% of the population was under the age of 18. The number of foreigners also surged from 298,546 to 687,082 during the same period.[16]

New classes and allegiances emerged in the light of these new social and economic realities. An elitist class of educated Kuwaitis, who could

---

[15] "Marahil al-Tʿlim fi al-Kuwait," Ministry of Education, 2012 (accessed 16 March 2014).

[16] Ibid.

be considered as the new intelligentsia, had returned with new ideas and trends from their college days in Cairo, Beirut and the United Kingdom; the working class remained small in both size and influence; a middle class that had shifted its domain of interest from handcrafts to office work soon became the largest class in Kuwait and finally, there was a class of merchants closely linked with the ruling family in addition to the traditional class of merchants and traders who had benefited from government contracts but were prompted to cement their relationship with the ruling family to safeguard their economic interests. This division may give the impression that there were very clear-cut boundaries between classes, but it was sometimes the case that an individual would belong to more than one class or was able to climb the social ladder in a small community where various individuals were linked to each other through blood, marriage or place of living.

Despite the multiplicity of Islamic, leftist, liberal, economic and sociopolitical ideas and schools of thought in Kuwait, it was Arab Nationalism that captured the hearts of the street in the 1950s and 1960s. The Egyptian President Jamal ʿAbdulnasser epitomised the calls for a secularist brand of Arab nationalism. The Arab Baʿthist party had a decent number of followers, especially as its main thrust did not initially conflict with Nasserite Pan Arabism. However, Nasser's endorsement of the Rogers Plan to tackle the Arab-Israeli conflict divided the nationalists in Kuwait, with the Baʿthists declaring their opposition to the plan; this led to the biggest split in the history of the Arab nationalists in Kuwait. The defeat of 1967 also put another nail in the coffin of Arab nationalism.

The rapid changes in society were signalled by the shift from old mud houses to new concrete buildings outside the old wall, a very exciting prospect for many Kuwaitis. Women's fashion saw Kuwaitis giving up the traditional ʿabayah and head cover, considered by many a symbol of patriarchy and backwardness, in favour of Westernised clothing under the influence of female Arab teachers who were seen as role models for Kuwaiti women.[17] The traditional clothes of the 1950s rapidly gave way to the more modern fashions of 1960s. The hairstyles and short skirts of the West and other Arab countries like Egypt and Lebanon also became very popular in Kuwait. Thus, these social changes were very rapid, having

---

[17] "Qissat Hayat Imraah Thairah ʿala al-Unuthah," *Majallat al-Kuwait*, 22 November 2011, issue 337 (accessed 16 March 2014).

begun with an incident when, in response to the rejection of their applications to study abroad, a group of Kuwaiti girls burned their ʿabayahs and head coverings.

This era was also marked by cultural developments guided by secularists who strove to spread their influence in the social domain and who become the intellectual and cultural reference for all Kuwaitis. Theatre performances flourished, especially with the arrival of Zaki Tulaimat,[18,19] and many young Kuwaitis joined this budding artistic movement. Some young men and women turned to acting in Gulf television drama series and plays. Other forms of art such as painting prospered with the increase in the number of museums and exhibition spaces like the Kuwait National Museum and Tariq Rajab Museum. The government established the National Council for Culture, Arts and Letters, which remains a secularist institution until this day. Secularist influence was also very evident in theatre and television where the budding artistic movement reflected the values of modernism and openness, in addition to glorifying Pan-Arabism. Kuwaiti art presented its vision for dealing with the transitional period the country was experiencing, which coincided with increased wealth and cultural openness. The latter was reflected in enthusiastic efforts to rid the country of traditions that encouraged backwardness and regression, especially in relation to the treatment of women who were being encouraged to break free from the control of men and seek education and independence.

According to Aman, Islamist movements considered all these changes a huge threat to social values derived from Islam. They had also lost their historic role in guiding the social and cultural domains. Several members of the Muslim Brotherhood moved to establish the al-Islah as a response to what they perceived as secularist infringement upon the social domain. They challenged figures like Zaki Tulaimat, whom they accused of belonging to the Egyptian Freemasonry movement, as well as

---

[18] Zaki Tulaimat (1894–1982) was a major figure in theatre in the Arab world, working in Egypt, Tunisia and Kuwait. Also, he had a positive influence on the theatrical movement in Kuwait when he moved therein.

[19] ʿAbdulmehsinal-Shammari, "al-Masrah fi al-Kuwait... Khamsun ʿAaman min al-ʿAtaʾ" (*Majallat alKuwait*, June 30, 2013). http://kuwaitmag.com/index.jsp?inc=5&id=2531&pid=112&version=27 (accessed 29 June 2013).

other icons of the artistic and cultural movement for their role in these changes.[20]

FORMING THE SOCIAL REFORM SOCIETY (AL-ISLAH) IN 1963 AND THE NEW ORGANISATION OF THE MUSLIM BROTHERHOOD IN 1968 AS A CULTURAL REACTION TO THE LOSS OF THE SOCIAL DOMAIN

Islamists frowned upon these social and political changes particularly those related to women's Westernised attire, and viewed these changes as a conspiracy against social and religious values. Proponents of Islamist movements were shocked by the speed of social change, and several rushed to hold meetings to address these urgent issues. A number of Muslim Brotherhood figures, headed by Abdullah al-ʿAli al-Mutawwaʿ, and several supporters of the group held a meeting on 8 June 1963 at Fahd al-Khalid's *diwaniyya* to "establish an Islamic entity in this wonderful country to defend religious and social values."[21] Three days later, the Social Reform Society (*Jamʿiyyat al-Islah al-Ijtimaʿi*) was born, a clear indication that the meeting had been held to garner support for the establishment of such a society.

The Society for Social Reform, or al-Islah, seemed like a natural extension of al-Irshad, and although reform followed in the footsteps of al-Irshad, there were several differences between the two. A close reading of their aims and objectives sheds light on their priorities. According to the basic laws of the al-Irshad, the society aimed to:

1. Offer clear, concise and simple overview of the basic tenets of Islam in a manner appropriate to the spirit of the modern age.
2. Free the mind and human reason from the shackles of ignorance.
3. Protect today's youth from intellectual and moral decline.
4. Raise the standards of living of Muslims.
5. Nurture the spiritual life of the individual.
6. Achieve social justice for all citizens and contribute to social welfare.

---

[20] Aman, interview.

[21] ʿAbdullah Al-Mutawwaʿ, "Muthakarat," 4–5.

7. Fully support Arab unity and work towards achieving an Islamic University in collaboration with Islamic groups in Muslim countries.[22]

On the other hand, al-Islah defined its aims and objectives as,

1. Combating social vices and immoral activities such as prostitution, drinking, gambling and usury.
2. Guiding youth onto the path of righteousness and teaching them useful pastimes.
3. Offering curricula to educational and media departments to encourage the dissemination of material that represents Islamic *shariᶜa*.
4. Finding solutions to some of the challenging dilemmas facing Muslim societies.
5. Safeguarding religion and spreading virtue among members of society to protect its mores and values.
6. Uniting the Umma under the principles of Islam and adopting such principles as a holistic way of life.[23]

Al-Irshad favoured spreading the message of Islam and its compatibility with modern times against the Western ideologies that were penetrating Muslim society and conservative and backward practice of Islam (Articles 1, 2, 6 and 7). Al-Islah, on the other hand, opted to focus on combating social vice and immorality and protecting society (Articles 1, 2, 3 and 5). The aims and objectives came as a response to the challenges facing the Islamist movement in Kuwait at that time; the end of the 1940s onwards was a time of great conflict with imported Western ideas which gravely defied Islamic thought, the latter being often described as backward, oppressive and not suitable for the needs of the modern age. The conflict at the end of 1950s and early 1960s revolved around social thought, especially concerning the role of women in society and gender relations in the public domain. Islamists felt that society during the 1950s was under attack from "immoral seculars," hence the urgent need to protect society.

---

[22] "ᶜAn Jamᶜiyyat al-Irshad," (*Majallat al-Irshad,* March 1957), 1.

[23] *Official Website of Jamᶜiyyat al-Islah,* "ᶜAn al-Jamᶜiyyah," Last modified 2012 (accessed 24 December 2013). www.eslah.com/ah/?page_id=65.

Combating the rise of secularism in the social domain took many forms and focused on several issues such as banning alcohol, mixed-gender education at the University of Kuwait, applying shariᶜa and amending Article 2 of the Constitution (which will be explored in detail in the chapter on political movements). Al-Islah attracted all those who supported Islamist movements and hosted many programmes and activities, such as lectures by prominent Islamists (Hasan Ayyub, Hasan Tannun, ᶜAbdulrahman ᶜAbdulkhaliq and ᶜUmar Al-Ashqar). Prior to the establishment of the 1968 Muslim Brotherhood (which was more organised and focused on educational activities), it was also a focal point for ad hoc activities. Thus, Islamist movements began to come together to face up to the threat of secularism in a new battle over the hearts and minds of Kuwaitis.

AL-ISLAH AND BANNING ALCOHOL IN 1964

The sale and consumption of alcohol were permitted in Kuwait, but in a conservative society that frowned upon the consumption of alcohol, it was on a limited scale. But as society became more liberal in the 1950s and 1960s and with the arrival of Christian foreigners, alcohol gained widespread acceptance. Gray Mackenzie and Co. Ltd monopolised the sale of alcohol and, in order to spare the Kuwaiti government any embarrassment, claimed that Westerners and Indians were its target customers. In practice, consumers included many Kuwaitis. Following Kuwait's independence on 19 June 1961, thousands of Kuwait citizens, backed by Islamists, petitioned the government to ban the sale of alcohol but to no avail. *Al-Raᵓi al-ᶜAam* newspaper criticised Gray Mackenzie for monopolising the sale of alcohol in a country which supposedly subscribed to the notion of a free economy.[24]

[24] Hamzah ᶜUlaiyyan, "Al-Khamr min al-Masmuh ᶜIla al-Mamnuᵓ" (*Al-Qabas Newspaper*, 27 January 2009).

The turning point came following legal consultation with the lawyer Hasan ʿAshmawi,[25] vice-president of the Fatwa and Legislations committee. Yusif Rifai, who was Minister of Post, Telegraph and Telephone Services, worked closely with ʿAshmawi and conveyed his recommendations to the Islamist movement. The two men drafted a law that would ban the import, consumption or sale of alcohol. Another milestone appeared in the form of Kuwaiti Airlines when, on 2 May 1964, six Kuwaiti MPs proposed to ban the serving of alcohol on the national airline and to confiscate and destroy all the alcohol in Kuwait. Ahmad alKhatib, representing the secularists, argued that Kuwaiti Airlines stood to lose some of its customers if the ban was introduced and requested more time to examine the matter. Other secularist members claimed that banning alcohol would increase demand and could prompt young men to drink perfume or home-made alcohol, both highly poisonous.[26] The law was unanimously passed and referred to the Emir for ratification. Secularists attempted to lobby the Emir to reject the draft law, while Islamists faced the challenging task of having to mobilise inside and outside the Parliament. In the end, their efforts were rewarded and the law passed, with only one MP voting against it. Most members could not openly oppose the law because Islam's stand regarding alcohol is clear, and there was no denying its negative impact on people's lives.[27] Islamists made the most of these facts to pressure MPs to back the draft law.[28]

[25] Hasan ʿAshmawi (1921–1972), an Egyptian lawyer, was a member of the Muslim Brotherhood. While Nasser was persecuting the Muslim Brotherhood, ʿAshmawi escaped to Switzerland, Saʿudi Arabia and Morocco, ending up in Kuwait where he worked as vice-president of the Legislation Department and was a consultant for the Ministry of the Defence and Ministry of Interior. He was linked to forgery in the Parliamentary elections in 1967. ʿAbdullah al-ʿAqil, "Al-Daʾiyah Hasan ʿAshmawi." *The Official Historical Encyclopaedia of the Muslim Brotherhood*, www.ikhwanwiki.com/index.php?title=العشماوي. Last modified 20 June 2012 (accessed 29 June 2013).

[26] Yusifal-Rifaʿi, *The Official Website of Saiyyid Yusif al-Rifaʿi*, Last modified1 March 2006 (accessed 29 June 2013). www.rifaieonline.com/ViewArticle.aspx?ArticleID=84.

[27] ʿAbdullah al-Mutawwaʿ, "Muthakarat," 4.

[28] Ibid.

The New Muslim Brotherhood Organisation and the Battle of Mixed-Gender Education

The issue of mixed-gender education at the University of Kuwait sparked very heated debates between secularists and Islamists and formed the core of the struggle over the social domain for more than five decades. The dispute began when the University of Kuwait was established in October 1966. Both the ruling family and the left-wing intelligentsia were very keen to establish a national university to train highly-qualified Kuwaitis for the new job opportunities arising in the newly-established state. Society viewed the university as the centre of values that could greatly shape and influence social principles in general. As such, it was important for all schools of thought at the time to control the intellectual and cultural directions of the university. Teaching began in November 1966 in the Colleges of Science and Arts, and the Women's College. A few months later, in April 1967, two more colleges were added – Law and Shariʿa, Business, and Political Science. The College of Medicine was established in July 1973 and the College of Engineering and Petroleum Studies in December 1974.[29]

Students' movements were already active prior to the establishment of the university. Young Kuwaiti students had begun to hold a number of cultural and intellectual activities at al-Shuwaikh Secondary School in 1957, and had also established the Union for Secondary School Students. Because of the lack of universities, the Ministry of Education and Higher Education used to send students to study abroad, chiefly in Baghdad, Lebanon and the United Kingdom, but the biggest cluster of Kuwaiti students was in Egypt where, with support from the Kuwaiti Ministry of Education, they established a centre called "Bait al-Kuwait" (the House of Kuwait) in 1945.[30] The centre was located in Zamalik in the former home of Fuʾad Sultan Pasha, and the opening was attended by the philosopher and Islamic scholar Ahmed Amin, who deputised for the Egyptian Minister of Education. The centre moved to al-Duqqi in 1958 and was reopened by the Egyptian President Jamal ʿAbdul Nasser himself in the

---

[29] *The Official Website of Kuwait University*, "About the University" (accessed 29 June 2013). www.kuniv.edu/ku/ar/ABOUTKU/ABOUTKU/index.htm.

[30] The number of Kuwaiti Students in Egypt jumped from 6000 in 1951 to 40,000 in 1960. Ibrahīm al-Melaifi, "Al-Harakah al-Tullabiyyah al-Kuwaitiyyah fi 40 ʿAaman (1)" (*Al-Qabas Newspaper*, 4 October 2008).

presence of the Shaikh Abdullah Jabir al-Subah. In addition to being a meeting place for Kuwaiti students, the centre was a hub of intellectual and cultural activities. Ideologically, it was controlled by nationalists who supported most of the Arab causes at the time. Kuwaiti students in Baghdad were greatly influenced by nationalist and Baʿthist ideologies that created a common denominator between them and Kuwaitis in Egypt. Kuwaiti students called for the establishment of a national union for students studying abroad, and on 24 December 1964, the National Union of Kuwaiti Students (NUKS) was founded with its headquarters in Cairo.[31]

Following the establishment of Kuwait University in 1966, a number of Kuwaiti students also decided to form a students' union at the university, and the NUKS-KU was established on 14 January 1969 with support from Kuwaiti students' unions in various Arab countries. The board of directors consisted of Abdullah al-Nafisi (president), Yusif al-Jasim (vice-president), Muhammad Al-Subaʿi (secretary general), Shaikha Al-Nibari (treasurer), and ʿAdnan Hussein, Faisal Al-Dawud, Fatima Shubaiki, Tamadur al-Nisif and Munir al-Fuzan (members).[32] Mixed-gender education was one of the first demands made by the Union; customarily, males and females were taught in separate buildings. The Union which was dominated by nationalist and left-wing elements, called for equality and for abandoning regressive and ultra-conservative modes of thinking. They argued that women were no different from men and deserved respect, freedom of movement and the right to make their own decisions, and that there was nothing better than a university context in which to instil those values. The Union organised a strike in 1969, along with a series of sit-ins, petitions and newspaper articles for the purpose of pressuring the University administration to put an end to gender segregation.

The Union's magazine al-ʾIthad, observed that,

> Since women are expected to share responsibilities at home with men, it is only natural that they also share education with them as well. Preventing them from do so is a stark infringement on their natural right

---

[31] Ibid.
[32] Ibid.

to equality and justice without discrimination on the basis of sex, language or religion.[33]

The magazine also called for a forward move in society's treatment of women by seeking inspiration from Western countries,

> The Kuwaiti society's traditional values were derived from within Kuwaiti society, not imported from abroad...These have placed great restrictions on women's freedoms who were treated as inferior creatures...The economic boom of the mid-1950s created a desperate need to revolutionise our value systems more suited for these great advances...Kuwait women have demanded that old traditional values be replaced with new ones.[34]

Islamist movements perceived these calls for mixed-gender education as a secularist assault on the moral fibre of society, and especially on young people. They reacted very strongly to what they described as attempts to Westernise young people and lead them astray. Al-Islah drafted a memorandum entitled "On Kuwait University," which they presented at the beginning of the academic year 1970/1971 to the Crown Prince and Prime Minster Shaikh Jabir al-ʾAhmad al-Subah, the Cabinet and Members of Parliament. The Society accused secularists of attempting to corrupt students at Kuwait University and warned the university against the danger of this "conspiracy." Al-Islah argued that,

> The aim behind establishing the University of Kuwait was to teach and educate a generation of Kuwaitis more superior to the generation that lost Jerusalem. A generation armed with values, virtue and morality. The founders did not dream that one day the university would adopt policies aimed at tearing at the moral fibre of society because they knew that society needed education not dancing, factories not clubs. Kuwaitis could split the atom if they wished and excel in medicine, engineering, etc. without mixed-gender education. There is no scientific link scientific progress, dancing and mixed gender education.[35]

[33] Muhammad J. Rida, *Maʿrakatal-Ikhtilat fi al-Kuwait* (Kuwait: Dar al-Rubaiʾān, 1983), 24.

[34] Ibid., 21–25.

[35] Ibid., 25–26.

The memorandum criticised secularist ideas, especially those pertaining to the liberation of women and the nature of the relationship between the sexes. It also criticised activities held by the Students' Union, such as mixed-gender trips, plays and parties. The memorandum called on the government to take all the necessary steps to put an end to attempts to corrupt society at the hands of the Union which

> … seeks to lure society away from Islam [and] intentionally or unintentionally [to] sour the relationship between society and the university [as well as to] lead Kuwaitis into the trap of mixed-gender activities and dancing which crush young people's talents, motivation and good qualities and eventually lead them down the path of drugs.[36]

The struggle between the two sides over control of the social domain through the issue of co-education escalated with time and remained open on the pages of magazines and newspapers. The Society levelled very harsh criticisms against ʿAbdulfattah Ismail, Director of the University, following a masquerade party held to celebrate the start of the academic year 1971/1972. *Al-Mujtamaʿ* journal expressed its dismay that such a party had been organised, and targeted the heard of the university who had attended what they described as "the party of sins."[37] *Al-Raʾi al-ʿAam* reacted equally strongly to these accusations on 12 November 1971 and demanded the government launch an immediate investigation into these claims and put an end to what they described as "the sword wielded in the name of religion."[38] Meeting on Sunday 13 November 1971 to discuss the accusations levelled against the Director, the University Council reached three decisions,

1. They fully supported the Director of the University.
2. The Council expressed its condemnation of the attacks against the university.
3. The University would file a defamation suit against *Al-Mujtamaʿ* Journal.[39]

---

[36] Ibid., 27.
[37] Ibid., 41.
[38] Ibid., 43.
[39] Ibid., 45.

Meanwhile, the Union had issued an invitation to students through *al-ʾIthad* magazine and *al-Ṭalīʾa* newspaper to attend a symposium about co-education on 13 November 1971; this coincided with the religiously-significant last ten days of Ramadan. The Islamists viewed the timing as a blatant provocation of Muslim sentiments during the holy month and as an attempt to corrupt society, both morally and intellectually. The scene was thus set for a clash between the two sides.

The Muslim Brotherhood decided to attend the symposium and called upon its members to be present, and Shiʿa Muslims rallied with the Muslim Brotherhood to defend conservative values against the secularists. Islamists filled up the hall, and as soon as proceedings started, they began chanting slogans and demanding to be given the floor to express their views. They objected to a number of speakers (Khalid Fahad, Fatimah Hussein, ʿAbdulʿaziz alSultan and Saʿad ʿAbdulrahman) who hailed from the same school of thought. The Islamist audience demanded to be allowed to participate and voice their opinion on the matter of co-education, and after a heated exchange, the organisers agreed to allow a representative from the Islamists to take part. The very tense atmosphere and the incessant interruptions from the two sides eventually prompted the organisers to cancel the symposium and switch off the microphones. In the ensuing tussle, both parties physically assaulted each other.

But the battle was not over yet. Newspapers supporting co-education fiercely attacked the Islamists. Front page headlines in *al-Raʾi al-ʿAam* read "The Battle of Kuwait University...Proponents of the Reform Society interrupts the discussions. Police intervention leads to injuries including 3 girls."[40] *Ajial* newspaper's front page read "Beating instead of dialogue at university...Guardianship under duress" and "A dangerous precedent by the Reformists to terrorise the opposition."[41] The most fervent attack was by *al-ʾIthad* magazine whose headline for Issue no. 48 was "Monkeys invade the university."[42] Islamists responded on the pages of *al-Mujtamaʿ* with a report entitled "Proponents of loose morality incite sedition by monopolising the platform."[43] As the dispute played itself out on the pages of newspapers and magazines, both the government and

[40] Ibid., 58.
[41] Ibid., 66.
[42] Ibid., 81.
[43] Ibid., 75.

society were stunned by what happened. On 14 November 1971, a day after the symposium, the government issued a number of decisions,

1. *Al-Mujtamaᶜ* Journal would be suspended for three months from 15 November 1971.
2. The university council was entrusted with taking the appropriate measures to address the situation on the basis of the educational and scientific mission for which the university had been established.
3. A fact-finding committee headed by the minister of education and the president of the university would be formed, and its final report filed as soon as possible.[44]

These decisions reflected the government's desire to contain the situation before it got out of control. They also contained an implicit criticism of the Islamists and a warning to the university's administration. The decision to suspend *al-Mujtamaᶜ* Journal stemmed from wide-spread anger over the inflammatory manner in which they had portrayed gender relationships on campus. The implied warning to the university administration was carried in the emphasis on its "educational and scientific mission" and the clear message that it should focus on education, not extra-curricular activities and programmes.

However, the government's dismay intensified further following a speech by the MP Muhammad al-Wasmi on the nature of mixed-gender education,

One day I saw a group of cars driving alone and when I asked, I was told it was mixed-gender university trip. I followed them to Nuwaisib and what I saw there was both sad and regrettable; boys and girls walking away in couples to secluded areas. I asked the driver and he told me it was quite normal.[45]

The President of al-Islah wrote a letter to the Minister of Education and the President of the University Council, Jasim al-Marzuq on 1 April 1972 demanding an end to mixed-gender university trips. The response was immediate, with the minister informing the university administration that

---

[44] Ibid., 87. See Appendix B.
[45] "Al-Ikhtilat" *Al-Mujtamaᶜ* (4 April 1972), 4.

mixed-gender activities were no longer allowed, clearly indicating that the government was perturbed by such activities.

The dispute then spilled into the corridors of the Parliament. Secularist MPs put a lot of pressure on the Islamists by drafting stricter legislations that targeting *al-Mujtama*ᶜ Journal, the Islamists and al-Islah. However, the government did not wish to aggravate the situation further and refused to issue more than the three decisions it had made earlier. The Secularists began to feel that the government was turning a blind eye to the Islamists, especially when both the government and the Parliament voted against listing the campus violence on the agenda for the parliamentary session on 16 November 1971, and with pressure from the secularists mounting, the Minister of Education was forced to clarify the government's position on the subject. MPs seized the opportunity to voice their views on this sensitive topic with more than 30 out of 50 MPs expressing their wish to speak. As expected, the Parliament was highly polarised, from the extreme left to the far right, respectively. Thus, ᶜAbdulᶜaziz al-Musaᶜid, editor-in-chief of *al-Ra'i al-ᶜAam* newspaper, demanded that the Interior Ministry should investigate the activities of al-Islah, arguing that it represented a danger to the state, and accused the ministry of colluding with the Society by supporting it morally and financially, while the MP Ibrahim Khuraibit warned the government about a war on Islam and implied that secularists were acting on behalf of Zionists who wished to destroy Islam.[46]

However, while awaiting the fact-finding committee's final report, the government insisted on its earlier position and the decisions it had made with regard to suspending the magazine and respecting the university's measures while emphasising its educational and scientific mission. The committee, headed by the Education Minister, presented its report to the Cabinet on 2 December 1971, and it was published in the newspapers on 8 December 1971. The speed with which the report had been prepared reflected the government's desire to resolve the matter as quickly as possible before the situation worsened.

The report concluded that while both sides were responsible for the fracas, Islamists were mostly to blame for planning to disturb the gathering in an undemocratic manner. The University Council, which had formed the fact-finding committee, recommended referring the matter to

[46] Ibid.

the Parliament, arguing that it would be unwise to drag students through the courts.[47] The government and the Parliament worked together to put a speedy end to the whole matter, and despite objections from secularist MPs, the Parliament voted on 28 December 1971 to hold both parties responsible and to punish the Islamists by suspending *al-Mujtama*ᶜ magazine for three months.[48]

Mixed-gender education was duly implemented at Kuwait University, especially following the university's decision to adopt a system of credit-hours, which would have made it too costly to offer the same courses in separate rooms for boys and girls. The number of female students was increasing because while most male students made use of the availability of scholarships to study abroad, many Kuwaiti families did not allow their daughters to study outside Kuwait. Moreover, the university argued that, as long as students adhered to social codes and values, there was no reason why mixed-gender education would not work. The Faculty of Business Studies was the first to implement the co-education policy, and other faculties soon followed suit.

Islamists persisted in criticising the policy in newspapers, under headlines such as "Co-Education... how we implement what the West has proved was a bad idea",[49] and "Mixed Gender Education in Business School."[50] The writer of the former article wondered, "How long are we going to follow in the footsteps of the West and adopt their mistaken policies, sins and moral decay?"[51] The writer of the second article stated that co-education was a form of corruption and would benefit only the enemies of the state who were doing their best to tear at the moral fibre of young people. Islamist MPs and those close to them launched a fierce campaign against the government following its decision to implement the co-education policy. MP Sayyid Yusif al-Rifaᶜi, proponent of the Islamists in the Parliament, argued that,

---

[47] Rida, *Maᶜrakatal-Ikhtilat*, 208.

[48] Ibid., 209.

[49] Ibid., 225.

[50] Walid al-Wehaib, "al-ʾIkhtilat fi Kulliyat al-Tijarah" (*al-Siyasah Newspaper*, 28 September 1973), 28.

[51] Ibid.

The soldiers of destruction and social corruption have begun an assault on Kuwait and their Freemasonry, Zionist and Crusader schemes aim to transform Kuwait into Beirut and Lebanon after Beirut and the American University of Beirut's role in the region have been exposed. They usually start with transplanting new values for old ones to cultivate a sick society. We can find these forms of invasion and corruption everywhere, fully supported and encouraged by the government; hotels, alcohol, dancing, night-life, entertainment seasons, corrupt media and co-education.[52]

However, the government had already made its decision and persisted in defending it against the onslaught of Islamists. In November 1973, the Ministry of Education issued a statement responding to Islamist accusations saying that the university was a place of learning under the supervision of teachers and social workers who would not allow any immoral behaviour.[53] The Education Minister also defended the government's decision during a parliamentary session,

The system at Kuwait University is not an American system.[54] It can trace its origins to education at al-Azhar in Egypt and has nothing to do with co-education or the US. It is a system that could be applied anywhere. Attacking Kuwait University in this manner is inappropriate and unacceptable. I have before me a leaflet describing the university in terms that would put a nightclub in Paris to shame. This tarnishes the reputation of our daughters who are honourable and chaste. We have more than 300 Kuwaiti girls studying in mixed-gender universities abroad and none have been criticised the way the Faculty of Business Studies has been. I hope we can exercise good judgement and wisdom in handling the matter.[55]

This was the government's position vis-à-vis co-education, and it prompted the Islamists to retreat somewhat and adopt a more mellow tone. The Muslim Brotherhood in particular reduced the level of their activities regarding the issue, having handled it so badly that they ended up losing part of the popular support they had enjoyed and some of their

---

[52] "Al-Ikhtilat" (*al-Siyasah Newspaper*, 23 June 1974), 17.

[53] Rida, *Ma'rakatal-Ikhtilat*, 226.

[54] The Minister asserted that the new system did not carry an American cultural project which threatened the identity of the society; it was a system to improve the management of Kuwait University.

[55] "Al-Ikhtilat," Al-Siyasah Newspaper, 23 June 1974, 17.

credibility. Instead, they shifted their focus to *da'wah* to encourage young university students to join them (in addition to seeking to take over the students' union).

The end of the 1970s and the 1980s represented a period of relative calm in terms of the issue of co-education as the Islamists became increasingly interested in other issues, such as the growing influence of Shi'as in Kuwait following the 1979 Iranian revolution. Islamists collaborated with the governments of the Gulf State to prevent the revolution from reaching the Gulf. Jihad against the Soviet Union in Afghanistan was another major concern at the time, and Islamist energies were directed towards these two causes, against the backdrop of the Iraq-Iran war which cast its shadow on an apprehensive society. Sunni Muslims demanded that the Kuwaiti government support Iraq amid criticisms from Shi'a Muslims, resulting in polarisation along sectarian lines. The Shi'as felt they were treated as second-class citizens and that their loyalty was brought into question, thereby preventing them from occupying sensitive posts in the interior and defence ministries and in the national oil company.

Kuwait also witnessed a number of unprecedented incidents, such as the bombing of a cafe in 1983, and the seven concurrent explosions on 13 December 1983 that targeted the American and French Embassies, a residential complex for Americans, a number of US companies, the airport control tower, oil interests in al-Shu'aibah Port and the control centre at the Ministry of Electricity and Water. In 1985, there was an assassination attempt against Shaikh Jabir al-Ahmad al-Subah, and in 1988, a Kuwaiti commercial flight was hijacked (another flight had been hijacked in 1986). Because of their links with the Iranian government, the Shi'a Iraqi Da'wah Party and Hizbullah were blamed for these incidents. Many saw the violent acts as a clear message to the Kuwaiti government that it should end its support for Iraq in its war against Iran. The Iraqi invasion of Kuwait on 2 August 1990 was without a doubt the biggest event in the country's history.

The events that followed the liberation of Kuwait on 26 February 1991 had preoccupied the Islamists, but as their power to influence increased (they had won an unprecedented number of seats in the 1992 parliamentary elections), attention once again shifted to issues like co-education at Kuwait University. This time the Islamists succeeded in reaching an agreement with the government of Shaikh Sa'ad al-Abdullah al-Subah on a formula that would ban co-education in general. The government's only condition was that an exception be made in the case of private schools, which would be covered in law by a somewhat vague article that explicitly banned mixed-gender education at the university and at the Public Authority for Applied Education and Training (PAAET).[56] The articles of the law were as follows,

Article (1) The government shall undertake during a period that shall not exceed five years from the day this law became valid to provide facilities and buildings at the colleges, centres and institutes of Kuwait University and schools of Public Authority for Applied Education and Training to prevent gender interaction by providing female students with special buildings, teaching halls, laboratories, libraries, and other services. All new buildings must conform to this law.

Article (2) Kuwait University and the Public Authority for Applied Education and Training shall amend their regulations and the conditions that school uniforms, student conduct and activities must meet in order to conform with Islamic *Shariʿa*.

Article (3) The Ministry of Education shall issue resolutions that regulate the work of private schools in a manner that conforms with the general objectives of education in the State of Kuwait and Islamic values.

Article (4) The Minister of Education and the Minister of Higher Education shall present an annual report outlining all the measures taken to implement this law.

Article (5) All ministries concerned shall implement the articles of this law which shall become effective on the day of its publication in the official gazette.[57]

Thus, the Islamists collaborated with the government in the absence of any real opposition from secularist Pan-Arabists who had been greatly weakened by the Iraqi invasion. Although, naturally, none joined the

---

[56] Jamal al-Kandari (MP in Kuwait National Assembly 1992–1996 and 2006–2008), interview by Ali al-Kandari, London, 30 January 2013.

[57] GCC Legal Network, "Law Number 24 for 1996 on Organizing Higher Education in Kuwait University, Public Authority for Applied Education & Training, and Private Schools." www.gcclegal.org/MojPortalPublic/LawAsPDF.aspx?opt&country=1& LawID=3682. Last modified 23 April 2013 (accessed 30 June 2013).

Islamists, many of them had sided with the government, while others had joined the Liberals with few remaining loyal to Pan-Arabism.

The conflict between Islamists and secularists extended beyond voting on the law banning co-education in 1996 because the secularists, who exercised total control over the university's administration, kept delaying implementation of the law since, according to them, it was not intended to be applied.[58] Anwar al-Nuri, the university's first General Secretary, remarked that "the law banning co-education is similar to passing a law that sets the speed limit at 60 km/hour on a highway! Do they expect anyone to implement such a law? Everyone knows it is impossible, just like the law banning co-education."[59] The university refused to implement the law using a variety of pretexts (e.g. the cost was too high, it was very difficult to find qualified lecturers, etc.). The Islamists pointed out that Kuwait was a rich country, and the university was not short of money to provide buildings and new lecturers; also the university was legally obliged to respect the decisions of the Parliament. The university did take some insignificant steps by providing segregated cafeterias and a few classrooms. However, the situation remains unresolved.

The Islamist-Secularist Conflict Over the Islamic Economic System and Usury

The economy was yet another field of struggle between Islamists and secularists. And although the economy is linked with both the political and social domains, the issues surrounding it in Kuwait took on a more socio-religious dimension. Islamists had declared from the outset that they were opposed to the capitalist system which, they argued, relied on usury (*riba*), a practice forbidden by Shari'a. Liberal secularists defended the capitalist system's reliance on interest since many of them belonged to the merchant class in Kuwait. They raised doubts that the Islamic economic system was capable of standing up to the power of international capitalism; they were also worried that Islamists might gain some leeway with the economy and pull the rug from under the feet of the Kuwaiti merchant class that historically had exercised total control over the economy. Before the discovery of oil, the merchant class had been

---

[58] Anwaral-Nuri, "Mudhakkarat Anwaral-Nuri," *Aafaq Magazine*, 21 April 2013.

[59] Ibid.

more powerful than the ruling family, but their influence had diminished dramatically once oil revenues had begun to flow. Oil had transformed Kuwait from a country with a very basic economy into a rentier state that brought all classes under the control of the ruling family. Having already lost a lot with the discovery of oil, the merchant class did not wish to relinquish what was left of its influence on the Islamists.

While an Islamic economic system initially seemed a far-fetched notion, a number of thinkers including ʿIsa ʿAbduh, and Muhammad Baqir al-Sadir, explored the possibility at length in their writings. Al-Sadir, a turbaned Shiʿa Imam, published his book "*Iqtisaduna*" [Our Economy] in 1961 as part of a series of Islamic studies re-examining Islamic civilisation in the light of contemporary challenges. Al-Sadir had already published, *Falsafatuna* [Our Philosophy], a book in which he outlined the pillars of Islamic civilisation and responded to secularist attacks on Islamic thought. He had planned to produce a third book entitled *Mujtamaʿuna* [Our Society] which would have explored Islamic view of social life,[60] but this was never published. In *Iqtisaduna*, al-Sadir criticised Marxist historical materialism and capitalism for their inability to regulate society's economic life. He compared these two systems with the Islamic economic system, remarking that this was a very basic attempt to explore the idea of an economic system based on the teachings of Islam with its rich philosophical heritage.[61]

ʿIsa ʿAbduh, who had studied economics in the West in the 1930s began, during his stay in Manchester, to write about why Islam had forbidden usury. His ideas developed over time, and he eventually called for the establishment of a network of Islamic financial institutions[62]; these would consist of a number of banks in many Muslim countries and would provide banking services without recourse to either direct or indirect usury.[63] ʿIsa ʿAbduh researched the issue at length in the 1940s and 1950s and began delivering lectures on related matters in a number of Egyptian and other Arab countries from the end of the 1950s and during the 1960s. He contributed to the establishment of the first Islamic bank

---

[60] Muhammad B. al-Sadir, *Iqtisaduna* (Beirut: Dar al-Tʿaruf, 1987), 25.

[61] Ibid., 32.

[62] ʾIsa ʿAbduh, *Silsilat Bunuk Bidun Fawayid: al-Faʾidah ʿAla Raʾs al-Mal Surah min Suwar al-Riba* (Cairo: Dar al-Fath, 1970), 13.

[63] Ibid., 29.

in the Egyptian city of Mit Ghamr and helped draw up its financial and banking rules. Between 1960 and 1967, ʿAbduh presented a number of television shows which played a role in disseminating information about Islamic banking to a wider sector of society in the Arab world. The Society for Social Reform invited ʿAbduh to deliver a series of lecture on Islamic Banking in 1965.[64]

Following the establishment of al-Manar Islamic library in 1960 by a number of Muslim Brotherhood figures (ʿAbdulwahid Aman and Abdullah al-ʿAqil) to spread Islamic thought, a number of serials directed at young people were published by the library. Series issued included "Towards a Just Islamic Law," "Towards an Ideal Islamic Education," "Towards a Stable Islamic Society" and "Overview of Destructive Movements", in addition to "Towards an Ideal Islamic Economy." Al-Manar wrote to a number of Muslim scholars asking them to contribute to these serial publications, and Al-Sadir and ʿAbduh were among those who wrote articles for the Islamic Economy series. These publications soon turned into the nucleus for an Islamic Banking Corporation. In 1968, Abullah Al-Mutawwaʿ, Abdullah al-ʿAqil, ʿAbdulwahid Aman, Jamal al-Dīn ʿAtiyyah, Humam al-Hashimi, Nizar Siraji, Ismaʾil Raʾfat, Muḥib al-Mihjari, Muḥī al-Dīn ʿAtiyyah, and ʿIsaʿAbduh, who became president of the group, met to form "The Preparatory Committee for the Kuwait Finance House." The committee invited Ahmed Irshad to talk about his experience as the founder of the first bank to operate without usury in Karachi, Pakistan. Irshad spoke about his experiences and the obstacles he had faced, which had eventually led to the bank closing down. The committee, and ʿAbduh in particular, began to formulate the details of a comprehensive project based on a close examination of the Kuwaiti market and existing banking laws. Al-Sadir published a study entitled "Non-Usury Islamic Banking"[65] which also served to support the project of an Islamic bank.

Two years later, a memorandum entitled "Kuwait Finance House" was issued to introduce the company. Various officials rejected the idea which they saw as being incompatible with international interest-based

---

[64] Ibid., 59–60.

[65] Muhammad B. al-Sadir, *al-Bank al-Laribawi fi Islam* (Beirut: Dar al-Tʿaruf, 1994).

banking systems.[66] However, the bank was finally established in 1977 with the support of ʿAbdulrahman al-ʿAtiqi, the Minister of Finance (and a former member of al-Irshad).[67] Al-ʿAtiqi presented the project to the Crown Prince Shaikh Jabir al-Ahmad al-Subah, while the Parliament was in recess so as to avoid a confrontation with secularist MPs. The Emir issued Decree No.72 for the year 1977 approving the establishment of the Kuwait Finance House (KFH), or *Baituk* [your home], as the bank liked to be called. The government owned 49% of the shares, the Ministry of Finance and the Ministry of Justice each owned 20% and the Ministry of Awqaf and Religious Affairs owned nine per cent. The remaining shares were sold on the stock exchange.[68]

Because the KFH did not impose interest on loans as other banks did, it had to formulate other methods, such as *mudarabah*,[69] *murabahah*[70] and *musharakah*,[71] to make profits and manage investments in a manner

[66] ʿAbdullah al-ʿAqil, "ʾIsa ʿAbduh Ibrahim: raʾid al-Bunuk al-Islamiyya," www.alaqilabu mostafa.com/chardetails_print.asp?CharId=12605. Last modified 25 April 2013 (accessed 30 June 2013).

[67] Ibid.

[68] *Official Website of Kuwait Finance House*, "Baituk ... Qissat Najah," http://www. kfh.com/ar/about/news/ArchiveNewsDetails.aspx?q=M9tbDDFfYL0L2XuYDoRT3w. Last modified 23 March 2010 (accessed 30 June 2013).

[69] *Mudarabah* is a special kind of partnership where one partner gives money to another for investing it in a commercial enterprise. The investment comes from the first partner who is called "rabb-ul-mal," while the management and work are the exclusive responsibility of the other, who is called "mudarib." See Kuwait Finance House, Official Website, "Financial Services." www.kfh.bh/ar/retail-banking/profit-rates. html, last modified 30 April 2013. (accessed 30 June 2013). Also see; *Islamic Banker*, "Musharakah & Mudarabah" at www.islamicbanker.com/education-resources/15.Last modified 2013 (accessed 8 September 2013); and *Islamic Banker*, "Murabahah," at www. islamicbanker.com/education-resources/17. Last modified 2013 (accessed 8 September 2013).

[70] Most Islamic banks and financial institutions use *murabahah* as an Islamic mode of financing, and most of their financing operations are based on *murabahah*. This is why this term has been taken up in economic circles today as a method of banking operations, while the original concept of *murabahah* is different from this assumption. See *Islamic Banker*, "Murabahah," www.islamicbanker.com/education-resources/17. Last modified 2013 (accessed 8 September 2013). See also *Official Website of Kuwait Finance House*, "Financial Services," www.kfh.bh/ar/retail-banking/profit-rates.html. Last modified 30 April 2013 (accessed 30 June 2013).

[71] *Musharakah* or *Musharaka* is a word of Arabic origin which literally means sharing. In the context of business and trade, it means a joint enterprise in which all the partners share the profit or loss of the joint venture. It is an ideal alternative for interest-based

that did not contradict Islamic teachings. The decree issued by the Emir bestowed upon the KFH a unique legal status that allowed it to diversify its activities. The new bank was not subject to the laws governing the operations of other banks under central bank supervision, which clearly reflected the high level of government support enjoyed by the KFH, while its individual legal status allowed it to enter the commercial sector, something that other banks were not permitted to do. Since the KFH was able to engage in selling and buying like any other company, it invested in a number of sectors especially property development. In the mid-1980s, almost 60% of its investments were in the Kuwaiti property market, but due to pressure from various parties, it had to lower its property portfolio to around 35%.[72] The KFH also invested abroad, especially in Muslim countries, and set up branches in Turkey, Bahrain and Malaysia. It is now Kuwait's second biggest bank after the Kuwaiti National Bank which is owned by the merchant class.

The writings of early thinkers like ʿAbduh and al-Sadir on Islamic finance aimed to introduce society to the values of Islam's economic system and to encourage people to abandon practices forbidden by Islam. They also aimed to effect change in the political domain to challenge Western capitalist hegemony over the economy, believing that imperial powers were exercising too much control over Muslim countries through this approach. The new Islamic economic mode succeeded in the social domain more than the political one. From its establishment in 1977 until the late 1990s, the KFH went through various phases of social change; the first was the birth of the idea itself, and the second was the dissemination of the idea.

During the first phase, the bank was keen to distinguish itself from other traditional banks. The KFH's first board of directors was headed by Ahmad al-Yasin, a former member of al-Islah, and the bank gave preference to employees who were members of Islamist movements (Muslim

---

financing with far-reaching effects on both production and distribution. In the modern capitalist economy, interest is the sole instrument and is used indiscriminately in financing of every type. Since Islam prohibits interest, this instrument cannot be used for providing funds of any kind. Thus, musharakah can play a vital role in an economy based on Islamic principles. See Islamic Banker, "Musharakah & Mudarabah," www.islamicbanker.com/edu cation-resources/15. Last modified 2013 (accessed 8 September 2013).

[72] Kristin Diwan, "The Kuwait Finance House and the Islamization of Public Life in Kuwait," in Clement M. Henry and Rodney Wilson (eds.) *The Politics of Islamic Finance* (Edinburgh: Edinburgh University Press, 2004), 175.

Brotherhood and others). The first branch had special sections for men and women, while the bank's uniforms were chosen to reflect the spirit of Islam (women were expected to be veiled). Smoking was prohibited. The Islamic identity of the bank could be discerned in the choice of furniture, the use of Islamic calligraphy and art and the prayer rooms that were provided for both employees and customers. The logo of the bank combined tradition with modernity as evidenced by the image of the mosque minaret and oil well.

From the outset, the KFH aimed to attract customers with Islamist leanings; it also targeted some of the major Kuwaiti tribes by opening branches in Jahraʾ, al-Raqqah and al-Fuhaihīl in addition to the main branch in Kuwait City.[73] The response was excellent, with 150 customers flocking to open an account on the first day of business. At the start of the twenty-first century, the percentage of Kuwaitis with an account at the bank (90% of whose employees were Kuwaitis), was nearly 40%.[74] In other words, if one assumed that the number of Kuwaitis working in the public sector was one million (i.e. 25% of the population, of whom 40% are below 20 years of age), the number of accounts at KFH would be around 100,000, in addition to the estimated two million other accounts. In 2003, deposits were estimated at around KD1.8 billon[75] (approximately US$6 billion), a figure that represented some 15% of the total bank deposits in Kuwait.[76] The following graph illustrates deposits between the yeas 1978–2001.

[73] Ibid., 173.
[74] Ibid., 174.
[75] KD = Kuwaiti dinar.
[76] Ibid., 173.

Consumer Deposits in the Kuwait Finance House, 1978–2001

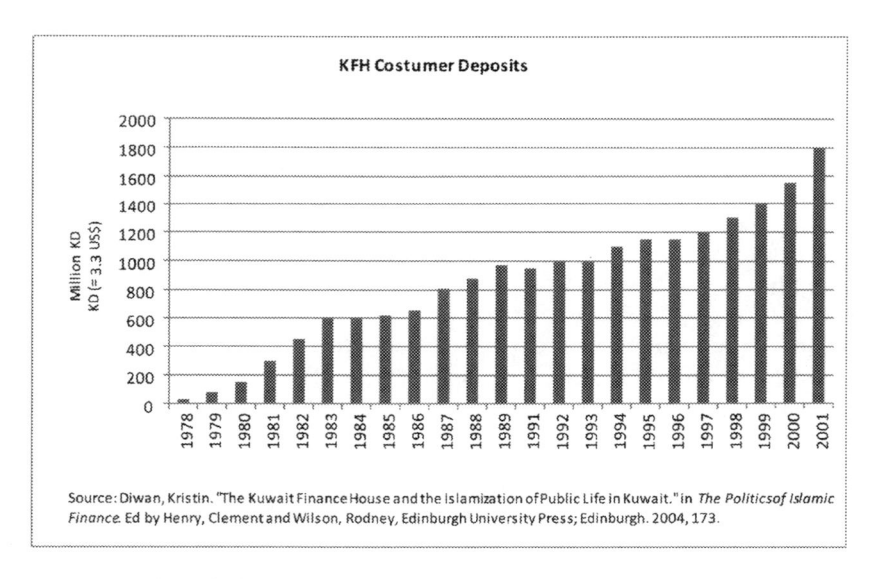

KFH Costumer Deposits

Source: Diwan, Kristin. "The Kuwait Finance House and the Islamization of Public Life in Kuwait." in *The Politics of Islamic Finance.* Ed by Henry, Clement and Wilson, Rodney, Edinburgh University Press; Edinburgh. 2004, 173.

To ensure that all financial and banking dealings conformed with *shariʿa*, the KFH established the Fatwa and Shariʿa Supervisory Department to devise financial and investment methods through examining *fiqh* and *shariʿa* and transforming Islamic teachings into modern tools and contracts. This department was also entrusted with adopting tools from international systems and adapting them to *shariʿa*. All contracts and investments had to be approved by the Supervisory Department which possessed powers of veto over the decisions of the Board of Directors and the Executive Director of the bank.

The presence of a number of renowned religious scholars in the Supervisory Department lent it greater legitimacy in Kuwaiti society. Promoting the services of the KFH usually began by emphasising the differences between it and other Kuwaiti banks which relied on the forbidden system of usury. Through its subsidiary, the Property Development Company, the KFH invested in a series of residential buildings designed to reflect Islamic architecture. The architectural plan for the apartments created special areas for families and single people. The floor plan itself was

Islamic; the kitchen was placed near the bedrooms away from the reception area or the living room used to receive guests so that the wife would not have to encounter her husband's friends. Al-Muthanna commercial and residential centre in heart of the capital, which is owned by the Property Development Company, is considered an Islamic complex suitable for families. Shops adhere to the rules and regulations of the company such as the ban on the use of mannequins which some argue are forbidden in Islam.[77]

These efforts popularised the notion of an Islamic economic system among Kuwaitis. The KFH's slogan was "Security and Reassurance" which it used in the face of wide-spread scepticism that it could succeed in its mission. The bank's huge profits served to increase its trustworthiness prompting devout clients and society at large to believe Allah was blessing their efforts.[78] The bank then began to employ Kuwaitis who were not devout Muslims or tribal members. The number of non-devout Muslims increased, tempted by high profits and excellent salaries. People joked that an Islamic bank was employing people who drank alcohol.[79] Many clients were also non-devout Muslims. This emphasised the extent to which the KFH succeeded in bringing about social change in the minds of Kuwaitis. As members of a conservative society, many Kuwaitis were very keen on *halal* investments after decades of being forced to seek the services of interest-based banks.

The economic activities of the KFH have undoubtedly had a great influence on Kuwaiti society, as an example of how the many ideas and principles advocated by the Islamist movement were transformed into a reality. Gender segregation, at the university and in the workplace, was widely acceptable, despite secularist scepticism, and did not pose any hindrance to progress. Islamic economic systems, Islamic entertainment and books, Islamic knowledge and other products benefited from the success of the KFH in a very technocratic and hostile environment. It became easier for the Islamist movement to propose initiatives on the basis of the success of the KFH, and over time, it increasingly gained popularity in the social domain.

[77] Ibid., 181.

[78] Ibid., 147.

[79] Kristin Diwan, "Culture and Capital: The Strategic Construction of Islamic Financial Institutions in the Gulf" (International Studies Association, New Orleans, February 2010), 12.

Islamic banks such as KHF and the Dubai Islamic Bank promoted the notion that anyone contributing to the success of these Islamic establishments would gain rewards in the afterlife, especially as they were standing up to the forbidden practice of usury and capitalism. This link between the value of work and the spiritual life is similar to Max Weber's exploration of the Protestant ethic with its emphasis on the value of work and how that contributed to the prosperity of Europe and the US. The Dubai Islamic Bank remarked in one of its leaflets that, "Work is a religious exercise just like Jihad on the battlefield. Both lead to the spread of Islamic principles and moral virtues in the soul of a Muslim... and indeed the world around him."[80]

The establishment of the KFH and its success certainly owed a lot to government support. The proposal to establish the KFH had been presented to the government several times after it was first drafted at the end of the 1960s, but it was vetoed every time. It had also been deemed in violation of the banking laws of Kuwait which were based on international financial institutions where profit was always based on accrued interest, while the traditional banks, unlike the KFH, were not permitted to engage in direct commercial transactions. Technocratic government administrations such as the Ministries of Finance and Trade, and the Central Bank of Kuwait, which had more affinities with the liberals and secularists than with Islamists, were not convinced the project could succeed.[81] But the project was destined to see the light at the hands of a merchant who wished to find an alternative to traditional banks. Said Lutah, a well-known merchant from Dubai, had secured oral approval from the Ruler of Dubai, Shaikh Rashid Said al-Maktum, to seek a substitute for the conventional bank, and embarked on his quest in the early 1970s. After reading some of al-Sadir's and ʿAbduh's writings, and following several trips to Greater Syria and Egypt to meet a number of Shariʿa scholars, Lutah could find no one better than ʿAbduh, who persuaded him to establish an Islamic bank. In establishing the Dubai Islamic Bank (DIB), ʿAbduh applied the findings of the preparatory

---

[80] The Manners and Approach of the Person Working in An Islamic Organization, (Employee Manual of the Dubai Islamic Bank), 9. Also, Kristin Diwan, "Islamic Finance and the Renewal of Awqaf" (The Eighth Annual Harvard University Forum on Islamic Finance, May 2008), 2.

[81] ʿAbdulraḥmanal-ʿAtiqi(former Minister of Finance and a Private Advisor of the Emir), interview by Ali al-Kandari, Kuwait, 5 May 2012.

committee's study for the KFH project, and Lutah convinced Shaikh Rashid of the importance of the project and won his full support in overcoming legal obstacles. Shaikh Rashid opened the bank in 1975 as the first Islamic bank in the region and in the wider Arab world.[82]

The success of DIB prompted the Kuwaiti Minister of Finance, ʿAbdulrahman al-ʿAtiqi, to present the KFH proposal to the Crown Prince and Prime Minister Shaikh Jaber al-ʾAhmad Al-Subah. The KFH was established with a royal decree and a special law, despite objections from government technocrats and secularists who saw the project as a direct interference in the Kuwaiti economy by a government-Islamist alliance. The government owned 49% of the shares which bestowed legitimacy upon the bank, and despite the decrease in government shares over the years, members of the ruling family continued to support it by retaining its services for various property and investment deals. They also owned big shares in the KFH, although this support came at a price, since the government exercised control over the names that could be appointed to the bank's board of directors and leadership positions. Despite the widespread misconception that the Muslim Brotherhood controlled the KFH, in reality they represented only ten per cent of the individuals in leadership positions over the years. It was the presence of Muslim Brotherhood figures in middle-management that entrenched the perception that they ran the KFH.[83]

The Islamist movement succeeded in penetrating into the Kuwaiti economic stronghold through an alliance between the government and the Islamists by way of the KFH. With the success of the KFH, the Islamist movement went on to establish a number of successful Islamic corporations and institutions. Shariʿa scholars played an important role in supporting and developing the idea of Islamic institutions through research, conference papers, symposiums and lectures. The same scholars who issued fatwas to people inquiring about personal and public matters advised Muslims to leave traditional banks and companies and move to Islamic banks, thus cementing the Islamists' power in both the social and the economic domains despite the fierce objections of secularists.

---

[82] Saʿid Lutah (founder of Dubai Islamic Bank), interview by Sami Kulaib, TV Show "Saʿid Lutah... Fikrat al-Masarif al-Islamiyyah," *Aljazeera Channel*, 8 March 2008 (accessed 30 June). www.aljazeera.net/programs/pages/190b3512-df1a-4160-a620-eff9a9dcd492.

[83] Aman, interview.

Even some traditional merchants began investing in Islamic companies in an important development that signalled the deterioration of secularist influence.[84]

THE RISE IN POPULARITY IN THE 1980S AND THE COMPETITION BETWEEN SALAFIS AND THE MUSLIM BROTHERHOOD OVER THE SOCIAL DOMAIN

As the end of the 1970s approached, the Islamist movement became well-entrenched with the success of Islamic institutions like the Society for Social Reform, the KFH and other smaller projects (*al-Manar* bookshop, *al-Mujtamaᶜ* Journal). Meanwhile, the 1967 defeat and the loss of Palestine followed by Jamal ᶜAbdulnasser's death had considerably weakened secularist nationalism. The alliance between the government and Islamists on a number of political and social projects boosted the status of the Islamists as that of the secularists gradually disappeared. The year 1979 proved to be a turning point in the region; following a series of protests against the Shah of Iran by various political and social powers headed by Islamic parties, the Shah was forced to relinquish his post on 16 January 1979, after which the opposition seized control.

On the first day of February, Khomeini arrived in Tehran on a flight from Paris, and in 1 February 1979, following a referendum on the constitution and a fierce struggle between various powers, the Islamists took over, and Khomeini was declared the Supreme Leader of Iran. The Iranian Revolution, with its distinctive Shiᶜa identity, created ripples in the region especially following its attempts to export the revolution to other countries. When Saddam Hussein succeeded Ahmed Hasan al-Bakir as Iraqi president in July 1979, he plotted a coup against Iran's new rulers with the help of several Iranian officers who opposed Khomeini, but the plot was uncovered, and Saddam was forced to wage a war against Iran to stem the tide of Shiᶜa politics.

---

[84] Ali Mohammed Thunayan al-Ghanim, the Chairman of the Kuwait Chamber of Commerce & Industry (KCCI), who is one of the main investors in Aayan Leasing & Investment Company, an Islamic company, mentioned that he was once asked why he was investing in an Islamic company; his reply was "because it makes money!" Ali al-Ghanim, interview by Ali al-Kandari, Kuwait, 25 September 2004.

Thus, the beginning of the Iraq-Iran war which lasted eight years and was the fiercest and most brutal conflict in the history of the region. Kuwait and other Gulf States supported the Iraqi regime in its war against Iran out of fear that the revolution would bring down their monarchies. Khomeini had been calling for the overthrow of all monarchies and oppressive regimes and for them to be replaced with an Islamic system of government, and his incitements and Shi^{c}a ideology were viewed as a huge threat to the Gulf's Sunni monarchical regimes. The alliance between Islamists and the government was further cemented by regional developments; Islamists launched a fierce attack against Shi^{c}as by casting doubts on their loyalty in the aftermath of the explosions carried out by Hizbullah against Kuwaiti and foreign interests and even the Emir himself. Salafis drew upon Wahhabist literature, especially accounts of the early Wahhabist struggles against Shi^{c}as in 1801, when Sa^{c}ud bin ^{c}Abdulaziz attacked Karbala and destroyed a number of Shi^{c}a trends and fads such as the dome constructed over the tomb of al-Hussein bin Ali.[85] The Salafis also employed fatwas issued by Sa^{c}udi Salafis declaring Shi^{c}a practices un-Islamic. Some scholars have argued that Sunni and Shi^{c}a beliefs can never be reconciled.[86] These fatwas were certainly instrumental in deepening the Sunni-Shi^{c}a rift in Kuwait.

Other political developments in the region also contributed to the spread of the Islamist movement in the 1980s. Juhaiman al-^{c}Utaibi's movement which flourished at the end of the 1970s was constantly persecuted by the Sa^{c}udi government especially after the movement had vandalised a number of shops in the mid-1970s that were displaying mannequins in Medina. The Sa^{c}udi authorities tried to rein in al-^{c}Utaybi's Salafi thinking, but he surprised everyone by breaking into the Grand Mosque in Mecca on 20 November 1979 and declaring that Muhammad Abdullah al-Qahtani was the Guided One (al-Mahdi).[87] Juhaiman and

---

[85] ^{c}Uthman bin Bishr, *^{c}Unwan al-Majd fiTarikh Najd* (Riyadh: King ^{c}Abdul^{c}aziz Foundation for Research and Archives, 1982), 257–258.

[86] There are many fatwas by Sa^{c}udi scholars such as ^{c}Abdul^{c}aziz bin Baz on this issue; these can be found at the official website of The General Presidency of Scholarly Research and Ifta: www.alifta.net/Default.aspx.

[87] For Sunnis, al-Mahdi is the Saviour and a descendant of the Prophet Mohammad whose anticipated return to rule the world will restore justice, peace and true religion. The Twelver Shi^{c}ites believe him to be the Twelfth Imam who is in occultation until his reappearance at the end of time. See, Said Amir Arjomand (December 2007). "Islam in Iran: The Concept of Mahdi in Sunni Islam". Encyclopaedia Iranica XIV

his followers were arrested and executed following a trial by shariʿa judges representing the official religious establishment. The incident left an indelible mark on the Islamists' psyche as it represented the first clash between Islamists and the government of a Gulf State. It also made Gulf governments aware of the need to contain Islamists by supporting state-backed Islamism against anti-government Islamists. Breaking into the Grand Mosque coincided with the Soviet invasion of Afghanistan on 25 December 1979 to support the pro-Soviet Afghan government against armed rebels. Backed by the anti-Communist West, the Islamists declared Jihad against the Soviet troops. Afghanistan became the ideal place in which to channel the energies of unwanted Islamists who became known as "Arab Afghanis."[88] Pakistan took on the task of training Afghanis and Arab Afghanis while the Gulf States, chiefly Saʿudi Arabia, provided financial support, and the United States provided logistical support, especially in the form of Stinger missiles which later tipped the balance against the Soviet aircraft. The war in Afghanistan took up all the time and attention of many Islamist movements and channelled their energies to the cause by intensifying Islamist calls for donations and volunteers.

These regional changes boosted the role of Islamists in the region who were widely viewed as a shield against the spread of Shiʿa Islam and the Iranian revolution. They were also instrumental in stemming the tide of Islamists who did not belong to any specific group, and the secularists who wished to overthrow all monarchies. The Islamist movements made the most of simple media such as books, leaflets, posters and newspaper articles to spread their message. But the greatest tool at their disposal was the cassette tape (known as the Islamic tape) which was widely used to reach as many young people as possible. Friday sermons and religious lessons would be taped and sold at bookshops. The low cost of the tapes and wide availability of tape players meant the messages were accessible to almost everyone. Preachers simplified their sermons and lessons and made them less cumbersome so they could reach a wider audience. Orators like Ahmed al-Qattan were highly skilled at inflaming people's passions and encouraging them to join the Jihad movement in Afghanistan and to resist

(Fasc. 2): 134–136. www.iranicaonline.org/articles/islam-in-iran-vi-the-concept-of-mahdi-in-sunni-islam (accessed 30 June 2013).

[88] Muhammad B. ʿAbdulʿati, Aljazeera Channel, "Al-Afghan al-ʿArab," Last modified 3 April 2004 (accessed 30 June 2013). www.aljazeera.net/specialfiles/pages/119d2e8f-080d-47e1-ad8b-82098360c304.

Iran and the Shiᶜas. The Islamic tape was more capable of tapping into the audience's hearts and minds than books, because the preachers often used local dialects to get closer to their listeners. Bookshops and record shops played an important role in marketing these tapes to enthusiastic young Muslims who began to adopt the ideas and the oratorical skills of the preachers.

Islamic tapes were not restricted to sermons and lessons but extended to the Islamic art of *Anashid* [Islamic chants]. The Muslim Brotherhood was very keen from the outset to utilise the power of art in the service of its ideas. *Anashid* were different from songs because the latter were usually associated with entertainment, music and sometimes forbidden pleasures. *Anashid*, on the other hand, had been known throughout Islamic history especially in Sufi traditions where the praises of Allah and his prophets are sung as part of spiritual sessions. The Islamist movement, especially the Muslim Brotherhood, revived the art and developed it further, using modern technology to include new topics like political issues, *Anashid* about fighting colonial powers, liberating Palestine and Jihad. Al-Banna himself was very interested in *Anashid* as part of the activities of the Muslim Brotherhood's Scout movement, in which a famous *nashid* was *al-Kataʾib* [the Militias].[89] The margin of freedoms and wealth in Kuwait allowed *al-Anashid* to be produced and distributed widely, and they became particularly popular during the 1980s to match the momentum of Jihad against the Soviet Union in Afghanistan, and the outbreak of the first Palestinian *intifada* [uprising] in 1987. *Anashid* then took on a more patriotic tone during and after the Iraqi invasion of Kuwait and throughout the 1990s.

THE SPREAD OF ISLAMIC CHARITABLE WORK

Charity work is one of the main features of Islamic efforts and has historically been associated with Islam as one of the most important channels for winning Allah's rewards. People would usually give their donations to religious scholars and trustees of charity organisations associated with mosques, who would then pass them on to those in need. Charity

---

[89] It was written by ᶜAbdulhakim ᶜAabdin and the full *nashid* can be found in ᶜAbdullah al-ᶜAqil, *The Official Historical Encyclopaedia of the Muslim Brotherhood*, "ᶜAbdulhakim ᶜAbdin." www.ikhwanwiki.com/index.php?title=عبدالحكيم ظمعابدين. Last modified 8 May 2013 (accessed 30 June 2013).

work developed over time, with endowment becoming one of its major features. Endowment was usually sourced from property (orchards, farms, private residences, wells, etc.) and was used to feed the poor, maintain mosques and teach children how to read the Qur'an. Judicial authorities were responsible for regulating and managing endowments. As old as Islam itself, endowments represent a unique model which combines social services with religious charity. Charity work and endowments developed throughout history to include the health sector (such as hospitals and centres), and education (libraries, universities and educational institutions during Abbasid rule), while the Mamluks and Ottomans expanded endowments to include religious and life studies and mosques in Mecca, Jerusalem and al-Medina.

As forms of charity, endowments were administered by civil society (mostly religious institutions) rather than by political authorities. In modern times, colonial powers chose to undermine religious institutions, accusing them of funding resistance movements. Targeting endowments was widely perceived as the best method for weakening religious establishment. The French colonial powers in Greater Syria issued special regulations to put an end to endowments, while the French in Algeria appropriated endowments and distributed them among the French. The British did the same and placed endowments under foreign administration. After the Arab countries had won back their independence, secularist governments followed the European model of weakening religious establishments, so that special ministries were established to regulate *waqf* and endowments.[90]

In Kuwait, the first endowment was bin Bahar mosque in 1695. Endowments have continued since, starting with mosques built by Kuwaiti citizens and charity work to feed and clothe the poor. Other examples included the "dinner endowment," Eid al-Adha endowment, school and university scholarships, printing books and publishing copies of the Qur'an. A number of private foundations (*Mabarrat*) managed, developed and distributed endowments in Kuwait and continued to do so even after the establishment of a government department for endowments that later became a Ministry for *Waqf* and Religious Affairs. These

---

[90] Muhammad al-Zuhaili, "Mulkiyyat A'yan al-Waqf baina Maqasid al-Tashri'wa Mathalib al-Saitarah" (Waqf Conference III, Medina, January 2010, 645–681), 663–666.

Mabarrat succeeded in remaining relatively autonomous, unlike those in many other Arab countries.[91]

The Islamic reformist movement took a great interest in charity work, establishing the Arab Charity Society in 1913 as noted in a previous chapter. The movement also established a special department for religious guidance in the field of social charity work in Kuwait and abroad. Al-Islah also invested heavily in charity, especially ones from oil revenues, and the Kuwaiti government invested heavily in the service sector so that most Kuwaitis began to enjoy the fruits of oil revenues, thereby leaving very few in need of charity. This meant that most endowments were spent abroad or given to some members of the foreign labour force in Kuwait.

In the 1980s, government support for charity work in Kuwait and abroad (especially in Afghanistan) gave it a further boost. Endowments extended to cover almost every aspect of life except for Jihad, from which many charity organisations, especially Muslim Brotherhood ones, steered clear. Because most Kuwaitis were well-off, most charity money went to spiritual and religious development. Charity organisations funded lessons for memorising the Qur'an, courses at Kuwaiti mosques and religious cassette tapes which were given away free of charge. They also sponsored *hajj* and *umra* trips for young Kuwaitis. Charity organisations played a role in supporting the activities of the KFH by opening all their accounts there, so that donations worth tens of millions of Kuwaiti dinars were deposited at the bank. They also benefited greatly from the experience of the KFH concerning the best (Islamic) methods for investing the charity money. Both the KFH and charity organisation thus collaborated to achieve the same goals: i.e. to spread conservative values and support the role of Islam in society.[92]

In her study on the renewal of *Awqaf* in Kuwait, Kristin Diwan examines the role of charity organisations in supporting political activities and the impact of charities on voting for the Muslim Brotherhood and Salafi candidates. This may apply to countries like Egypt, Greater Syria, Iraq and pre-oil Gulf States, but cannot be generalised to cover post-oil Gulf societies. The fact that the government takes care of citizens throughout

---

[91] *Official Website of Kuwait Awqaf Public Foundation*, "Waqf in Kuwait," Last modified 8 May 2013 (accessed 30 June 2013). www.awqaf.org.kw/English/AboutEndo wment/EndowmentHistoryInKuwait/Pages/default.aspx.

[92] Kristin Diwan, "Islamic Finance beyond the State: The Renewal of Awqaf" (MPSA Annual Conference, Chicago, 31 March–3 April 2011), 9–10.

their lives means that the impact of charity is negligible. The Muslim Brotherhood in Kuwait saw their mission as supporting Islamic work all over the world, and this trumped political reforms in Kuwait, since charity work associated with the Muslim Brotherhood cannot be tied to political manoeuvres and short-term electoral gains. Those responsible for charity work were very well aware of the dangers of conflating charity with political activities, so a decision was made to distance charity work from Kuwaiti political life. It was the fact that the Islamist movement's political participation expanded at around the same time as charity work that led many to the misconception that the two were related. So although both contribute to the propagation of conservative values and the spread of the message of Islam, they are not organically linked.

COMPETING WITH SALAFIS OVER THE SOCIAL DOMAIN

The Salafi movement did not enjoy any real influence due to the attacks launched by the Wahhabi movement with support from the Saʿudi government between 1926 and 1930. The strength of the anti-Wahabbi al-Hasa school and its sway over Kuwaitis meant that Salafis did not get far. But Kuwaitis of Najdi decent were sympathetic to the Wahhabi ideology and the founder of Saʿudi Arabia, ʿAbdulʿaziz al-Saʿud. During the second half of the 1960s, a number of young men, influenced by the Wahhabi Salafi sect, began to gather at mosques in various areas of Kuwait (Kaifan, al-Qadsiyyah and al-Fayhaʾ) to attend religious lessons given by independent shaikhs such as Hasan Ayyub and Hasan Tannun. With the arrival of ʿUmar al-Ashqar and ʿAbdulrahman ʿAbdulkhaliq, both of whom had been influenced by the Salafi Wahhabi ideology in addition to the Muslim Brotherhood, from Saʿudi Arabia in the summer of 1965, the scene was set for the rise of Salafis. Although they were initially very similar to the Muslim Brotherhood, Salafis gradually began to distinguish themselves by meeting separately and organising their own programmes which were not different from those of the Muslim Brotherhood (Qur'an readings, praying at the mosque and reading Islamic books).

Compared to the Muslim Brotherhood, these Salafi groups were small and quite limited. The Muslim Brotherhood had been well established since 1968 with its own organisation, the Society for Social Reform, and it had maintained a presence in Kuwaiti society since the end of the 1940s while the Salafis did not appear until the end of the 1960s.

The Salafi group remained small until Muhammad Ahmed al-Rashad had a major disagreement with ʿAbdulrahman ʿAbdulkhaliq in 1974. The incident led to the gradual departure of ʿAbdulkhaliq to the Salafi camp which lacked any religious or intellectual leadership, so that ʿAbdulkhaliq seemed the perfect candidate to lead the group. As a result, major intellectual disagreements emerged between the Muslim Brotherhood and the Salafis who did not appreciate any aspect of the Sufi heritage that the Muslim Brotherhood seemed to be quite fond of in their educating and training of young people. The rift between the Muslim Brotherhood and the Salafis grew even wider with time until the end of the 1970s when a number of regional events such as the breaking into the Grand Mosque, the success of the Iranian revolution and the declaration of Jihad in Afghanistan against the Soviets gave Islamists and especially the Salafis a big push forward. After the incident with the Juhaiman Salafi group, the Gulf States were careful to contain all other Salafis to prevent a recurrence of any attempts to overthrow their ruling families.

With the rise of Iran's sectarian ambitions and the threat of exporting the Iranian revolution to the Gulf States, the Islamist movement, especially the Salafis, seemed the best weapon against the spread of Shiʿa ideology. The Muslim Brotherhood eyed the Islamic revolution with great respect despite their apprehensions about Iranian influence, while the Salafis had no qualms about branding the Iranian regime blasphemous especially since history and Salafi tradition supported this divide with the Shiʿa sect. The governments of the Gulf States used the Islamists, especially the Salafis, to agitate the masses to support Jihad in Afghanistan since the Salafi Wahhabi ideology was represented by a number of Afghani factions, and a significant number of Arabs in Afghanistan subscribed to the Salafi school of thought.

The Kuwaiti government had a vested interest in supporting the Salafi movement in order to create a split in society by not allowing the Muslim Brotherhood to steer the hearts and minds of Sunni Muslims.[93] The government therefore backed Salafi efforts to establish their own organisation and al-Islah for the Revival of Islamic Heritage came into being in 1981.[94] Among those who established what came to be known as the

---

[93] Aman, interview.

[94] "Al-Taʿrif bil Jamʿiyyah," *the Official Website of Jamʿiyyat Ihya al-Turath al-Islami* (accessed 17 March 2014).

Revival of Heritage were Abdullah al-Sabt, Tariq al-ʿIsa, Khalid Sultan bin ʿIsa, Dakhil al-Jassar and ʿAbdulrahman ʿAbdulkhaliq. Shaikh Fahad al-Ahmad al-Subah, the youngest brother of the then Emir of Kuwait, was one of the founders and supporters of the Society. The Salafi momentum increased with their clear-cut positions vis-à-vis regional and local issues when compared with the Muslim brotherhood with their less extreme views.

Salafis were also more inclined to be strict with regard to certain aspects such as the general appearance of individuals. They adhered strictly to the growing of beards, wearing short clothes, and using a *miswak* for cleaning teeth, and wearing a headdress without *ʾIgal* in a fashion similar to that of Saʿudi Salafis, as well as other individual fashions that distinguished Salafis from other members of society. Salafi women also had their own style of dress to distinguish them from Muslim Brotherhood women and wore a black *niqab* that covered the whole face in addition to the black *ʿabayya* to hide the whole body. Muslim Brotherhood women wore a black *ʿabayya* with white head cover with the face left bare. Salafis criticised the Muslim Brotherhood for subscribing to the *fiqh* opinion that women were allowed to expose their faces, while Saʿudi jurists such as bin Baz and bin ʿOthaimin issued fatwas against women revealing their faces, a view opposed by the Syrian Salafi Shaikh Nasser al-Din al-Albani.

In addition to the differences in the domain of *fiqh*, major disagreements between Salafis and the Muslim Brotherhood were intellectual and doctrinal. From the end of the 1970s until the first decade of the new millennium, most of the heated debates and conflicts between the two groups centred on these issues. The most important among these debates was the disagreement between al-Rashid and ʿAbdulkhaliq over the relationship with the "Other," such as Sufi traditions. Al-Rashid was much more forgiving while ʿAbdulkhaliq refused to deal with this tradition, considering it impure and a hodgepodge of true Shariʿa and heresy so that the best thing would be to reject it altogether, just to be on the safe side.

Salafis also disagreed with the Muslim Brotherhood over the relationship with Shiʿas, as mentioned above, as well as other trends within the Islamist movement. Salafis were much more intolerant of the "Other." Kuwaiti Salafis had a great affinity with Wahhabis and their brutal rejection of the "Other" without allowing room for compromise. As far as they were concerned, any creed or thought that was not Salafi contradicted the teachings of Islam.[95]

And although they classified other Islamist movements on the basis of how closely related they were to Salafi thought, all Islamists were harshly criticised by Salafis, including movements such as al-Tahrir, al-Tabligh, Sufis close to Sayyid Yusif al-Rifai and other groups interested in religious scholarships such as the Shaikh Hasan Hītu group. This Salafi attitude prompted them to criticise a saying of Rashīd Rida's that was later adopted by the Muslim Brotherhood as one of their guiding principles in dealing with others; "We shall cooperate on those issues over which we agree and excuse each other over things we disagree about," because even when Salafis agreed to cooperate with Others on issues they approved of, they failed to justify or understand differences, especially when those were related to *fiqh* or doctrine. Salafis sought to purge Islam from heresy and fads as a first step towards spreading the message of true Islam. Thus, Salafis found themselves in direct conflict with almost all Islamic groups to the extent that their struggle against other Islamists became more notorious than their conflict with secularists, with their fiercest clashes being with the Muslim Brotherhood.

In addition to criticising the Muslim Brotherhood for their so-called tolerance of Sufi heresy, Salafis levelled other intellectual and *fiqh* criticisms against the group. They argued, for instance, that the lack of a clear doctrinal vision among members of the Muslim Brotherhood made it easier for other suspect approaches like Sufis and Muʿtazila and other controversial doctrinal issues like Tawassul (pleading) and Tafwīd (delegating) to lead them astray. Salafis drew upon the writings of Hasan al-Banna and Sayyid Qutb to wage these accusations, which proved to be particularly popular among the Salafis in Saʿudi Arabia from where Kuwaiti Salafis drew their inspiration. These condemnations affected the status of the Muslim Brotherhood who lost many supporters, especially tribal members who were more inclined towards Salafi ideology.

More importantly, casting such doubts started to affect members of the Muslim Brotherhood themselves who experienced certain doubts about their belief systems. A prominent Muslim Brotherhood figure, Jasim Muhalhal al-Yasin, wrote a short paper to elaborate on the Muslim Brotherhood intellectual tradition and to refute Salafi claims. Al-Yasin is

[95] Imad al-Marzuqi, "al-Ikhwan wa al-Salaf fi al-Kuwait," *al-Rai Newspaper*, 4 March 2012 (accessed 17 March 2014).

widely considered a leading Muslim Brotherhood intellectual and religious scholar. As a mature charismatic figure, he was different from the first generation of very young Muslim Brotherhood members in Kuwait whose leader ᶜAbdulwahid Aman was as old as their fathers. Al-Yasin had received his religious education at al-Imam Muhammad bin Saʾud Islamic University, graduating with a BA and an MA degree in Shariᶜa studies in 1980 and 1986, respectively. He was very close to ᶜAbdulrahman ᶜAbdulkhaliq, the Salafi Shaikh in Kuwait, and attended many of his lessons. Because of this Salafi educational background, Al-Yasin was widely respected by the Salafis. Moreover, his education was reflected in the paper he wrote to refute Salafi claims.

A pamphlet entitled "*Lilduʾat Faqat: Daᶜwat al-Ikhwan Haqaʾiq...Shubuhat...Tamaniyyat*" [For Preachers Only: The Muslim Brotherhood; Facts, Misconceptions and Hopes] clearly indicated from the title that its intended audience was the members of Islamist movements, since the misconceptions raised by Salafis impacted on Islamists more than the rest of society who had a different set of issues. Al-Yasin emphasised in the pamphlet that the Muslim Brotherhood's doctrine was not different from Salafis in being inspired by the traditions of the orthodox Sunna. In a section entitled "The Doctrinal Approach of the Muslim Brotherhood,"[96] he quoted extensively from the writings and lectures of al-Banna to demonstrate that the Muslim Brotherhood was essentially Salafis.[97] Al-Banna remarked in the sixth principle out of the Twenty that "no one is infallible except for the Prophet (pbuh) and that the Muslim Brotherhood embrace all the intellectual legacy of the Salaf if it does not contradict the teachings of the Qurʾran and the Prophet (pbuh)."[98] In explaining this principle, Al-Yasin included Shaikh Saʾīd Hawwa's comments on al-Banna's statement. Hawwa remarked that no source was infallible except for the Qurʾan and Sunna. Otherwise, one had to exercise caution in adopting the views of others, such as Imams, preachers and scholars.

---

[96] Jasim al-Yasīn, *Lilduʾat Faqat: Daᶜwat al-Ikhwan Haqaʾiq... Shubuhat...Tamaniyyat* [For Preachers Only: The Muslim Brotherhood; Facts, Misconceptions and Hopes] (Kuwait: Dar al-Daᶜwah, 1990), 34.

[97] Ibid.

[98] Ibid., 35.

Al-Yasin also elaborated on the statements of al-Banna that concurred with Salafi thought to stress the Salafi nature of the Muslim Brotherhood from a doctrinal perspective, in addition to other literature that confirmed the Salafi dimension of Muslim Brotherhood thinking. Al-Yasin explained in detail the great care the Muslim Brotherhood took in indoctrinating their young cadres. The Salafis had also raised the issue of the names and qualities of Allah and al-Yasin once again emphasised that the Muslim Brotherhood was in agreement with the Salafis on that front. He quoted al-Banna who argued that it was forbidden to describe Allah with adjectives or qualities not mentioned in the Qur'an or Hadith even if such descriptions denoted perfection. Thus, it was *haram* to say "the engineer of the universe" or "the general manager of human affairs" as absolute terms to describe Allah, but it was acceptable to use them in the context of a general conversation in order to explain the power of Allah to simple people. Indeed, it would be preferable to avoid them altogether. Al-Banna further commented that it was best to follow the opinion of the Salaf in refraining from such terms in any context.[99] After stressing the Salafi nature of the Muslim Brotherhood, al-Yasin explained the phrase "and we excuse each other over things we disagree about" by quoting al-Banna's division of people on the basis of their perception of the Muslim Brotherhood, and not their intellectual or doctrinal affiliations.

When speaking about other Islamists, al-Banna emphasised the spirit of tolerance between them, despite intellectual differences. He commented that the Muslim Brotherhood's position regarding Islamists, irrespective of their intellectual traditions, was one of respect, love, cooperation, loyalty and brotherhood. Al-Banna also pointed out that the Muslim Brotherhood always stove to bridge the gap between various Islamist movements in the spirit of cooperation and love, and further acknowledged that it would be impossible to attain consensus in matters related to religion, and indeed this would go against the very nature of religion. Thus, al-Banna continued, the Muslim Brotherhood movement found it completely understandable that others would disagree with them on some minor matters and that this should by no means be seen as an obstacle to good relations with others. He remarked that even Prophet Muhammad's

[99] Ibid., 53–54.

Companions disagreed over some fatwas with that being a cause of resentment, disunity or hate, and reminded Muslims of the debate regarding ʿAsr prayer among members of Bani Quraida tribe.[100]

Although al-Yasin laid much emphasis on the Muslim Brotherhood's spirit of tolerance of those who disagreed with them on some branches of Shariʿa, he devoted considerable space to a number of issues that Salafis had raised, such the Muslim Brotherhood's treatment of Sufi traditions. As al-Yasin argued, al-Banna did not approve of all Sufi practices but had criticised some of them despite his great admiration for that tradition, as evident in the third of the Twenty Principles. Al-Banna remarked that,

> True faith, true worship of Allah and Jihad possess a light that Allah throws into the heart and mind of anyone He wishes to, but inspiration, thoughts, visions and dreams are not incontrovertible evidence and should never be taken into consideration if they conflict with religious tenets.[101]

In the 13th Principle he commented that,

> The love and respect we have for the pious and their great deeds are a form of a worship …The miracles they perform may be acceptable but under very strict *shariʿa* conditions … Having said that, I do believe that they cannot do themselves much harm or good without Allah's will, let alone be able to benefit others.[102]

In this instance, al-Yasin focused on the statements that reflected al-Banna's criticisms of Sufi practices without mentioning them explicitly, evidence that the Brotherhood did not wholly embrace Sufism.

In the same paper, al-Yasin remarked that Salafism should be viewed as a general approach to which any Muslim could subscribe, and described himself as a Salafi. In this sense, Salafism ceases to be a group or a party that one could belong to but rather a way of thinking which no group is entitled to monopolise or exclude others from. Al-Yasin comments,

> Salafism is not a group in the same sense as the Muslim Brotherhood is a group. Salafism represents a certain understanding of Islam among many

---

[100] Ibid., 63.

[101] Ibid., 119.

[102] Ibid.

other perspectives which had deviated from the true way. This kind of understanding exists when an Islamic state becomes a reality. Indeed, the norm is for all preachers to adopt Salafism as a theoretical and practical mode. Thus, Salafism is not a group or a party.[103]

With this perspective on the matter, al-Yasin was said to be sending a clear message to the Salafis that they did not possess some inalienable right to monopolise Salafism and doubt the Muslim Brotherhood's commitment to Salafi thought. Nor, since the Salafi approach was not possessed exclusively by one group in particular, did Salafis have the right to level criticisms against others because they did not have the right to classify and evaluate other groups. Thus, the Muslim Brotherhood succeeded in bypassing the doubts cast on the legitimacy of the movement and the soundness of its doctrines and approaches. This had the effect of boosting morale and enhancing the Muslim Brotherhood's belief in what they represented and what they stood for, in addition to reining in the Salafi momentum that had been slowly spreading among members of the Kuwaiti society.

Kuwaiti Salafis did not find this response very convincing, but it did help alleviate some of their criticism. The pamphlet did not put an end to the bickering between the Muslim Brotherhood and the Salafis, nor did it prevent disagreements between them from deepening over all aspects of intellectual, political and activist life. The differences between the Salafis and the Muslim Brotherhood became glaringly obvious, starting with the institutions that represented them and the magazines in which each one of them set out to publish their views.[104] But the fiercest competition was over the social domain, especially control of mosques which were considered the most important locations for Sunni Islamist movements to maximise their outreach to the average and the more pious Muslims. Imams or whoever happens to wield a great deal of influence in mosques can make the most of mosques to win over the sympathies and support of those who perform prayers. Such support could with time turn into moral and financial help or even joining the movement.

Mosques were also at the heart of the operations of the Islamist movements, such as attracting young people and introducing them to the ideas of the Muslim Brotherhood or the Salafis. Upon joining the group,

---

103 Ibid., 94.

104 Aman, interview.

young people used mosques as a launching pad to attract peers to their movement. Because of the important role of mosques, the Muslim Brotherhood and the Salafis were locked in a fierce struggle to control as many mosques as possible in Kuwait, either by securing the appointment of an Imam sympathetic to one group's cause or by increasing their presence in mosques and thus forcing the hand of the other side. In the context of this race over mosques, no technique or method was spared; both sides tried to cast doubt on the educational and doctrinal soundness of the other side's approach. While the Salafis criticised the Muslim Brotherhood for what they perceived as their lax approach to religion and indifference to "purifying it from impurities," the Muslim Brotherhood criticised the Salafis for their training strategies which were based on destructive criticism without due attention given to moral training and tolerance of others. Clashes intensified in the 1980s due to the relatively youthful age of the two groups and their reliance on enthusiastic young people; this exacerbated the tensions and conflict between the two sides for control of the Sunni social domain they shared. With the rise of the Salafis, the Muslim Brotherhood had lost their monopoly as the sole Islamist movement.

The Iraqi Invasion 1990–91 and the Social Domain

The Iraqi invasion of Kuwait was a turning point in changing the social landscape of the Kuwaiti society which, overnight, found itself catapulted from a state of complacency and great material comfort to one of crisis and fear. The predicament and the tough circumstances the Kuwaitis had to endure brought them all closer, and overshadowed any ideological differences they might have had prior to the invasion. The common fate that awaited them required them to be united in their social and political efforts to liberate the country, provide basic services to Kuwaitis inside and communicate with the government of Kuwait abroad. Movements worked closely together to provide basis services to the community through committees established for that purpose. The work of these Islamist movements (Muslim Brotherhood, Salafis and Shiʿas) was largely focused on ensuring that the service sector remained operational, in addition to some pockets of resistance that functioned in their areas of influence.

The critical security situation did not allow for any attempts to exercise control over the social domain, but the work done by these movements, especially the Muslim Brotherhood which was the most organised and widespread in Kuwait, naturally increased their popularity among Kuwaitis. Despite the short span of the occupation which lasted around seven months, it had a great impact on society and changed its view of Islamist movements which now entered a new era marked by less conflict.[105]

The post-liberation phase followed by state-building enabled the Islamists to become more politically engaged, especially as the invasion had allowed them to become more integrated with the society as it got to know them better. The Muslim Brotherhood had the lion's share of post-invasion progress, when the movement announced the establishment of a new political entity called "The Islamic Constitutional Movement" (ICM), the first of its kind in Kuwait and the Gulf. The Muslim Brotherhood were given a free hand at the Ministry of Awqaf and Religious Affairs and were also permitted to set up a number of organisations such as the General Secretary of Awqaf. The Muslim Brotherhood expanded other social organisations like the Committees of Good Companionship, Social Work committees and others that helped them cement their status as a formal movement.

Their aim was to make the most of the post-liberation momentum in Kuwait and abroad. They were also very keen on becoming more integrated into society and spreading their message to all sectors and classes of the Kuwaiti society. But the Muslim Brotherhood was unable to break away from the organisational mould of secrecy that had been their mantra for a very long time. This prompted some of their new sympathisers to abandon the Brotherhood because they felt they were mere tools in the hands of the upper leadership with no decision-making powers. This meant that the Muslim Brotherhood had really not changed much, apart from having acquired some new privileges and rights.

[105] For details of the work of the Muslim Brotherhood during in the invasion see Chapter III.

CONCLUSION

The Muslim Brotherhood in Kuwait succeeded in reinstating the influence of Islamist movements on the social domain after decades of domination by the secularists. This could not have been achieved without the Muslim Brotherhood's alliance with the government with the explicit aim of reducing the influence of the secularists on both the social and political domain. Various events in the region also contributed to the spread of Muslim Brotherhood ideas, especially when popular discourse found itself in harmony with government discourse. Islamist movements, chiefly the Muslim Brotherhood, were caught up in fierce intellectual clashes with the secularists but succeeded in imposing their ideology on the social domain and rolling back the influence of secularists.

But the biggest threat to Muslim Brotherhood authority and influence came from a totally unexpected source: the Salafis. The Salafi movement emerged as a major contender in the battle for the hearts and minds of Sunni Muslims in Kuwait. Indeed, it could be argued that the biggest problem the Muslim Brotherhood faced in the social domain was the Salafis, rather than any other movement or party. The Salafis themselves had their own set of issues and problems due to internal conflict over a number of issues. This led to deep divisions within the Salafi movement which found itself splitting into various groups such as the Jihadist Salafis who believed that all political regimes in Muslim countries were heretical, including the ruling families of the Gulf States and another Salafi group which issued fatwas that it was forbidden to criticise leaders in any way. Between the extreme views of these two groups, a number of other Salafi movements emerged, further complicating the scene. Undoubtedly, the Salafis' internal politics were much worse than any conflict they had with the Muslim Brotherhood, but the scope of this book does not allow for further elaboration.

CHAPTER 5

Muslim Brotherhood and Politics

INTRODUCTION

For the Kuwaiti Islamists in general and the Muslim Brotherhood in particular, politics takes priority only after social activism. In fact, the reason for entering politics was to spread the Islamist influence throughout the social domain. The Muslim Brotherhood participated in parliament in order to introduce laws and legislation on the basis of Islamic Shariᶜa and to minimise the influence of the secularists who had already introduced much legislation that violated Islamic teachings. The Muslim Brotherhood in coalition with other Islamists and tribal forces succeeded in passing much Islamic legislation such as the law banning the consumption and selling of alcohol, the decree establishing the Kuwaiti Zakat House and the Personal Status law.

HISTORICAL BACKGROUND

Politically speaking, the discovery of oil came at a very opportune time for both the ruling family and the people, who were suffering from economic hardships and deep political problems. The introduction of Japanese cultured pearls in the late 1920s had all but ruined the lives of those dependent on pearl diving, while small maritime transportation businesses were undermined by modern cargo ships, First World War having ended with Britain gaining full control over the region's trade routes in order

© The Author(s), under exclusive license to Springer Nature Singapore Pte Ltd. 2023
A. A. Alkandari, *The Muslim Brotherhood in Kuwait*, Contemporary Gulf Studies, https://doi.org/10.1007/978-981-99-3050-0_5

to protect its own interests. The 1930s was a period of vigorous political activism demanding democratic changes but was met by fierce repression from the ruling family. The mid-1940s and onwards witnessed a great deal of international stability following the Allied victory and the reinvigoration of industries, especially the oil industry. Oil-exporting countries, including Kuwait, witnessed a great economic revival. Both the ruling family and the people of Kuwait breathed a sigh of relief when the economic wheel rolled on at new and unprecedented speeds.

Political life shook off its inertia with the arrival of Shaikh Abdullah al-Salim, but the honeymoon came to an abrupt end after an event held by the Nationalist Cultural Club to celebrate the withdrawal of British troops from Port Said after the Suez Crisis. The event took a surprising turn when Jasim al-Qatami, a prominent Nationalist leader, harshly criticised the tribal system of government in Kuwait in front of important members of the ruling family, including Abdullah al-Jabir. The backlash from the al-Subah ruling family was quite severe and many civil society organisations and media outlets were shut down as the al-Subah tightened their hold on every aspect of economic and political life. The indications of Kuwaiti independence from Great Britain, and Shaikh Abdullah al-Salim's need for popular support to ensure that the process would go smoothly, compelled him to ease the pressure on the Nationalists in order to win their support for his efforts to secure Kuwait's independence.

Independence from Great Britain on 19 June 1961 brought with it the promise of a new, modern and stable state, but was not without detractors; for example, the Iraqi president ʿAbdulkarīm Qasim had demanded that Kuwait be annexed to Iraq. The Soviet Union's support for this demand made it harder for Kuwait to secure international recognition and join the United Nations. Qasim's threat to annex Kuwait by force was especially problematic in a country that lacked a democratic system that would reflect the views and aspirations of the average Kuwaiti, but various political movements in Iraq expressed their unconditional support for the ruling family against Qasim's threats. These were also rejected by Britain, which dispatched a military force to thwart Iraq's ambitions in Kuwait.[1]

---

[1] Abdullah al-Hajeri, "Citizenship and Political Participation in the State of Kuwait: The Case of the National Assembly (1962–1996)" (PhD diss., University of Durham, 2004), 60.

The newly-independent state of Kuwait soon won international recognition and joined the Arab league and the United Nations.[2] A grateful Abdullah al-Salim returned the favour and ordered the establishment of an elected legislative council after Qasim had withdrawn his claims, and Kuwait was granted much-coveted membership in the UN. A new constitution was drafted to regulate the relationship between the ruling family and the people of Kuwait, and this set the stage for the modern state.

Throughout the modern history of Kuwait, the country's traditional political establishment proves that it has been always very powerful and that it became even more powerful with the rise of the petro-dollar. Abdullah al-Salim worked hard to rein in the traditionalists through the new constitution. With the progress made by Kuwait in civil services and education came a corresponding improvement in political life, assisted by developments in the region and by Abdullah al-Salim's sound treatment of the Kuwaitis who had supported him by adding legitimacy to his rule before the international community. The parliament and the constitution were established under unique circumstances that had been difficult to attain for more than six months by any national political powers, as evidenced by the parliament of 1938. The ruling family had responded very negatively to the establishment of a parliament, believing that it would reduce their supremacy and increase the power of the people. Thus, the new parliament was a great advance in the Kuwaiti system of government, but it was not enough, especially given the influence of tribal affiliation, boosted even further by oil money, and Kuwait's transformation into a rentier, almost communist state that provided all its citizens' needs from birth to death. Traditional seats of power remained firmly in place, due to the economic developments that prioritised welfare over citizenship and entrenched the value of state generosity rather than people's rights.[3]

Despite their calls for political reform, the reformist Islamists, represented by Yusif bin ʿIsa, did not profess any political antagonism towards the ruling family. Yet, as previously mentioned, when the ruling family came into conflict with movements calling for political reforms, the Islamist movement did not wish to jeopardise its influence over the social domain by appearing hostile to the ruling family, especially as its objective was social rather than political reform. Thus, in any conflict between social and political reform, the former would take precedence at the expense of the latter. This idea passed on from Yusif bin ꜥIsa to the Muslim Brotherhood through ꜥIsa's student ꜥAbdulaziz al-Ali al-Mutawwaꜥ. The Muslim Brotherhood and the Society for Social Reform focused on reforming the social domain alongside some tentative, sporadic political activities because the memory of the clash between the reformists and ruling family was still fresh in everyone's minds.

POLITICAL ACTIVITIES OF AL-IRSHAD

Although al-Irshad emphasised an avoidance of politics, as stated in the introduction of al-Barnamaj al-Tawjihi, it interacted indirectly with the local political currents. An example of such indirect interaction was the personal relationship of senior members with the al-Subah ruling family. ꜥAbdulaziz al-Mutawwaꜥ had a close relationship with Abdullah al-Jabir al-Subah, brother of the former Emir and cousin of the current Emir at that time, who attended some lectures at al-Irshad. Al-Mutawwaꜥ also become close to the Emir Abdullah al-Salim, for whom he acted as an adviser. Other members of al-Irshad such as ꜥAbdulrahman al-ꜥAtiqi and Ali al-Jassar, also had unique relationships with the ruling family. Al-ꜥAtiqi was the personal adviser of the Emir, while al-Jassar was the wedding cleric for many members of the ruling family. However, some members of al-Irshad took an opposing view of the ruling family; Mohammad al-ꜥAdsani was one member who adopted a radical method of dealing with the government and the ruling family.[4] These contradictory views and acts between the two strongest figures in al-Irshad led to a huge conflict within the society and as a result, weakened its future.

In dealing with the wrongdoings of the government, ꜥAbdulaziz al-Mutawwaꜥ followed the quietest methods of his teacher Yusif bin ꜥIsa by providing advice to the ruler and abandoning all violence or harsh criticism. In 1953, when anti-government brochures that were directly and harshly critical of the government were being distributed in the streets, ꜥAbdulaziz al-Mutawwaꜥ wrote in the *al-Irshad* journal that "honest work which pleases Allah should serve the country by working under the sun, not by distributing brochures in the darkness of night, and the rulers of

---

[4] This could be related to the history of his family in opposition especially what happened in 1938.

this country are not isolated from the people but are of them and love to hear from any honest citizen to change the wrong do the right thing."[5]

However, this quietist attitude did not prevent him from indirectly criticising the government. For instance, al-Irshad censured the government's policies on the immigration of foreign labour in Kuwait, and ʿAbduaziz al-Mutawwaʿ wrote an article in *al-Irshad* journal entitled "The Immunity of the Nation," decrying the uncontrolled increase of foreign workers, both blue-collar and white collar, and the negative social effects on youth, noting that:

> The microbes of moral depravation are spreading their poison in the body of the nation to weaken its immunity with this influx of different backgrounds of people into the society. You can see the result of this uncontrolled influx on the beach with naked bodies and on the streets with those beautiful foreign girls begging for money! Where the morality police to confront what are is going on here and there? Why are our borders open for this corruption? This is a fact on the ground, and we want a swift reaction and effective treatment of this disease before it becomes uncontrollable.[6]

In another article, al-Mutawwaʿ attacked the government for allowing women immigrants with no profession or qualifications to enter Kuwait, by which he meant the danger of prostitution which not only destroyed the nation's youth but also distorted the society's Arab and Islamic identity. Al-Mutawwaʿ also presented the numbers of immigrants and their countries of origin; there were "…40,000 Iraqis, 12,000 Syrians, 3500 Jordanians and Palestinians, 2400 non-Muslim Indians, 1500 Pakistanis, and an unknown number of Iranians because of the absence of a governmental Census Bureau."[7]

Al-Irshad was also disparaging about a number of the government's educational policies, such as allowing co-education in a Kuwaiti school in Bombay.[8] In addition, an article in *al-Irshad* journal on "Girls and Sports" asserted that Islam was not a backward religion; however, Islam

---

[5] ʿAbdulʿazizal-Mutawwaʿ. "ʿAn al-Nasharat," Majallat al-Irshad (August 1953), 66.

[6] ʿAbdulʿaziz al-Mutawwaʿ. "Manaʿat al-Ummah," *Majallat al-Irshad* (August 1953), 65–66.

[7] Ibid., 76–77.

[8] Al-Ruwaishid, interview.

did not permit girls to show certain parts of their bodies such as their thighs, chest and the private parts (which in Islam constitute the area between the navel and the knees), according to the saying of the Prophet that "man should not look at man's private parts neither woman look at private parts of woman."[9] Therefore, according to the article, the Department of Education should prevent girls from wearing short skirts or shorts in front of their male counterparts.[10]

Last but not least, al-Irshad raised several issues such as unemployment in Kuwait, the necessity of establishing a Ministry of Awqaf, and the lack of basic infrastructural needs and services (water, electricity, paved roads, etc.). It also commented on internal and external political issues such as the article by al-Mutawwa^c concerning municipal elections and the open letter addressed to King Sa^{c}ud in the introduction to *al-Irshad* Journal's edition entitled "*Ya Hukkamana*" [O Ye, Our Rulers].[11]

The Relationship of al-Irshad with Other Social and Political Constituents

Al-Irshad followed an open-minded policy towards other societal constituents and was influenced by the progressive school of Rashid Rida, who had a marked influence on Hassan al-Banna and on religious reformists and al-Irshad in Kuwait. ^{c}Abdul^{c}aziz al-Mutawwa^c always repeated Rida's famous saying: "let us work on what we agree upon, and let us excuse each other for what we disagree on."[12] He practised this axiom faithfully, exercising his tolerant stance in his interactions with different ideological and religious groups such as the Shi^{c}a and Hizb al-Tahrir.

Many Shi^{c}i Kuwaitis participated in activities held in al-Irshad and some of them, such as Abdullah al-Khars and Sayyid Hussain ^{c}Abdulsamad, wrote numerous articles in *al-Irshad* journal. In return, members of the Shi^{c}a community invited some leading figures from al-Irshad to lecture in their Hussainiyya. With regard to Hizb al-Tahrir, although it was in

---

[9] ^{c}Abdul^{c}aziz Al-Mutawwa^c. "Al-Banat wa al-Riyadah," *Majallat al-Irshad* (March 1954), 92–93.

[10] Ibid.

[11] "Ya Hukkamana [O Ye Our Rulers]." *Majallat al-Irshad* (December 1953), 55.

[12] Al-Banna mentions this saying several times in his letters to the Muslim Brotherhood and made it a guiding principle for the movement.

confrontation with the Muslim Brotherhood at that time, al-Irshad maintained a volatile relationship with Hizb al-Tahrir but never reached the conflict point, as occurred in other countries. Indeed, some members of al-Irshad, like Sayyid Yusif al-Rifaʿi and Rashid al-Farhan, actually joined Hizb al-Tahrir; this bridged the gap between the two Sunni Islamist groups and improved relations between them.

However, the relationship with the Nationalists was weak even before the clash that occurred in Egypt between the Muslim Brotherhood and President Nasser. Sayyid Yusif al-Rifaʿi, Khalid al-Masʿud and ʿAbdulrahman al-ʿAtiqi, who were all members of al-Irshad, arranged a meeting with Mohammad al-Barrak, President of the National Cultural Club, and his vice-President Ahmad al-Khatib, along with other leading members Jassim al-Qatami and Ahmad al-Munayyis. Nevertheless, the Nationalists remained hesitant about establishing any connection with al-Irshad, and when al-Khatib became the Club's President, he refused to have any connection with al-Irshad because of the radical divergence between his Communist ideas and the Islamic ideology of al-Irshad.

Al-Irshad's political positions were in practice meant to serve their agenda in the social domain, of which the Islamists saw themselves as guardians. There were demands to ban foreign women from migrating to Kuwait as well as mixed-gender education in order to protect society, especially young people, from moral corruption. Since demands for basic services were also considered part of their remit within the social domain, al-Irshad was thus a purely social organisation even in its political demands. Al-Irshad's position vis-à-vis politics and the ruling family was met with great dismay by Muhammad al-ʿAdsani and Najib Juwaifil, with several young ʾIrshad members being incited by Juwaifil against the leadership of al-Mutawwaʿ; this, as discussed above, was to culminate in a period of internal strife.

The clashes between the revolutionary wing (influenced by the National Bloc) and the pacifist wing (of Yusif bin ʿIsa) affected al-Irshad. This conflict was undoubtedly a natural outcome of the divergent and varied ideas circulating among al-Irshad members. In the end, no party could claim complete victory, which further weakened al-Irshad and lent more legitimacy to the secularists. Media pressure was also compounded by security pressures in Egypt and Iraq. Islamists in Kuwait shared the plight of the Muslim Brotherhood movement in other countries. And although Islamists in general and the Muslim Brotherhood members in particular were never targeted by the security apparatus, they nonetheless suffered from social and media isolation.

However, this pressure on the Islamists did not stop them from participating in politics. Yusif al-Rifaʿi, an Islamist candidate, ran unsuccessfully for the Constituent Assembly elections of 1962, but in the first parliamentary elections held in 1963 he did secure a seat, for reasons probably unrelated to his Islamic affiliation, such as being a descendant of the Prophet, since the Shiite vote contributed to his win. Neither did ʿAbduallah al-Ali or Ahmad Bzeiʾ al-Yasin, the two other candidates fielded by the Islamists that year, win seats in 1963. In fact, the Islamists lacked any prominent political figures who could represent them in parliament. Nor can Muhammad al-ʿAdsani, who won a seat in 1963, 1967 and 1981 and later (1981–1984) became Speaker of the House, be regarded as an example of Muslim Brotherhood electoral success, since he had renounced much of his Muslim Brotherhood ideology, especially the political aspects. His status as an independent national figure can be attributed to his family name and his opposition to many government policies, especially the rigging of elections in 1967.

AL-ISLAH IN THE POLITICAL DOMAIN

Both Ghabrah and Tahhan argue that al-Islah was an early participant in the political domain as a means towards serving its social goals. For instance, al-Islah had triggered the battle against the selling and consumption of alcohol in Kuwait, issuing statements and organising lectures about the damaging effects of alcohol on society and the importance of drafting legislation that would ban alcohol in Kuwait completely. The existence of a civil society institution like al-Islah was instrumental in opening a wider debate about the issue, especially within the parliament. Alcohol had been legal in Kuwait prior to 1964, with the British company Gray, MacKenzie & Co. holding a decades-old monopoly on the alcohol trade, while Christians were issued with ration cards permitting them to purchase liquor.[13] Al-Raʾi al-ʿAam newspaper mocked Gray, Mackenzie & Co's monopoly by referring to the company as "Shaikh Mackenzie's" company (due to its policy of selling alcohol at very high prices). The ban on alcohol was gradual and followed some heated

---

[13] Hamzah ʿUlayyan, "Qissat al-Khumur fi al-Kuwait min al-Mamnuʿila al-Masmuh" (Al-Qabas Newspaper, 26 January 2009).

debates within society and in parliament. Initially, in accordance with Penal Code No. 16 for 1960, the ban applied only to trading in alcohol and penalties were applied to the act of importing and selling alcohol but not to its consumption. However, in 1964, Article 206 was added to Law No 46 for 1964 banning the consumption of alcohol in any public place. Article 206 was further amended in 1983 (under Law No. 9) to include tougher penalties for both traders and consumers.[14]

The other issue adopted by al-Islah was Article 2 of the Kuwaiti Constitution which stipulated that "Islamic Shariʿa is a main source of legislation." The Society demanded that this article be amended to read "Islamic Shariʿa is *the* main source," and this has remained a bone of contention between Islamists and secularists. The Constituent Assembly records reveal the many heated debates surrounding the amendment of Article 2 of the Constitution. MP Khalifa al-Jeri, who petitioned the 19th session of the Constituent Assembly on 11 September 1962 to amend Article 2, is recorded as saying that "Kuwait is a Muslim country and there is no source but Islam. This amendment would guarantee that we adhere to our religious values, achieve social justice and protect freedoms according to Allah's teachings." A number of MPs supported the proposal (including Ahmad Khalid al-Fawzan, Naif al-Dabbus, Saʿud ʿAbdulrazzaq and Mubarak al-Hasawi).[15] However, other MPs opposed the suggested legislation for several reasons. For instance, Ahmad al-Khatib, the vice-president of the Constituent Assembly, enquired about the meaning of the proposed rewording of the text and whether it would be applied literally (e.g. to the as chopping off of thieves' hands and demanding an eye for an eye); and if that was indeed the case, what would be the fate of banks, companies and the rest of the economic structure whose local and international dealings were not based on Shariʿa law? Humud Zaid al-Khalid then enquired about hereditary rule which, he noted, contradicted Islamic Shariʿa. This issue in particular struck a chord with the ruling family despite the falsehood of the whole premise. The Assembly then sought the advice of the Egyptian constitutional expert ʿUthman Khalil ʿUthman, who was of the opinion that amending the text of the article and introducing the definite article "the" would make it virtually

[14] Ibid.

[15] Ahmad Baqir, *Dirasah ʿAn al-Maddah al-Thaniya fiDustur Dawalat al-Kuwait* (No Publisher: 1994), 1013.

impossible to draw upon other sources. He added that the article of the law in its current format gave prominence to Shariᶜa without restricting the legislator to one source only, especially in drafting laws best suited for new realities on the ground. In response to a question from al-Khatib as to whether rewording the text would mean the literal adherence to Shariᶜa or simply that Kuwait, as a Muslim country, must remain true to the spirit of Islam, ʾUthman answered that the definite article "the" would make it legally binding to adhere to Shariᶜa and nothing else, but that the current text allowed for several sources, including Shariᶜa.[16] Although the article was not amended, the issue was destined to resurface several times over the next few decades in 1973, 1975, 1980, 1981, 1992, 1997 and 1998.[17]

THE 1968 ORGANISATION AND POLITICS

To begin with the 1968 Organisation did not have any political presence, let alone political goals, due to the relatively young age of its members and the desire of its founders to steer clear of politics. But these wishes were short-lived; the nexus between social issues and politics meant the movement could not turn inwards to focus on capacity building and re-establishing their dominion on the social domain. Very early on, the Muslim Brotherhood found itself embroiled in political struggles despite all attempts to avoid political engagement. The Muslim Brotherhood supported al-Islah in its various political campaigns, especially the Islamisation of the constitution by amending Article 2, in addition to other moral issues.

Islamising Kuwait University and Teachers' Association

The Muslim Brotherhood also sought to change reality from the bottom up, starting with the University of Kuwait which they considered as the "locus of moral depravity." Because the National Union of Kuwaiti Students (NUKS) was widely perceived as influential in student life, the Muslim Brotherhood invested a lot of time and effort to control it. This

[16] Official Website of Kuwait National Assembly, "Minutes of the Founding Assembly in Kuwait. Minute No. 19 (11–09-1962)."

[17] Muhammad Nasser, "Tarikhal-Mutalabat bi Taghiir al-Maddah al-Thaniya" (*Al-Anbaʾ* Newspaper, 16 February 2012), 24.

put them in direct conflict with the secularists who at the time dominated the Union. It was only after the mixed-gender education incident of 1973 that the Muslim Brotherhood realised the importance of the NUKS and the ferocity of the battle with the secularists over controlling it. This prompted them to regroup and collaborate with those who shared their line of thought on the issue. In 1977, *al-I'tilafiyyah* [Coalition List] appeared, which consisted of the Muslim Brotherhood and other sympathetic groups at the university. The NUKS list from the Faculty of Law, the Moderates list from the Faculty of Business and the Independent list were thus unified under one list to represent the Islamists in the NUKS elections at the University of Kuwait branch.

Al-I'tilafiyyah declared that it represented "every Muslim who loves and respects Allah's laws, every citizen who wishes the best for his country and every student who aspires to a better university."[18] Thus, the list identified itself as both nationalist and Islamist. Al-I'tilafiyyah contested the 1978 elections which were rigged and therefore led to widespread protests. Security forces had to intervene and NUKS was suspended for a whole year. A new round of elections was held in 1979 and secured a landslide victory for the Muslim Brotherhood. Al-Wasatal-Dimoqrati [The Democratic Centre List], which represented the secularists, came third in what was perceived as huge blow, especially since the Sunni Muslim Brotherhood had come first, while the Shiites came second.[19]

Al-I'tilafiyyah has since dominated the leadership of the Student Union at the University of Kuwait. In 1981, the Muslim Brotherhood also succeeded in dominating foreign branches of NUKS in the UK and the United States. Capitalising on their success, the Muslim Brotherhood used the Union as a platform for spreading the ideas of the Muslim Brotherhood among students in Kuwait and abroad, and sought to Islamize the student community by focusing on raising religious consciousness. This was done through the work of the Committee for Religious Awareness which organised religious lessons, Qur'an contests and ʿUmra trips to Mecca. Al-I'tilafiyyah also pressed officials, especially within the university administration, to meet their demands for special places of worship and prayers and for imposing the ban on mixed-gender education. These

---

[18] Ibrahim Al-Mulaifi. "Al-Harakah al-Tullabiyyah al-Kuwaitiyyah fi 40 ʿAaman (3)" (*Al-Qabas* Newspaper, 6 October 2008).

[19] Ibrahim Al-Mulaifi. "Al-Harakah al-Tullabiyyah al-Kuwaitiyyah fi 40 ʿAaman (2)" (*Al-Qabas* Newspaper, 5 October 2008).

efforts to change the social reality at the University of Kuwait coincided with their work to serve the student community and had the effect of making the al-I'tilafiyyah and its Islamist ideas much more popular among students as well as among Kuwaitis in general. Al-I'tilafiyyah also succeeded in changing the identity of NUKS by amending parts of the Union's constitution to reflect the thinking of its new Islamist leadership. A paragraph in the preamble was changed from,

> We, the university students of Kuwait, being fully aware of the importance of union work and its role in securing a better future for our people and nation for the purpose of defending human causes, have decided to establish the National Union for the Students of Kuwait a pioneer project and beacon of hope for the future.[20]

To,

> We, the students of Kuwait, having attended the 8th Convention of the National Union for the Students of Kuwait and being fully aware of the importance of union work and its role in securing a better future for our people and nation on the basis of the principles of Islam, have decided to safeguard the National Union for the Students of Kuwait as a pioneer project and beacon of hope for the future.[21]

The amendments were introduced during the Eighth Convention of the Union held in 1981 to debate ways of re-imagining the Union and the nature of its role within a mainly Islamic identity. Article 2 of the Constitution was amended and the word "democracy" was replaced with "*shura*" (the Islamic notion of consultation). Two articles (6 and 7) were also added to the constitution, Article 6 says:

> As a student organisation that operates according to the principles of *shura*, the Union aims to: (1) Be fully committed to the principle of *shura*; and (2) Work towards implementing *shura* in all walks of life in Kuwait.[22]

And Article 7 says,

---

[20] Al-Mulaifi, "Al-Harakah al-Tullabiyyah al-Kuwaitiyyah fi 40 ʿAaman (2)."

[21] Ibid.

[22] Ibid.

The Union as an Islamist organisation aims at: (1) Raising religious awareness; (2) Exposing the plans of the enemies of Islam; (3) Unifying and supporting Muslim student movements; and (4) Boosting ties with Gulf, Arab, Muslim and international student organisations.[23]

Al-I'tilafiyyah succeeded in Islamising the student community and fought many battles against the university administration over several issues, such as mixed-gender education as outlined in the previous chapter. One of the main causes of controversy was a course entitled "Islamic Education" which the Faculty of Law and Shariᶜa decided to suspend in February 1981 for two semesters because of disagreements over the course content. The university supported the Faculty's decision, thereby prompting an angry response from the Union's new leadership which objected vehemently to the decision.[24] The Union also objected to the manner in which the university's administration had dealt with the matter since the Department of Shariᶜa had not been notified of the Faculty's decision even though it was the department that usually offered the course. Their stand revealed there had been prior coordination between the Union and the Department of Shariᶜa professors, and the confrontation between the Union and the university eventually culminated in a student strike.

The Union issued a statement explaining that it could not find any proper justification for suspending the Islamic Education course on the pretext that it needed extensive modifications, since the same did not seem to apply to hundreds of other courses at the university.[25] Al-Wasat al-Dimoqrati and several nationalist professors condemned the Union's handling of the whole issue and demanded that students comply with the university's scientific decisions. The standoff lasted for two weeks during which time the Union insisted on the student strike. Finally, the Crown Prince and Prime Minister Shaikh Saᶜad al-Abdullah met Union members and promised to form a committee to examine the matter. The Islamic Education course was offered that same semester with a few minor changes to the syllabus. This small victory for the Islamists demonstrated the importance of retaining full control over NUKS in order to continue the process of Islamising the University and to stem the tide of secularists.

[23] Ibid.
[24] Ibid.
[25] Ibid.

The success of the Muslim Brotherhood in gaining control of student unions in Kuwait and abroad encouraged them to try their luck at professional associations and syndicates which traditionally were nationalist strongholds. The Muslim Brotherhood battled with nationalists in several professional associations and unions and managed to control some of them, with the Teachers' Association[26] being one of those in which the Muslim Brotherhood gained a foothold. Having always considered education and the educational system at the heart of any social order, the Muslim Brotherhood viewed education as inseparable from their religious mission and therefore competed strongly with secularists in their attempts to control the Teachers' Association. In 1976, the Association's board of directors was dissolved, following the board's harsh criticism of the government for dissolving the parliament, and was replaced by a government-appointed board headed by Abdullah al-ᶜUbaid.

When four years were up, the Muslim Brotherhood decided to support the group that had run the Association between 1976 and 1981. The Muslim Brotherhood therefore collaborated with the Salafis and al-ᶜUbaid's group to ensure that Shiites and Nationalists did not win any seats. In this, they were partly successful and a new board was formed in 1982, with al-ᶜUbaid as its president. The 1984 elections saw major victory for the Muslim Brotherhood, the Salafis, and al-ᶜUbaid group against their Shiite and nationalist rivals. For the first time, Islamists were the majority on the board of directors, with Faisal al-Jaber, Bader Burḥama and Jamal al-Kandari representing the Muslim Brotherhood and Bader al-Shamroukh, Salem al-Muhanna and Faisal al-Yaqut representing the Salafis, in addition to al-ᵓUbaid as president for a third term.

Despite the disagreements between the Muslim Brotherhood and the Salafis, they managed, albeit reluctantly, to work together especially in the face of their common enemy, the Nationalists and the Shiites. However, in contesting the 1986 and 1988 elections, the Muslim Brotherhood and the Salafis excluded the al-ᶜUbaid group and divided the seats among themselves. They concerned themselves with a number of issues related

---

[26] The Teachers' Association was established in 1951 by number of Kuwaiti and Arab teachers and intellectuals who were influenced by modern education. The association was apolitical in its early years but was closed down by Emiri decree in 1959 after the famous speech of al-Qatami. However, the nationalists re-established the Teachers' Association in 1963 and controlled it until 1976. Yaqoub al-Ghunaim, Kuwait News Agency (KUNA), "Nadi al-Muᶜallimin min Aqdam Andiyat al-Kuwait," see also the official website of Jamᶜiyyatal-Muᶜalimin, "About Us."

to Islam that directly affected teachers' lives, but due to irreconcilable differences the fragile alliance between the Muslim Brotherhood and the Salafis did not last long.

The Muslim Brotherhood therefore decided to run without Salafi support, and in 1990, they won the majority of seats, especially with the help of female teachers who were extremely organised. The Iraqi invasion temporarily halted the Association's activities, but soon the Muslim Brotherhood resumed its activities and succeeded in winning all the seats.[27]

The Battle Over the Constitution and Legislations

With the success of the Muslim Brotherhood in taking over the Teachers' Association in addition to other professional associations, the movement entered the political domain through the parliament. Although Abdullah al-Mutawwaᶜ contested the al-Salmiyya seat in 1963 and Mishari al-Khashram the Faiha' seat in 1967, they ran as independents rather than a party list and failed to win any seats. The new Muslim Brotherhood movement did not participate in parliamentary elections until 1981 but habitually supported Islamists or pro-Islamists such as Yusif al-Rifaᶜi, ᶜAbbas Mnawir and others who were sympathetic to the Muslim Brotherhood and Islamic causes in the parliament, such as the banning of alcohol in Kuwait and the mixed-gender education debate. The 1976 parliament having been unconstitutionally dissolved, and the government decided in 1981 to hold parliamentary elections according to new electoral district divisions. Under the new system, each of the 25 constituencies would be represented by two MPs. The Muslim Brotherhood debated whether to field their own candidates or restrict their efforts to supporting Islamists and those close to them. Those who favoured direct participation argued that the Muslim Brotherhood should be in parliament at the heart of legislative power in order to introduce laws and legislations on the basis of Islamic Shariᶜa. They remarked that the secularists had already introduced much legislation that violated Islamic teachings and had refused to amend Article 2 of the Constitution. Those opposed to contesting the elections were of the opinion that Islamists would not be able to form a majority in the parliament, due to the new electoral system that meant

---

[27] Jamal al-Kandari, interview.

in effect that they would succeed in passing many laws that required a majority. They also felt it was still too early for them to become more politically active because they were not yet ready for an experiment that would require a lot of time, effort and manpower.

The experiences of other Muslim Brotherhood organisations in countries like Iraq where they clashed with the government also served to turn Kuwaiti Brotherhood members away from politics. However, the Muslim Brotherhood in Kuwait sent delegations to Muslim Brotherhood branches in other countries and eventually decided to heed the advice of the Jordanian Muslim Brotherhood because of the similar nature of the ruling systems in their respective countries. Jordanian Muslim Brotherhood members advised them to take part in the elections but to avoid any ministerial posts since these were usually of no consequence and consisted mainly of carrying out orders that could breach Islamic teachings. The Kuwaiti Muslim Brotherhood eventually fielded three candidates: Abdullah al-ʿAtiqi in al-Khalidiyya constituency, Humud al-Rumi in al-Faiha and al-Nuzha, and ʿan al-Shahin in al-Rawda. Both al-Rumi and al-Shahin won seats but al-ʿAtiqi lost by a small margin.

Through their MPs, the Muslim Brotherhood succeeded in putting a lot of pressure on the government in parliament to meet their demands regarding several laws and articles. For instance, Article 4 of the Nationality Law, which opened the door to giving the Kuwaiti passport and nationality to anyone regardless of his/her religion, was opposed by Islamists who pushed for the Article to be amended to propose that only Muslims could become Kuwaiti nationals. Article 4 was duly altered to read.

A decree, upon the recommendation of the Minister of Home Affairs, may be issued granting the Kuwaiti nationality to anyone who has reached the age of majority if the following conditions are met:

1. If the applicant has been a resident of Kuwait for at least twenty consecutive years or at least 15 years if he is an Arab from another Arab country. Any periods of time spent abroad on official business shall not prejudice his application for nationality but periods spent abroad on unofficial business shall be subtracted from the required period of stay.
2. The applicant shall be employed in legitimate business, be in possession of good record and must not have been charged with any felony.

3. The applicant must know Arabic.
4. The applicant must possess skills that are needed by the State of Kuwait.
5. The applicant shall be a Muslim by birth or have officially converted to Islam at least five years before being granted the Kuwaiti nationality. His nationality shall be revoked in cases where he renounces Islam. This shall apply to all his family members who acquire the nationality through their relation with him.[28]

This amendment was perceived as an important step towards preserving the Islamic identity of Kuwaiti society and combatting attempts to westernise it.

In addition, the Islamists in the parliament worked on passing new Islamic laws. Drawn exclusively from Islamic Shariᶜa, the new Personal Status law came into effect in October 1984. This law covered all aspects of family law such as marriage, divorce and inheritance. Many saw the 60-page code as a guarantee that social affairs would remain governed by Islamic teachings. Moreover, a decree establishing the Kuwaiti Zakat House followed the submission of two proposals by two independent MPs—both of whom were merchants—Jassim al-Khurafi and Mishari al-ᶜAnjari. Their proposals were merged and referred to the Ministry of Awqaf, which prepared a study and presented it to the parliament for approval. Law No. 5 for 1982 was issued on 16 January 1982.[29] Zakat House was financially and administratively independent but came under the jurisdiction of the Minster of Awqaf and Islamic Affairs, who was also president of the board of directors at Zakat House. Despite being a government-controlled entity, Zakat House played a substantial role in spreading the values of charity and *zakat*.

The Relationship with the Government

Not far from Ghabrah's argument, the relationship between the Muslim Brotherhood and the government was harmonious and mutually beneficial since both made gains at the expense of nationalists and secularists

[28] GCC Legal Network, "Marsum AmiriRaqm 15 Lisanat 1959 bi Qanun al-Jynsiyyah al-Kuwaitiyya (151959)."

[29] Kuwait News Agency (KUNA), "Dhikra Murur 20 ᶜAaman ᶜAla Taᵓsis Bayt al-Zakat al-Kuwaiti."

who were hostile to the Muslim Brotherhood and the government. The government supported the Muslim Brotherhood's demands for various services and legislation that protected society from moral decay through the calls for banning alcohol, and protected the Muslim Brotherhood's members from prosecution in the co-education symposium incident at the University of Kuwait. The government also issued an Emiri decree establishing the Kuwait Finance House (KFH) despite objections from technocrats and secularists, and in addition backed a number of proposals for Shariᶜa inspired laws in the 1981 parliament.

In return, the Muslim Brotherhood and other Islamists refrained from echoing the demands of Nationalists for greater political freedoms and reforms, and also refused to discuss the election rigging incident of 1967 and the unconstitutional dissolution of the 1976 parliament. The division of power was clear; Islamists were interested in wielding more influence in the social domain through their work at mosques, schools and the university and succeeded in controlling many of those at the expense of the Secularists. The government, on the other hand, was more concerned with reducing the influence of Nationalists by encouraging tribes and Islamists to enter the political domain and to side with the government against the Nationalists.

The honeymoon was soon over and the collaboration between the two sides faced some serious, though not fatal, challenges. The Muslim Brotherhood continued to participate in parliamentary elections and gradually increased the number of its candidates in various constituencies. Other Islamists with close ties to the Muslim Brotherhood also won seats. A serious standoff ensued between the parliament and the government when the former demanded that the Central Bank be placed under the jurisdiction of the parliament. Hamad al-Juᶜan had been selected to head the investigation committee into the stock market crisis (Souq al-Manakh Crisis) which had badly shaken the Kuwaiti economy.[30] When al-Juᶜan asked for the minutes of the meeting of the Central Bank's board of

[30] Souq al-Manakh was a highly speculative parallel stock market which started up in the late 1970s and reached its peak in 1980–81. Because of the lack of checks and balances, the default of one trader led to the collapse of the whole al-Manakh edifice in 1982, which in turn triggered a major national financial crisis, since debts arising from the crash reached about US $94 billion. The crash led to an economic recession, a deep social calamity and a serious political crisis. Abdulghani A. Elimam, Maurice Girgis, and Samir Kotob, "The Use of Linear Programming in Disentangling the Bankruptcies of Al-Manakh Stock Market Crash," *Operations Research*, 44, No. 5 (1996): 665–676.

directors, along with other documents, the government refused to comply with his request; a series of interrogations was therefore begun that was meant to put the government under pressure. The matter was referred to the Constitutional Court which ruled that the parliament was within its legal rights to monitor the activities of the Central Bank. On 3 July 1986, the parliament was unconstitutionally dissolved and several articles in the Constitution were suspended leaving the country in the middle of a political crisis alongside the economic crisis with which it was already struggling. Throughout 1989 and 1990, MPs from the 1985 parliament sought to revive parliamentary life and enforce the 1962 constitution by holding extensive meetings known as "Monday Diwaniyyas." Twenty-six MPs, in addition to prominent figures from civil society, condemned the unconstitutional dissolution of the parliament.

The Muslim Brotherhood sided with the opposition against the government, especially with regard to the dismal manner in which the government had handled the stock market crisis. Mubarak al-Duwaila and Abdullah al-Nafisi conducted separate enquiries that were later presented to two ministers from the ruling family. Al-Duwaila, al-Juʿan and Ahmad al-Rubʿi participated in the cross-examining of Shaikh Salman al-Subah, the Minister of Justice and Legal Affairs, while al-Nafisi, together with Jasim al-Qatami and Mishari al-ʿUsaimi, interrogated Shaikh Ali al-Khalifa al-Subah, the Minster of Oil and Industry.[31] The Muslim Brotherhood attended the famous "Monday Diwaniyyas" in response to the general mood which was highly critical of the government's performance and its failure to bring corrupt officials and those responsible for the economic crisis to justice.

Following the dissolution of the parliament, a number of political parties stepped up their efforts to reinstate parliamentary life according to the 1962 Constitution, and nationalist, secularist and merchant powers mobilised to achieve this aim. Ahmad al-Khatib, representing 32 MPs, presented a petition to the Emir demanding the reinstatement of the parliament and the Constitution. The Emiri Court rejected the petition on the pretext that it did not follow the proper channels of reference.[32] Political efforts faltered between 1986 and 1988. On 22 February 1988,

---

[31] "Diwaniyyat al-Ithnain: al-Hadathlaisa Baʿidan wa la yumkin nisyanuh (1)" (*Al-Jarida* Newspaper, 5 February 2009).

[32] "Diwaniyyat al-Ithnain: al-HadathLaisa Baʿidan wa la Yumkin Nisyanuh (2)" (*Al-Jarida* Newspaper, 9 February 2009).

MP Humud al-Rumi was entrusted with the task of presenting a petition with the same demands, only for that to be rejected as well.[33] Following these rejections, the conflict escalated when the opposition encouraged people to sign a popular petition. More than 20,000 signatures were collected, chiefly through the efforts of the Muslim Brotherhood-led University Union.[34] Popular movements had gained momentum in 1986 with a greater focus on tribal areas. The "45 Committee" was formed to represent the interests and demands of merchants, Islamists and secularists from both Shiite and Sunni backgrounds.[35] When the committee's request to meet the Emir was rejected, it supported the opposition which held public meetings in the *diwaniyyas* of Jasim al-Qatami, Mishari al-ʿAnjari, Muhammad al-Marshad and Faisal al-Saniʿ.[36] Meetings were also held at tribal *diwaniyyas* such as the *diwaniyyas* of Ahmadal-Shriʿan in al-Jahra and ʿAbbas Mnawir in Farawaniyya. A meeting was scheduled at the *diwaniyya* of Saʿad Tami in al-Riqqa but was cancelled because of security concerns.[37] Following a series of confrontations between security forces and the opposition, the latter called for a truce while the government decided to launch a national dialogue. The Crown Prince and Prime Minister Shaikh Saʿad met the chief editors of Kuwaiti newspapers on 29 January 1990 to present the government's views of the events at the "Monday Diwaniyyas,"[38] while a second meeting was held with the Islamic delegation representing Islamists who did not belong to

---

[33] Ibid.

[34] "Al-Itihad al-Watani li talabat al-Kuwait Yantasir Lilhuriyyat" (*Sabr Electronic* Newspaper, 13 February 2013).

[35] Members of the Muslim Brotherhood such as Jamal al-Shihab and Bader al-Sumait participated in the '45 Committee'.

[36] "Diwaniyyat al-Ithnain: al-HadathLaisa Baʿidan wa la Yumkin Nisyanuh (3)" (*Al-Jarida* Newspaper, 10 February 2009).

[37] "Diwaniyyat al-Ithnain: al-Hadath Laisa Baʿidan wa la Yumkin Nisyanuh (6)" (*Al-Jarida* Newspaper, 11 February 2009). "Diwaniyyat al-Ithnain: al-Hadath Laisa Baʿidan wa la Yumkin Nisyanuh (7)" (*Al-Jarida* Newspaper, 12 February 2009). "Diwaniyyat al-Ithnain: al-Hadath Laisa Baʿidan wa la Yumkin Nisyanuh (11)" (*Al-Jarida* Newspaper, 17 February 2009).

[38] "Diwaniyyat al-Ithnain: al-Hadath Laisa Baʿidan wa la Yumkin Nisyanuh (8)" (*Al-Jarida* Newspaper, 13 February 2009). "Diwaniyyat al-Ithnain: al-Hadath Laisa Baʿidan wa la Yumkin Nisyanuh (9)" (*Al-Jarida* Newspaper, 15 February 2009). "Diwaniyyat al-Ithnain: al-Hadath Laisa Baʿidan wa la Yumkin Nisyanuh (10)" (*Al-Jarida* Newspaper, 16 February 2009).

any groups like the Salafis or the Muslim Brotherhood.[39] This meeting was also attended by representatives from charity organisations dominated by Islamists, such as Yusif al-Hajji from the Abdullah Al-Nuri Charity Society, Ahmad al-Jasser and Ahmad Bezeᶜ al-Yasin from al-Najat Society (both organisations were closely affiliated with the Muslim Brotherhood), Abdullah al-ᶜAtiqifrom al-Islah and ᶜUmar al-Ghrair from the Teachers' Professional Association (both controlled by the Muslim Brotherhood).

Salafis were represented by Sultan bin ᶜIsa and Rashid al-Misabbahi from the Society for the Revival of Islamic Heritage. The Islamic delegation issued a statement following the meeting in which they stressed the importance of national dialogue and the urgent need to reinstate parliamentary life in accordance with the 1962 Constitution and without changing election laws. The statement mentioned that there was a proposal to amend the Constitution which the delegation insisted should only be done by the parliament in a manner that did not violate the Constitution.[40] The meeting with the Islamic delegation was followed by a number of meetings with MPs from the 1985 parliament who reiterated their demands.[41] But the government eventually decided to replace the parliament with the National Council, only half of which was elected (50 seats) while the rest of the seats were filled by government appointments.[42]

The opposition responded by calling for a boycott of the National Council elections that were held in June 1990.[43] The turnout was very low and none of the major parties participated. More than 194 prominent figures signed a petition known as the "'Abdulᶜaziz al-Saqir Petition," which emphasised the sense of hope and expectation that had prevailed before the government had decided to establish the National Council and ignore public demands for reinstating the old parliament. The petition

---

[39] Hamad al-Mishari, ᶜAbdulᶜazizᶜAbdulrazzaq al-Mutawwa, Hamad Yousif al-Rumi, Abdulwahab al-Faris and Abdullah al-Sharhan participated but were not members of Salaf or the Muslim Brotherhood.

[40] Ibid.

[41] "Diwaniyyat al-Ithnain: al-Hadath Laisa Baᶜidan wa la Yumkin Nisyanuh (16)" (*Al-Jarida* Newspaper, 23 February 2009).

[42] "Diwaniyyat al-Ithnain: al-Hadath Laisa Baᶜidan wa la Yumkin Nisyanuh (18)" (*Al-Jarida* Newspaper, 25 February 2009).

[43] "Diwaniyyat al-Ithnain: al-Hadath Laisa Baᶜidan wa la Yumkin Nisyanuh (19)" (*Al-Jarida* Newspaper, 26 February 2009).

noted that the relationship between the ruling family and the people was one that had been inspired by the spirit of democracy since the establishment of Kuwait,[44] and renewed the opposition's demands that the 1962 Constitution must be reinstated and that any changes to the parliamentary process should also be done according to the constitution.[45] Signatories announced they were boycotting the National Council elections.[46] The petition reflected the demands made by the MPs of the 1985 parliament. The political crisis persisted until 2 August 1990 when the Iraqi invasion created more urgent and pressing realities.

Signatories on the 1985 parliament statement included Brotherhood MPs (Humud al-Rumi, Mubarak al-Duwaila), while members of the Muslim Brotherhood who also signed the petition included Mubarak al-Duwaila, Adil al-Subih, Bashir al-Rashidi, Muhammad al-Muqatiʾ, Faisal al-Khatrash, Bader al-Sumait and ʿAbdulmuhsin al-Khurafi, as well as Abdullah al-Nafisi and Jamal al-Shihab.[47] Despite the participation of the Muslim Brotherhood in these opposition efforts, a number of their leaders did not sign some of these petitions; chief amongst them was Abdullah al-Ali al-Mutawwaʿ who sent Abdullah al-ʿAtiqi to represent him as part of the Islamic delegation. Al-Mutawwaʿs good relationship with the ruling family, especially Shaikh Saʿad, was the reason why he did not sign the petition, although he attended many opposition meetings.

The political crisis had placed the Muslim Brotherhood in an untenable position. On the one hand, they enjoyed excellent relations with the government, but on the other, they were careful not to alienate the population, who had been angered by the government's decision to dissolve the parliament. The Muslim Brotherhood's participation in the opposition occurred only through politicians and some members of professional association, with the result that the movement was accused of double standards, over their insistence on maintaining good relations with the government while engaging opposition efforts. These accusations undoubtedly affected their popularity.

[44] Ibid.
[45] Ibid.
[46] Ibid.
[47] Ibid.

THE MUSLIM BROTHERHOOD DURING THE IRAQI INVASION

The Iraqi invasion of Kuwait put the constitutional crisis on the back-burner as Kuwaitis struggled to deal with the unprecedented reality of the occupation. The Muslim Brotherhood reacted quickly by re-grouping and reformulating their objectives to suit the needs of the times and played a central role in providing basic services to local communities, especially through mosques. The Muslim Brotherhood's social role during the invasion was outlined in the previous chapter. In the political domain, the Muslim Brotherhood was instrumental in maintaining links between the political leadership in Taif and Kuwaitis inside Kuwait through the correspondence carried by various Muslim Brotherhood members (Ismail al-Shatti, for example, represented Kuwaitis inside at the Jeddah conference). The Muslim Brotherhood had access to satellite services, which they used for communicating with the government. Their most important contribution during the invasion was organising the Jeddah conference and reconciling the opposition with the government in order to reach a consensus and put up a united front before the international media.

THE JEDDAH CONFERENCE

The Iraqi President Saddam Hussain claimed that Kuwait's ruling family, Al-Subah, lacked any legitimacy and that its decision to dissolve the parliament and suspend democratic institutions had been done to hide other serious issues, such as the disagreements over the Iraqi-Kuwaiti borders and the joint oil fields between Kuwait and Iraq, and Iraq's attempts to drive up oil prices by reducing OPEC production in order to prop up its ailing economy, drained by years of war with Iran. Saddam Hussain had also requested that Gulf States cancel Iraqi debts in return for preventing the Iranian Revolution from spilling into their countries. Irrespective of the reason, Saddam Hussain used democracy as a pretext to occupy Kuwait, prompting the French President François Mitterrand to question the legitimacy of al-Subah family among Kuwaitis.[48]

---

[48] Judith Miller, "CONFRONTATION IN THE GULF; Iraqi Pullout? Election in Kuwait? Prospects Worry Hawks" (*The New York Times*, 8 October 1990), (accessed 17 March 2014), http://www.nytimes.com/1990/10/08/world/confrontation-in-the-gulf-iraqi-pullout-election-in-kuwaitprospects-worry-hawks.html.

In the light of these serious allegations, the Kuwaiti government rushed to hold a conference to assert popular support for al-Subah family, and Shaikh Saʿad invited representatives from all political and social forces to attend the conference. Opposition groups seized the opportunity to bargain with the Taif government for the return of the parliament, the reinstatement of the 1962 Constitution and the formation of a national unity government. The second point was the bone of contention that almost caused the Jeddah conference to fail. The Muslim Brotherhood acted as mediators between the two stubborn sides, with al-Mutawwaʿ playing a central role in thawing the ice between them. The Taif government agreed to the opposition's demands for the revival of the 1962 constitution. Another debate ensued over who would deliver a speech in the name of the Kuwaiti people, with one side favouring the Speaker of the dissolved parliament, Ahmad Saʿdun, and the other proposing Yusif al-Hajji. Eventually, neither was chosen and ʿAbdulʿaziz al-Saqir was selected to deliver the speech.[49] The Conference was held between 13 and 15 October 1990 under the slogan "Liberation: Our slogan, our path, our aim."[50]

The Muslim Brotherhood represented by Abdullah Al-Mutawwaʿ was instrumental in managing and organising the conference. Al-Mutawwaʿ made a few modifications to al-Saqir's speech by adding the word *shura* next to democracy and a number of phrases to emphasise the Muslim aspect of Kuwaiti identity. Among the phrases he added were the following:

> ...The second pillar I would like to emphasise is Islam. The new Kuwaiti order must focus on Islamic education, moral codes and social practices to raise a generation of pious and committed young people who believe in the greatness of Islam and its causes. They must also be aware of Islam's spirit of tolerance and fully versed in its teachings, ready to defend it and encourage others to embrace Islam without prejudice or bias.[51]

Al-Saqir agreed to the changes and included them in the speech he gave after the Emir of Kuwait, Shaikh Jabir al-Ahmad al-Subah, and the Crown

---

[49] "Mubarak al-Duwailah Yastathkir Dhikrayat al-Ghazw al-Iraqi waMuʾtamar Jeddah," interview with Mubarak al-Duwailah on *al-Yawm* channel.

[50] "Muqtatafat min MuʾtamarJeddah," The Opening Ceremony of Jeddah Conference.

[51] Ibid.

Prince and Prime Minister, Shaikh Sa'ad al-Subah, had delivered their own speeches. Al-Shatti participated in the Jeddah conference with a speech on behalf of the Kuwaiti people under occupation (having carried the speech across the Kuwaiti-Sa'udi borders). The conference succeeded in stressing the legitimacy of al-Subah rule, the importance of the 1962 Constitution and the democratic process, which left the media with a very positive impression of the Taif government. It also served to emphasise the Islamic aspect of Kuwait identity.

The Muslim Brotherhood played a pivotal role in mediating between the opposition and the government and made very positive contributions to the organisation of the conference and its themes, as evidenced by al-Saqir's speech and the final statement. The government also relied on them and other political parties to present the Kuwaiti point of view to the rest of the world. Sixteen delegations were formed and dispatched to various countries. Tariq Suwaidan, a Muslim Brotherhood member, was on the delegations sent to the United States, Canada, Mexico, Cuba, Venezuela and Ecuador. Suwaidan also headed the International Committee for Kuwaiti Solidarity, which was established by Brotherhood members studying abroad, mainly in the United States.[52] Yusif al-Hajji was in the delegation dispatched to the Soviet Union, Bulgaria, Romania, Czechoslovakia, Yugoslavia, Austria and Poland. Bader al-Sumait was in the delegation to China, South Korea, Japan, North Korea, Malaysia, the Philippines and Singapore. Abdullah al-Mutawwa' joined the delegation to the Gulf States, while Nasser al-Sani', Ismail al-Shatti and Ahmad al-Qattan went to countries of North Africa. Mubarak Duwaila represented the Muslim Brotherhood in the delegation to Egypt, Syria, Jordan, Lebanon, Yemen and Sudan while 'Abdulwahab al-Huti joined the Kuwaiti delegation to Ethiopia, Kenya, Somalia, Uganda, Djibouti and Tanzania.[53] The UK and Ireland branch of the Kuwaiti Students Union led by the Muslim Brotherhood launched the "Free Kuwait" campaign. They were the first to issue a statement condemning the Iraqi invasion and later ensured that Kuwaiti students in the UK continued to

[52] Marzuq al-Harbi, "Al-Hai'ah al-'Aalamiyya Liltadamun ma'a al-Kuwait" [International Institution of Solidarity with Kuwait]" (*Al-Watan* Newspaper, 25 February 2013).

[53] Wafa'i Diyab, *Watha'iq al-Ihtilal wa Haqa'iq al-Tahrir* (Lebanon: al-Mu'assasah al-Arabiyyah al'Urubiyyah Lilsahafah wa al-Nashr, 1991).

receive government funds; these were handled by Shaikh Khalid al-Subah who distributed them to students all over the UK.[54]

During January and February, the Muslim Brotherhood became increasingly confident that Kuwait would soon be liberated, which prompted them to prepare for the regaining of independence. Several meetings were held to determine the aims and objectives of the post-independence period, chiefly how to capitalise on the increasing popularity of the Muslim Brotherhood in the light of their exemplary aid and relief efforts during the invasion. The Muslim Brotherhood remained wary of coming out into the open, although this seemed on the face of it an ideal time to do so. It was decided therefore to establish a number of fronts for the Muslim Brotherhood, in addition to the Society for Social Reform.

THE LIBERATION AND THE ESTABLISHMENT OF THE ISLAMIC CONSTITUTIONAL MOVEMENT (ICM)

The first entity to be founded was the Islamic Constitutional Movement (ICM), to represent the political wing of the Muslim Brotherhood in Kuwait. Brown asserts that the name of the movement reflected the Muslim Brotherhood's commitment to the Constitution and its Islamic identity, a controversial contention since Article 2 of the Constitution did not specify Islamic Shariʿa as the main source of legislation.[55] However, the Muslim Brotherhood had revealed in a statement during the invasion that ICM would strive to amend the second article of the Constitution. The establishment of the ICM was an unprecedented step in the political history of Kuwait, since while most social and political movements were known to the Kuwaiti society, there had been very little political institutionalisation. Other political movements followed suit, thus imposing a new reality in Kuwaiti political life, especially since this shift was spearheaded by the Muslim Brotherhood which enjoyed good relations with the government.[56]

---

[54] Al-Obaidly, Interview.

[55] Brown, "Pushing Toward Party Politics," 3.

[56] Many political fronts were announced such as al-Minbar al-Dimuqrati [the Democratic Forum], al-Iʿtilaf al-Islami al-Watanni [the Nationalist Islamic Coalition], al-Tajammuʿ al-Islami al-Shaʿbi [the Populist Islamic Group], al- Tajammuʿ al-Dusturi

The establishment of ICM was announced during a press conference one month after the liberation of Kuwait, on 31 March 1991 at the Fatima mosque in the Bayan Area, which had been the headquarters of the Muslim Brotherhood during the invasion.[57] During the press conference, ICM outlined its principles and objectives in a memorandum entitled "The Islamic Constitutional Strategy for Rebuilding Kuwait"; this was to include establishing the rule of just law in the country; equality between citizens; adopting the *shura* principle in accordance with Islamic teachings; calling for more political participation; and amending the Kuwaiti constitution to reflect the noble principles of Islam.[58] ICM also contributed to the drafting of a paper entitled "Future Vision for Rebuilding Kuwait" which was signed by a number of prominent Kuwaiti figures, mainly Shiite and Sunni Islamists.[59] The paper remarked that the great sacrifices of the Kuwaiti people would go down in history as befitted their courage, resilience and commitment in resisting occupation. The paper commented on the tremendous spirit of cooperation and solidarity among Kuwaitis during the long months of occupation and concluded that faith in Allah had helped people to pull through and remain steadfast in the face of adversity; this demonstrated the importance of both absolute faith in Allah and His abilities, and the application of Islamic Shari'a and the 1962 Constitution.

As Brown argues, most of the Muslim Brotherhood's political literature and the outlets they contributed to, such as the statement read out by al-Saqir at the Jeddah conference and the ICM memorandums on "The Islamic Constitutional Strategy for Rebuilding Kuwait," and the "Future Vision for Rebuilding Kuwait," stressed the importance of adopting Shari'a law as a source of legislation while maintaining the political gains of the 1962 constitution and working to increase them through

[the Constitutional Group], Takattul al-Nuwwab [Parliamentarians Bloc] and Takattul al-Mustaqilin [Independent Bloc].

Official Website of ICM, "Dirasah ʿAn Majhudat al-Harakah al-Dusturiyyah al-Islamiyya Athnaʾ al-Ghazw al-Iraqi al-Ghashim."

[57] Ibid.

[58] "Al-Istiratijiyya al-Dusturiyyah al-Islamiyyah li Binaʾ al-Kuwait," Islamic Constitutional Movement ICM, 31 March 1991.

[59] Signatures on the paper included Mohammad al-Adsani and Yousif al-Nisif from al-Irshad; Khalid Sultan al-Iysa and Nathim al-Misbah from the Salaf; and Sayyid Adnan Abdulsamad and Abdulhadi al-Salih from Shia Islamists, in addition to Abdullah al-Naibari and Ahmad al-Dyain as secular figures. Ibid.

a new law for political parties. In addition to their social projects, the Muslim Brotherhood was now making huge leaps in the political domain. They called for the separation between the posts of Crown Prince and Prime Minister, and for more media and political freedoms, in addition to the reinstatement of the 1962 Constitution. The Muslim Brotherhood had emerged as important political player in Kuwaiti life and as an important constituent of the opposition. The latter, however, began to falter and disintegrate, due to major ideological differences between its Islamist and secularist constituents. The government also played an important role in fostering disagreements among opposition parties by supporting some and antagonising others. The first of these clashes occurred very soon after the liberation of Kuwait and was again centred on amending Article 2 of the Constitution and mixed-gender education at the University.

Post-Liberation Islamists' Issues in Parliament

The amending of Article 2 of the Constitution was the Muslim Brotherhood's top priority in parliament. Following the original debate in the 1962 National Assembly, the subject had been broached many times over the decades with special attention given to debate in the 1981 and 1992 National Assemblies. According to Article 174 of the Constitution, which outlines how amendments are to be made:

> The Emir and a third of the members of the National Assembly may propose amendments to the Constitution by amending, adding or revoking articles. If the Emir and the majority of the members of the National Assembly vote to discuss amendments, the assembly shall debate each article separately. Amendments shall be approved by two thirds of the votes and require the Emir's ratification to come into effect with the exceptions of Articles 65 and 66 of the Constitution. If the Assembly votes against discussing the amendments, a whole year shall pass before the same proposal is submitted again. No changes shall be made to the Constitution until five years have passed from the day the Constitution came into effect.[60]

There were two attempts to amend Article 2. The first was in 1981 when 26 MPs submitted an amendment proposal which was rejected by the

---

[60] *Majmuʿatal-Tashriʿat al-Kuwaitiyyah (1): al-Dustur al-Kuwaiti wa Mudhakkiratih al-Tafsiriyyah* (Kuwait: Ministry of Justice, 2011), 48.

Emir in accordance with Article 174 of the Constitution granting him the right to reject any attempts to debate the issue—an absolute right that could not be vetoed. A similar proposal was signed in 1984 by 46 MPs, but the proposal was rendered moot by the dissolution of parliament.

The proposal to amend Article 2 submitted by the 1981 National Assembly contained the proposed text of the article as amended, and postulated that "Islam is the religion of the state and Islamic Shariʿa is the source of legislation,"[61] instead of "Islam is the religion of the state and Islamic Shariʿa is the main source of legislation."[62] The proposal explained that although the original article encouraged legislatures to rely on Islamic Shariʿa as a source of legislation, as evidenced by the statement: "The article of constitution urges the legislators to rely on Islamic Shariʿa whenever possible and makes this an explicit request,"[63] it was not sufficiently binding[64] and thus "it became imperative to make Shariʿa law the only source rather than one of the sources and to forbid any legislation that violates Shariʿa."[65]

The proposal was thus intended to confirm Islam as a legal and social guide. The proposal refuted all claims made by secularists that these changes would annul all legislation not drawn from Shariʿa, that they posed a threat to the monarchical form of government in Kuwait, or that they created a conflict with international economic and financial laws in light of Kuwait's commitment to several international agreements. The response to the first claim was that these changes would not in any way hinder the resorting to general laws or legislation as long as they did not breach Shariʿa laws.[66] The response to the second claim was that the changes did not allude to the monarchical system which had been decided by *shura* and popular consensus.[67] As for the third claim, the proposal argued that these could be considered necessary laws to ensure the smooth running of daily life.[68]

---

[61] Baqir, 26.

[62] *Majmuʿatal-Tashriʿat al-Kuwaitiyyah (1)*, 16.

[63] Ibid., 61.

[64] Baqir, 27.

[65] Ibid.

[66] Ibid.

[67] Ibid.

[68] Ibid.

In July 1994, 39 members from the 1992 National Council submitted yet another proposal for amending Article 2 of the Constitution, and once again the Emir rejected it, thereby marking an end to all attempts to amend the article.[69] Some half-hearted attempts were made subsequently, but were not actively pursue by the Islamists who had become firmly convinced the ruling family was not interested in amending the Article. However, Shaikh Jabir al-Subah was eager to please the Islamists as he had been back in 1981 when he allowed several items of Islamic legislation to be formally codified. He therefore issued Decree Number 139 for the year 1991 for establishing the Higher Advisory Council to Work towards Applying Islamic Shariʿa. This body was entrusted with the task of examining how various pieces of legislation could be Islamised, and under the leadership of Shaikh Khalid al-Mathkur, it presented a number of studies and reports to the parliament, some of which were duly adopted. The Islamists may have failed to amend Article 2 of the Constitution, but they did succeed in Islamising many laws and regulations. They also became increasingly convinced that amending Article 2 did not mean that society would, by default, become more Islamic. Egypt served as a perfect example of a country which had amended an Article 2 to make Shariʿa the source of legislation without that leading to the application of Islamic teachings across the board.

The second issue which preoccupied the Islamists was that of mixed-gender education at the University of Kuwait.[70] After years of struggle, they succeeded in forcing the hand of the University and its secularist administration, who were obliged to conform to parliamentary legislation that had been adopted in cooperation with the government. The ICM, represented by Jamal al-Kandari, headed negotiations with the government and the Crown Prince and Prime Minister, Shaikh Saʿad al-Subah. Once the Islamists realised they were not going to win the battle to amend Article 2, they decided to focus their energies on trying to make other laws more Islamic. The debate over mixed-gender education was part of their battle to ensure that these laws were implemented.

The relationship between the government and the Muslim Brotherhood following Kuwait's liberation from the Iraqi occupation remained

[69] See Appendix C.

[70] See Chapter 4.

warm and amiable despite the Emir's rejection of the Muslim Brother-hood's proposal for amending Article 2 of the Constitution. A number of laws presented by the Islamists were approved by the government, which also offered alternatives to projects that it did not approve—hence the establishment of the Higher Advisory Council to Work towards Applying Islamic Shariᶜa. With help from the government, the Islamists also succeeded in increasing their influence in the social domain and became increasingly powerful in the political domain at the expense of secularists.

Nevertheless, this close relationship came at a price, with the Islamists remaining silent amid calls for investigating the government's responsi-bility in the events that had culminated in the invasion. Many called for the government to be held accountable for mishandling the earlier signs of the impending crisis with Iraq in the summer of 1990, but instead of the judiciary being entrusted with the task, a parliamentary fact-finding committee was set up to investigate the Iraqi invasion of Kuwait. The government formed the committee in coordination with the Islamists, and a ballot was held on 8 December 1992 to select the members of the committee. Saleh al-Fudalah was elected president, Ahmad Baqir was secretary general, and the members included Ismail Al-Shatti, Khalid al-ᶜAdwa, Fahad al-Meeᶜ, Talal al-ᶜAyyar, Yaqub Hayati and Abdullah al-Naibari. Al-Shatti and al-ᶜAyyar resigned on 16 November 1993 and 30 November, respectively, and were replaced by Mubarak al-Duwaila and Khalaf Dmaithir al-ᶜAnizi. The list of members reflects the level of government-Islamist coordination. The committee, which began its work on 10 December 1992 and finished on 14 August 1995, met 96 times, with the military, political and financial aspects of the invasion being discussed during these meetings. However, despite the detailed report that outlined the events leading up to the invasion and the ensuing occu-pation, its causes, major events and outcomes, no party was singled out for any recriminations. The only person to be held politically accountable was Shaikh Sabah al-Ahmad al-Subah, who had been Kuwait's foreign minister on the eve of the invasion; he was ousted from the Cabinet between 1992 and 1996 but was later reinstated.

Notwithstanding the good relations between the Islamists and the government during the 1990s, a few skirmishes did occur between them, especially over the issue of granting women the right to vote and to run as candidates. Article 1 of Kuwait's Election Law states that only Kuwaiti males over the age of 21 are eligible to vote.[71] Attempts to grant women access to political participation had begun in 1971, when MP Salem al-Marzuq submitted a draft law that would grant women the right to vote; however, only twelve MPs voted in favour. The law did not fare any better in the 1975, 1981, 1985, 1992 and 1996 National Assemblies, but on 16 May 1999, the government announced that the Emir wished to grant women the right to vote and to stand for elections. A royal decree was issued that deleted the word "male" from the first Article of the Election Law, but the approval of the National Assembly was still required before it could pass into law. The 1999 National Assembly narrowly rejected the Emir's decree, which failed to pass by only two votes.

Six years later, on 16 May 2005, the parliament passed a government proposal that granted women the right to vote and contest elections. The government had coordinated efforts with secularists, independents and Shiites within and outside the parliament to ensure that the draft law would pass. It also persuaded Islamists and tribal representatives to vote for the law by agreeing that the text of the law could have an "Islamic" addition, to the effect that,

> Article (1) Any Kuwaiti over the age of 21 shall have the right to vote. This excludes nationalised citizens who were nationalised less than twenty years prior to the elections being held according to Article (60) of the Emiri Decree Number (15) for the year 1959. Women may vote and stand in elections as long as they respect the teachings of Islamic shariᶜa.[72]

Thus, the Islamists succeeded in making the legislation more "Islamic" through an understanding with the government.

POLITICAL OPPOSITION WITHIN THE MOVEMENT

The Muslim Brotherhood in Kuwait, similar to any other movement, witnessed differences of opinion among its leaders especially in the absence of any clear vision or political goals. The movement's leaders in Kuwait al-Ali and al-ᶜAdsani differed over how to deal with the ruling family. Shaikh Abdullah al-Jaber al-Sabah wished to become an honorary

---

[71] "Qanun al-Intikhab" [Elections Law], *The Official Website of the Kuwait National Assembly* (2013) (accessed 17 March 2014).

[72] Ibid.

member in al-Irashd. Al-Mutawwa' who enjoyed great relations with the ruling family welcomed the idea, but al-'Adsani was completely opposed to it.[73] Al-Mutawwa' and al-'Adsani also disagreed over how to respond to Nasser's campaign against the Muslim Brotherhood in Egypt. The former adopted a neutral stand while the latter declared his support of the Muslim Brotherhood. Despite there being previous disagreements between the two over a number of issues, it was political issues that deepened the division between the two men.

The 1968 organisation faced similar challenges. Following the government's decision to reinstate the parliament in 1981 after it was suspended in 1976, members of the Muslim Brotherhood engaged in heated debates about whether to field candidates or not, an unprecedented step in the history of the movement. Most of those Muslim Brotherhood members who had contested the elections ran as independents. The debate centred on whether parliamentary elections conformed with Shari'a especially in view of the controversy surrounding Article 2 of the constitution.[74] Some members were sceptical that any real change could be affected through the parliament. The movement held several meetings and consulted with Muslim Brotherhood in other countries such as Iraq, Egypt and Jordan after which it was decided they would field candidates and make Article 2 of the constitution the focus of their campaign in addition to other legislations. It was not an easy decision especially since many members of the organisation were opposed to participating in the elections. Those members including Musa'id al-'Abduljadir were of the opinion that the Muslim Brotherhood was a social and education movement and should not involve itself in politics.[75]

During the second half of 1980s, especially during the Monday diwanyyias, a general sense of dissatisfaction with the Muslim Brotherhood's involvement in political life through the parliament and the Kuwait University Student Union, the conduit through which the movement fought its political battles against the government. This could be attributed to the fact that the president of al-Islah Abdullah Al-Mutawwa' enjoyed very close and warm relations with the ruling thanks to his brother 'Abdul'aziz. He was particularly close to the Crown Prince and

---

[73] Al-Rifa'i, interview.

[74] Yousif al-'Atiqi, interview.

[75] Al-'Abduljadir, interview.

Prime Minister Shaikh Sa'ad. The struggle between the movement and their members in parliament intensified following the movement's decision to expel Abdullah al-Nafisi because he did not heed the movement's orders. He ended up publishing a series of articles in al-Qabas Newspaper, later collected in book entitled "al-Harakah al-Islamiyya: Thagharat fi al-Tariq" [The Islamic Movement: Gaps along the Way], in which he criticised the movement and the way it was being run.[76] Al-Nafisi criticised what he perceived as the political, strategic and social shortcomings of the movement. On the political level, he condemned the movement for failing to develop a clear political vision and carve a place for itself on the political stage. Socially, he expressed his disapproval of the fact that the movement did not open up to the public and work remained limited to a select few. He remarked this meant that members of the public were put off by the movement's air of mystery and lack of clear goals.[77] Al-Nafisi also accused the movement of being stagnant and of refusing to indulge in any form of self-criticism or dialogue with the other.[78] He reserved his harshest criticism for the leadership which he described as "tiresome, patriarchal, old, dictatorial and stuck in time."[79]

The disagreements with the movement's leadership result in the expelling of some members such as al-Nafisi and the retirement of others.[80] This was considered the most serious division in the history of the movement in Kuwait but did not lead to the collapse of the organisation which was mainly social and educational and therefore insulated from the political bloc. In general, political issues were debated within the movement and decisions were issued by the Shura Council. Members were expected to abide by these decisions.

[76] Abdullah al-Nafisi, "*al-Harakah al-Islamiyya: Thagharat fi al-Tariq*" (No Publisher: Kuwait, 1992).

[77] Ibid., 7–9.

[78] Ibid., 14–23.

[79] Ibid., 62.

[80] Yousif al-ʿAtiqi, interview.

CONCLUSION

After the establishment of the Muslim Brotherhood in Kuwait in the 1950s, the movement focused on social reform and the Islamisation of society. It sought to achieve these objectives through supporting Islamist MPs and other MPs sympathetic to its causes after Kuwait had won back its independence and a National Assembly had been established. Muslim Brotherhood members failed to win any parliamentary seats as independents, but as a movement, they succeeded in fielding several successful representatives in 1981; this was almost 14 years after the establishment of the new movement whose young members were now in their thirties. During the 1980s and the 1990s, the Muslim Brotherhood entrenched itself as an important political player in Kuwait, especially following the 1990 Iraqi invasion of Kuwait when it became the central player in the post-liberation period. Their position was cemented by their establishment of the Islamic Constitutional Movement (ICM).

Following the invasion, the Muslim Brotherhood and other political movements imposed a new reality, and from the early 1990s, the Muslim Brotherhood began to make political demands, such as its calls for the legalisation of political parties, increasing political freedoms and so on. Their social and religious demands naturally remained more pressing and more urgent in their discourse than their political demands.

Kuwait's Islamists, especially the Muslim Brotherhood, are unique among their counterparts in other countries in that they have enjoyed very good relations with the government and the ruling family. Kuwait had retained the old ruling system from the days of the Umayyads; this was predicated on dividing the Islamic state into a political power (concerned with running the country, its finances, army, international relations and other political affairs under the direct control of the ruling family, the army chief and other politicians and sometimes the merchants as was the case with Kuwait) and a social power (concerned with the judiciary, issuing fatwas, education and charity work). Although social services were shared by both the political and the religious powers, the latter had greater influence on providing services through its direct links with the Waqf and its allocations (e.g. in building schools and hospitals, and helping the poor). The boundaries were clear between these two sorts of power, and that status quo was maintained for a very long time. This should not be understood to mean that there were no clashes between political and religious powers.

Thus, the political system in Kuwait remained quite stable, unlike in several Arab countries where nationalist secularist movements overthrew old systems and replaced them with secularist ones, causing traditional ruling families and religious institutions to lose power. The biggest shock occurred when, after centuries of control, leadership of the social domain by religious institutions was appropriated. In Egypt, for example, al-Azhar's lands and Waqfs were nationalised in the 1950s to weaken it economically and bring it under the control of the new secularist government. A number of western-style universities were established to pull the educational rug from under al-Azhar's feet, and Nasser cracked down on the Muslim Brotherhood for fear they might mobilise the masses against him. He enlisted the help of secularists, socialists and nationalists in his war against the Muslim Brotherhood, who became engaged in an existential battle against an authority that was intent on wiping them out. The Muslim Brotherhood viewed this as a war against Islam and insisted on the need to replace the new regime with one that was more Islamic. The struggle between the Muslim Brotherhood and the regime persisted throughout the tenure of both Sadat and Mubarak.

The situation was quite similar in other Arab countries like Iraq, Syria and Tunisia, and secularist movements in Kuwait attempted to do the same thing by imposing their own political agenda on the ruling family to pressure them to make changes to the ruling system. The secularist agenda was keen to imitate the changes in Egypt, which resulted in the leading ruling family and the Islamists taking steps to resist these political and social threats to their existence. It was therefore quite natural that the interests of the government and the Islamists should converge to enable them to deflect the secularist threat and ensure the survival of the old system.

In spite of its good treatment and tolerance of Islamists, the Kuwaiti government was nevertheless quite wary of them. The Islamists had been drawn upon as a balancing power in the conflict with the secularists, but the government remained constantly aware of the status of the Muslim Brotherhood as a regional power. These fears were further aggravated by the rise in their popularity during the invasion by Iraq and afterwards, as the Muslim Brotherhood forged ahead with building their social institutions in addition to the dynamic nature of the ICM in various social and political issues. All of this prompted the government to reject any amendments to Article 2 and to several other proposals by the Islamists. The authorities also sought to keep a more watchful eye on the activities of the general secretariat of the Waqf by introducing non-Brotherhood members and deposing Muslim Brotherhood ones.

Other policies were used to contain the influence of the Muslim Brotherhood during the 1990s, and when the Muslim Brotherhood joined efforts with the opposition in the 1980s and the 1990s, the government opted for a "divide and rule" tactic by pitting the opposition groups against each other, especially as the opposition incorporated elements from secularist as well as Islamist movements (both Sunni and Shiʿi). In addition to this successful tactic, the government encouraged the emergence of "service MPs" (MPs renowned for their skill and prowess in dealing with government red tape). Such privileges were extended to pro-government MPs only, thereby prompting voters to elect service MPs who would be able to help them process their paperwork much more rapidly.

Thus, the relationship between the Islamists and the government remained in a state of ebb and flow without any real confrontations occurring. Indeed, following the attacks on New York on the "events of 9/11," the Islamists were fiercely defended by the Kuwaiti government in the face of accusations levelled against them by the United States, especially criticisms against their charity organisations.

CHAPTER 6

Conclusion

The Muslim Brotherhood movement in Kuwait undoubtedly had a great influence on Kuwaiti society, especially in the social domain which the Muslim Brotherhood sought to dominate. The Muslim Brotherhood's interest in the social domain stems from their conviction that Islam is the society's cultural compass and the repository of values and identity. For centuries, Islam has been the major component of the society, through the efforts of the religious establishment actors such as scholars who worked in schools and the judiciary. The Muslim Brotherhood's impact on the political domain was quite minimal due to the lack of any clear political project and the defensive position it adopted to protect its dominance over the social domain. From its establishment until 2005, the movement limited its political engagement to occasional collaboration with other political forces to demand certain political reforms. Although the difference between their role in the political and social domains emerges quite clearly when the two are compared over the first four decades of the movement's activities in Kuwait, the Muslim Brotherhood has become increasingly influential in the political domain over the last two decades following the establishment of the Islamic Constitutional Movement (ICM) as their political wing in 1991. It is expected that the Muslim Brotherhood's political role will witness even more dramatic changes as their activities intensify.

A. A. Alkandari, *The Muslim Brotherhood in Kuwait*, Contemporary Gulf Studies, https://doi.org/10.1007/978-981-99-3050-0_6

These are the main conclusions reached during the course of book: first, the Muslim Brotherhood organisation in Kuwait is originally a social movement that sought to dominate the social domain which had historically been under the control of religious institutions. Inspired by the thinking of Islamist renaissance scholars such as Jamal al-Din al-Afghani, Muhammad ʿAbduh and Muhammad Rashīd Rida, the Muslim Brotherhood grew in influence as a reformist movement in some parts of the Arab world by regarding itself as a continuation of, or even a replacement, for religious establishment especially since its members hailed from all walks of life (preachers, scholars, teachers, etc.) who had previously been part of such establishment. The organisation attracted members from new segments, such as academics and businessmen, making it the most comprehensive movement in terms of covering both the social and political domains. In Kuwait, the efforts of all its members were directed towards serving the social goals of the movement (cultural education and moulding social and individual identity) especially after the secularist trend succeeded in controlling those aspects from the 1950s to the 1980s. The educational sector, originally under the control of the religious establishment, was gradually secularised, and secularists also exercised a great degree of influence over the media which replaced mosques. As far as Islamists were concerned, the biggest danger posed by Secularists was the introduction of several secularist articles into the Kuwaiti Constitution which ceased to consider Shariʿa "*the* main source" of legislation and instead regarded it as "*a* source of legislation."

Second, the original Muslim Brotherhood movement in Kuwait was inspired by the mother organisation in Egypt, but after being greatly weakened, the movement sank into oblivion at the end of the 1950s. In 1968, ʿAbdulwahid Aman, a Kuwaiti who had been raised in the traditions of the Iraqi Muslim Brotherhood re-established the organisation. A number of Muslim Brotherhood members, such as Abdullah al-ʿAqil, relocated from Zubair in the south of Iraq to Kuwait where they spread the movement's philosophy and ideas. Muhammad Ahmad al-Rashid, who was a member of the Muslim Brotherhood in Baghdad, was the chief theorist of the Muslim Brotherhood in Kuwait. Thus, it can be argued that the Iraqi Muslim Brotherhood had the biggest influence on its sister movement in Kuwait starting from 1968. It is worth noting that the Muslim Brotherhood of Iraq was a highly secretive and vigilant movement which took great care in selecting its new members. Noted for its highly organised structure, it was renowned for the moral and religious training its members had to undertake, in addition to being schooled in the art of leadership and management to help shoulder the movement's grand task of educating society. The Iraqi model was so effective that Muslim Brotherhood movements everywhere strove to emulate the standards of their Iraqi counterpart. The Iraqi Muslim Brotherhood members transposed their experiences onto the Kuwait branch of the Muslim Brotherhood, thus establishing a solid, well-structured organisation whose members were carefully selected and trained. The 1968 Kuwaiti Muslim Brotherhood organisation, too, opted not to carry out its activities in the open to the extent it eventually became overly secretive and complicated in a society known for its open and simple way of life. Despite the success of the Muslim Brotherhood in establishing this well-organised movement, it became gradually more accommodating of Kuwaiti realities by publicly announcing its activities and the identity of its members, and even exposing its political wing, the ICM.

Third, the Muslim Brotherhood had originally participated in political life indirectly through their links with conservatives or Islamic politicians as evident from the legislation banning alcohol and attempts to amend Article 2 of the Constitution. The Muslim Brotherhood then engaged with union activities, usually a precursor to full political participation. They succeeded in dominating a number of professional associations and organisation such as the National Union of Kuwaiti Students. In the 1980s, the Muslim Brotherhood won two parliamentary seats, thus consolidating their influence over the social and political domains. They established the ICM, their political wing, but this foray into the political was intended only to serve their aim of dominating the social domain, since they were convinced, they needed political gains in order to protect their influence in the social domain. All the issues the Muslim Brotherhood fought for politically were of a social nature such as banning alcohol, amending Article 2 of the Constitution, banning mixed gender education and outlawing usury. However, none of this prevented the Muslim Brotherhood from joining other political forces in mobilising for political issues. A special understanding between the Muslim Brotherhood and the ruling establishment was born out of the realisation that the secularists were a mutual enemy that they had to combat, especially as the secularists were attempting to control both the social and political domains. The Muslim Brotherhood refrained from opposing the government except in very rare cases and on a limited scale. The real enemy was presented in the shape of the secularists who posed a danger to both the Muslim Brotherhood and the government in the political domain, especially since secularists had the backing of their counterparts in other Arab countries. Even so, the ruling establishment did not give free rein to the Islamists, as it did not wish to replace its secularist enemy with an Islamist one.

Fourth, the Muslim Brotherhood employed several methods to control the social domain by establishing a number of successful social organisations, the most prominent and successful being al-Irshad, followed by al-Islah. The activities of these two organisations included charity work, training and educating the youth, da*wah and media activities (*al-Irshad* and *al-Mujtama*^{c} journals), in addition to some indirect political activities. The Muslim Brotherhood focused on effecting change at the grass roots level; hence their objective of putting together a base of members from all specialisations. Social activities such as education and religious scholarship were the main avenues through which the Muslim Brotherhood pursed their interests in the social domain, and explains why schools and mosques were their main field of operations. They gradually succeeded in reshaping social identity by pulling society more towards the conservative right, especially during the 1980s and 1990s. The *hijab* is a very clear example; during the 1970s, there were very few girls donning the Muslim head cover, but in the 1990s, the number of women wearing the hijab far exceeded those who did not.

Fifth, the Muslim Brotherhood's brand of activism is best represented by Munson's theory of integrating thought with structure, and Asef Bayat's theory of social movements. Bayat's theory of "imagined solidarity" explains the spread of Islamic thinking throughout society, but he did not elaborate on the mechanisms for spreading those ideas. Munson, however, covers this aspect in his examination of the Muslim Brotherhood in Egypt, argues that the movement integrated its intellectual sources into the structure of the organisations. Munson further comments that da*wah is the best example of synthesising Islamic teachings with organised work. This explains why the Muslim Brotherhood has been so successful in spreading their ideas, despite the security and political challenges they have encountered from Arab governments everywhere. When applying these two theories in the Kuwaiti context, that of "imagined solidarity" explains the spread of the general acceptance of Islamic ideas in the society, especially after the 1967 War when Islamists used the defeat to put the blame on the Secularists. Islamists also used "imagined solidarity" to prohibit alcohol consumption when they waged a strong campaign against it. Islamists, especially the Muslim Brotherhood, also used da*wah to spread their message in the society starting from the young generation in schools and at Kuwait University. Both theories were used by the Muslim Brotherhood to control the social domain and spread Islamic ideology in the society.

As a dynamic movement capable of adapting to new realities, the Muslim Brotherhood in Kuwait will engage with the political domain in a new manner that reflects its ability to change and shift according to the needs of the time. This is a natural progression for a movement which has always aimed to enforce certain social values. Now, with the introduction into the Muslim Brotherhood's discourse of values such as freedom, social justice and democracy, these notions have acquired an Islamic identity. The relationship between the Muslim Brotherhood and the ruling establishment is also bound to change as fresh realities create the need for new alliances.

As the Muslim Brotherhood movement in Kuwait advanced in age along with its solid base on which the movement was founded and as the number of its members increased and it became quite active in the political domain during the 1990–1991 Iraqi invasion of Kuwait, it was inevitable for the movement to progress into a new and more complex phase. On the one hand, the Muslim Brotherhood's relationship with the ruling family and society at large became more multifaceted and complex since 1991. The horizontal spread of Muslim Brotherhood ideas helped them reach both urban and tribal areas. At the same time, the Muslim Brotherhood itself was also influenced by the environment into which it was born. In tribal areas, for example, the Muslim Brotherhood was influenced by tribal structures as evident from the fact that several Muslim Brotherhood members contested parliamentary seats on tribal platforms during the 1990s, a move which in principle contradicts with the tenets of their membership. This gave rise to several dilemmas; should the member heed the Movement's or the tribe's political opinions? Social and tribal pressure intensified on tribal members who were also Muslim Brotherhood members in addition to some Muslim Brotherhood affiliates complaining of the strict need for secrecy, especially among the much older members who refused to obey orders unless there was an acceptable rationale behind them.

The biggest hurdle to overcome was the generational conflict which also plagued other branches of the Muslim Brotherhood. In the Sudan, for example, young members rebelled in 1999 against Hasan al-Turabi, the founder of the movement. As the original base of the movement continues to be controlled by the older generation, young members find themselves unable sometimes to impose their own fresh vision on the movement. Since 2005, the height of the confrontation occurs in the field of politics where the younger generation in Kuwait grapples with issues such as freedoms, pluralism and political participation, issues that the older generation did not allude to. Thus, the pressing question is: how can young Muslim Brotherhood members compete with the ruling family over its long-held control of the political domain which the Muslim Brotherhood had for decades conceded to the ruling family in return for full control over the social domain.

Undoubtedly, the examination of the Muslim Brotherhood experience in Kuwait is important for understanding the dynamics of Islamic movements in the Gulf, especially for scholars who are interested in studying the political and social history of Islamic movements. In addition, such a study helps examine how Western theories of social movements could be modified to apply to non-Western contexts.

Appendix A: Petition Addressed to ʿAbdulʿaziz al-Ali al-Mutawwaʿ by the Members of al-Irshad

Dear honourable Brother ʿAbdulʿaziz al-Ali al-Mutawwaʿ
General Observer of Jamiʿiyyat al-Irshadal-Islami in Kuwait

Assalamu alaikum wa rahmatu Allah wa barakatuh..

We have been sad since we read your letter in Al-Biʿtha Journal about your will of resigning from the burden of leading al-Irshad. How could our older brother resign and the beginning of the road of spreading God's word among people? How can he resign after giving him our trust and leadership as a brother, a friend and a leader who promised his solders to be with them in good times and bad times and in return they promised him to obey him in what they like or hate until God fulfils his promise to believers. We all know about your responsibilities and business; however, our belief in your sincerity, responsibility, your preference for the hereafter rather than this ephemeral life as God says "And who is better in speech than one who invites to Allah and does righteousness and says, "Indeed, I am of the Muslims."" (44:33), and your fulfilling of leadership qualifications as Islam explains makes you the best person who can take this responsibility which is still in around your neck.

Therefore, in the name of our brotherhood and this holy mission, we ask you to write back Al-Biʿtha Journal that you are still with us on the road as a leader of this organisation. Also, we would like to mention to you that your request for withdrawing your nomination for the election of choosing the General Observer of al-Irshad is not accepted because

A. A. Alkandari, *The Muslim Brotherhood in Kuwait*, Contemporary Gulf Studies, https://doi.org/10.1007/978-981-99-3050-0

people choose who they want to represent them, who they trust and love, and whenever a person is chosen by people he cannot reject them. Thus, consolidate your determination to walk with us on this road that God chose for us. May Allah bless you and guide you to righteousness.

Assalamu alaikum wa rahmatu Allah.
[Signatures of 45 members of al-Irshad][1]

---

[1] A copy of the letter is in possession of Ahmad ʿAbdulʿaziz al-Mutawwaʿ.

Appendix B: Report of the Fact-Finding Committee on the Events Surrounding the Symposium on Mixed-Gender Education at the University of Kuwait

The committee held four meetings on 22, 23, 27 and 30 November 1971 at the conference room of the University Council. The meetings were presided over by the Minister of Education, the President of the University and the following members:

Mr Anwar al-Nuri	University Secretary General
Mr Jasim al-Saqir	University Council Member
Mr Hasan al-Ibrahīm	Lecturer at the Department of Political Science
Mr Yusif al-Sumaiṭ	Teaching assistant at the Geography Department

The committee examined the case thoroughly and conducted a number of interviews to gain deeper insight into the events that occurred at the symposium. Members listened to statements from students, organisers of the symposium, students opposed to holding the symposium and some members of the audience from outside the university; some opposed to and some who support the idea of mixed-gender education. The witnesses were:

1. **Students:**

A. Naji ʿAbdulʿaziz al-Ibrahim al-Muʾawwad	Economics (Third year)
B. Ghassan Nisif al-Yusif al-Nisif	Business (Fourth year)
C. Badir ʿAbduwahab Sayyid al-Rifaʿi	Science (Second year)
D. Bashir Saleh Thnian	Science (First year)
E. Muhammad Mahmud al-Raḥmani	Law (Fourth year)
F. Hamad Falih Humud al-Rushaid	History (Fourth year)
G. Hamīd Mansur Qasim (ʿAbdulamid al-Sarraf)	Law (Third year)
H. Wadha al-Khali	Economics (Second year)

2. **Others:**

A. Mr Muhammad Musaʿid al-Saleh	Lawyer
B. Mr Sulaiman al-Mutawwaʿ	Employee at the KOC
C. Mr Ali Maʿrafi	Assistant Librarian Kuwait University
D. Mr Yusif Qattan	Employee, Min. of Electricity & Water
E. Mr Humud al-Mudian	Director of an Orphanage
F. Mr ʿAbdulwahid Aman	Employee at the Municipality

The committee listened to a tape recording of the symposium, examined many photographs taken during the incident and reviewed all the discussions at the parliament and on the pages of newspapers.

The committee discussed the following points:

- The right of the National Union of Kuwaiti Students (the University of Kuwait branch) to hold the symposium as part of its cultural and social activities.
- Students opposed to the symposium and their right to voice their opinions, the manner to do so and how opinions were actually expressed during the symposium.
- The type of audience who attend the symposium and their role in what occurred.
- The causes behind the ensuing state of tension and disorder.
- The accusations that arose in the parliament that the symposium had included offensive statements about the Qurʾan.

The Committee concluded the following:
The National Union of Kuwaiti Students (Kuwait University branch) was established three years ago and is supervised by an annually-elected administrative body. The Union organises many social and cultural activities. It has held a number of social and entertainment gatherings and several cultural symposiums, the latest being the symposium on mixed-gender education to which the following were invited to speak:

MP Khalid al-Masud, Dr. Saʿad ʿAbdulrahman, Mrs Fatimah Husain, Dr ʿAbdulʿaziz Sulṭan.

As is the case with any society, big or small, or a group of people, and even members of the same family, several points of view are bound to emerge. Some might support a certain opinion while others oppose it. In a democratic system like the one we have in Kuwait, the opposition represents the views of the minority, and if with time it succeeds in convincing the masses of the validity of its opinions, it becomes the majority and the other side becomes the opposing minority. This is what elections are for.

The student community at the University of Kuwait includes some students who are opposed to the administrative body of the National Union of Kuwaiti students-University of Kuwait branch. As such and because they oppose the principle of mixed-gender education seeing that they are very conservative and religious, they seized the opportunity to express their views at the symposium and to stand up to the National Union of Kuwaiti Students (Kuwait University branch), especially in view of the fact that none of the participants was opposed to the notion of mixed-gender education.

None of the opposition contacted the organisers of the symposium or any university official to request they be extended the opportunity to speak and express their opinions. Nor did they follow procedure by waiting for the floor to open in order to express their opinions and debate their views as part of the discussion that follows the end of speeches. Nor did they resort to any other democratic means such as holding their own symposium or conference to present the opposition's point of view backed up by evidence. Indeed, the opposition did not resort to any of these democratic methods but four of them: Bashir Saleh Thnian, Muhammad Mahmud al-Rahmani, Hamad Faleh Hamad al-Rushaid and Hamīd Mansur Qasim chose to voice their opposition as soon as the symposium started and before any of the other participants had the chance to utter a single word. They took advantage of the tension in the hall and the type of audience in attendance who supported their shouting and screams, and before anyone knew what was happening, some members of the audience had pushed forth two other members (Muhammad Mahmud al-Rahmani and Hamad Faleh) and demanded they be allowed to participate.

The organisers of the symposium did not wish the situation to spiral further out of control and so decided to break with tradition and give in to the shouts and demands of the audience to add Muhammad Mahmud al-Rahmani and Hamad Faleh to the panel of speakers. They had no intention of allowing them actually to speak and so when it was their turn to take the floor, electricity was cut off to their microphones because the organisers were not happy with the way these two speakers were foisted upon them by an unruly audience.

In the meantime, a member of the audience (Mr Yusif al-Qattan who works at the Ministry of Electricity and Water) leapt onto the podium with a copy of the Qur'an in his hand and waved it in the air as evidence against mixed-gender education. He placed it in front of the participants and left it there before getting off the platform and allowed Muhammad Mahmud al-Rahmani to take his place. This behaviour only served to aggravate the tension in the hall.

In the light of these unfortunate events and the disorder and chaos that ensued during which expletives were exchanged between the two sides, especially since the moderator Badir alRifaʿi was in a very bad state of agitation after being interrupted, one of the participants (Mr Khalid al-Masud) decided to quit the session, while another participant (Mrs Fatimah Husain) refused to speak. Only Dr Saʿad ʿAbdulrahman and Dr ʿAbdulʿaziz Sultan agreed to address the audience. Despite the participation of the opposition, the chaos continued until the noise drowned the speakers' voices. This left the impression that the opposition was there simply to wreak havoc and voice their objections regardless of the opinions being debated.

The events that transpired have required the committee to examine a number of factors: the subject and timing of the symposium, who was invited and how, and the finally the circumstances that aggravated the existing tensions between the various groups.

With regard to the subject of the symposium, some of those interviewed contended that the subject encouraged mixed-gender education which is morally corrupt and contravenes the teaching of Islam. They also objected to the symposium being held in the last days of the holy month of Ramadan which are considered very sacred to Muslims.

Others pointed out that the neither the topic nor the timing of the symposium were offensive and that all topics should be debated within the realm of science and religion. They also remarked that the topic had already been debated on national television with the participation of two members of parliament and a lawyer. Similarly, the Alumni Club had held another symposium two years before with the participation of the Society for Social Reform. Thus, the symposium was not guaranteed to approve of mixed-gender education.

Yet the symposium became the subject of heated debates on radio shows during the holy month of Ramadan, in Friday sermons and during religious tutorials in which Imams and religious scholars condemned the central premise of the symposium. They encouraged their followers and students to attend and many impressionable young people responded to these calls (see photographs 1 and 2 of the audience). They showed up in groups quite early in the day to occupy their seats in the hall. It was very evident they were neither university students nor regular members of the audience who usually attend cultural events at the university's auditorium. Nor did they attend out of interest in religious matters; just one week before on the 19 of Ramadan, a symposium entitled "A Journey with the Qurʾan" with the participation of Professor of *Sharʿia*, Dr Muhammad Salam Madkur, was held and only the front rows were occupied. Young people were further agitated by the attack launched by *al-Mujtamaʿ* Journal against the university, its administration, Council, students and Students' Union, prompting the Union to issue a formal response.

Some witnesses said that Mr ʿAbdulahid Aman who was among those present would signal to the audience to shout or desist and they would obey his cues. Aman denied the accusations.

It is worth mentioning that the invitation to the symposium, similar to any other cultural symposium held in Kuwait, was not by special invitation. Several newspapers (*al-Siyasah*, 13 November 1971, *al-Taliʿah* 13 November 1971) had printed the invitation on its pages. The symposium received a mention on television in addition to the symposium being advertised by word of mouth.

It was against the backdrop of these tensions that the symposium was held and the audience attended. When the opposing students began to shout and challenge the speakers in the manner outlined above, the two sides got caught up in a shouting and cursing match (see photograph 3). As the situation got gradually out of control, members of the audience were shouting from all directions, especially members of the opposition. The symposium organisers felt compelled to call the police and request troops to keep order for fear the situation might worsen. The interruptions and the shouting continued even after two of the opposition were allowed to take a seat on the podium. Only two of the original participants were able to speak (Dr Saʿad ʿAbdulrahman and Dr ʿAbdulʿaziz Sultan). The chaos persisted, a clear indication that the opposition was quite intent on thwarting the symposium rather than taking part in it. The organisers advised the Union's students to suspend the symposium to avoid any further deterioration of the situation. The president of the National Union called upon the Union's members and female students to leave the hall. The opposition tried to object to their departure so the organisers turned off the microphones and switched off the lights. People rushed to the doors and the staircase in a great state of agitation. Some members of the audience got into a fist fight which resulted in two minor injuries.

Based on all the evidence and the statements made by witnesses from both sides, the committee hereby confirms that the Holy Qur'an was not desecrated in any way. It is Allah's book that everyone takes great care in protecting.

The committee is honoured to present the results of its investigations to the esteemed Cabinet.

Minister of Education and President of the University
Jasim Khalid al-Marzuq[2]

---

[2] Rida, *Maʿrakatal-Ikhtilat,* 195–203.

APPENDIX C: PROPOSAL FOR AMENDING ARTICLE 2 OF THE CONSTITUTION OF KUWAIT

After reviewing the Constitution, especially Articles 2, 174 and 175 thereof, the National Assembly hereby ratifies the following Constitutional Law.

> Article (1)
> Article (2) of the Constitution of the State of Kuwait shall be amended as follows: "Islam is the religion of the state. Islamic Shariʿa is the source of legislations."
> Article (2)
> The prime minister and ministers concerned shall implement this amendment which shall become valid on the day of its publication in the Official Gazette.

A memorandum explaining the text of the law was published to ensure that the law was interpreted as intended. The memorandum read as follows:

Almighty Allah has commanded in many verses of the Qur'an that Shariʿa should be the source of legislation; "And whoever does not judge by what Allah has revealed - then it is those who are the disbelievers" (5:45), "But no, by your Lord, they will not [truly] believe until they make you, [O Muhammad], judge concerning that over which they

© The Editor(s) (if applicable) and The Author(s), under exclusive license to Springer Nature Singapore Pte Ltd. 2023
A. A. Alkandari, *The Muslim Brotherhood in Kuwait*, Contemporary Gulf Studies, https://doi.org/10.1007/978-981-99-3050-0

dispute among themselves and then find within themselves no discomfort from what you have judged and submit in [full, willing] submission" (5:65), "Legislation is not but for Allah" (12:40). These verses and many others demonstrate that it is forbidden to drawn upon any other source of legislation or consider it equal to Shari'a. It is well-known that Allah almighty knows what is best for people and has enacted legislations that ensure their stability, security and peace of mind in all aspects of their lives. Secular laws that violate Allah's laws are incapable of tackling all the problems people face in their daily lives and often lead to intractable problems.

In addition to this, Allah's laws are as perfect as Allah's abilities and knowledge and suitable for times and places. It is comprehensible covering all aspects of political, economic and social life. Allah says "This day I have perfected for you your religion and completed My favour upon you and have approved for you Islam as religion" (5:4).

The Constitution promulgated in 1962 postulated that "Shari'a is a main source of legislations," not that "Shari'a is the source of legislations." All efforts exerted by the Foundational Council and later National Assemblies to adopt the more binding version of the law failed miserably.

As such, the degree to which Shari'a should be the source of legislation was left to the discretion of lawmakers as shown by the Explanatory Memorandum which stated that "the text of the law in the Constitution calls upon lawmakers to draw upon Shari'a as much as they can." Yet despite this explicit prompting, after 19 years no serious efforts had been undertaken to adopt the dictates of Islamic Shari'a.

The passage of time demonstrated that the promptings of the explanatory memorandum to rely on Islamic Shari'a as a source of legislation was not sufficient to make Shari'a the sole source. It would thus seem imperative that a more constitutionally binding article of law would need to be incorporated to prohibit any source but Shari'a from being adopted.

This amendment would put an end to the dispute among jurists by placing Islamic Shari'a at the forefront of legislation. In other words, Shari'a would be considered the only main source from which all legislations derived their provisions while other sources would become secondary, to be used only when there were no relevant provisions in Shari'a law.

The current text of the Constitution which stipulates Shari'a as a source of legislation is not binding and leaves matters to the discretion of lawmakers. What is required is a law that codifies that injunction. This would protect the country from legislative chaos and would not leave the door open for appealing the applications of Shariᶜa. Making the necessary amendments to Article 2 would embody the spirit of Islam which encourages gradual change.

The term Islamic Shariᶜa refers to the Qur'an, the Hadith, Consensus and Ijtihad.

Ijtihad or "independent reasoning" is the method by which Shariᶜa is made suitable for all times and places.

The new text of the Constitution does not prohibit regular lawmakers from adopting secular laws or other legislations, as long as they do not violate the principles of Shariᶜa and serve the interests of the country, Muslims and justice. Nor would the new text propose changes to the current system of rule since Islamic Shariᶜa does not specify how a ruler is chosen; rather, it commands Muslims to follow the principles of *shura* in selecting their rulers.[3]

---

[3] Baqir, *Dirasah*, 26–31.

Bibliography

Primary Sources

Publications

Al-ʿAdsani, Khalid, *Mudhakarat Khalid Sulaiman al-ʿAdsani* [Memoirs of Khalid Sulaiman al-ʿAdsani), unpublished undated typescript.

Al-Nuri, Anwar, "Mudhakkarat Anwar al-Nuri [Memoirs of Anwar al-Nuri]," *ʾAafaq Magazine*, 21 April 2013. http://afaq.kuniv.edu/contents/current/details.php?data_id=5529. Accessed 30 June 2013.

Allison, Mary, *Doctor Mary in Arabia*, Houston: University of Texas Press, 1994.

Ayyub, Hasan, "Biography of Hasan Ayyub," Official Website of Hasan Ayyub. www.hasanayoub.com/. Last modified 22 August 2013. Accessed 22 August 2013.

Al-Barnamaj al-Tawjihi, Beirut: ʿIbad al-Rahman, No date.

Al-Banna, Hasan, *Rasaʾil al-Imam Hasan al-Banna* [The Letters of Imam Hasan alBanna], Egypt: Dar al-Kalemah. 2005.

GCC Legal Network, "Marsum Amiri Raqm 15 Lisanat 1959 bi Qanun al-Jinsiyyah alKuwaitiyyah (15-1959) [An Emiri Decree No. 15 Year 1959 About Kuwaiti Citizenship Law (15-1959)]." www.gcclegal.org/MojPortalPublic/LawAsPDF.aspx?opt&country=1&LawID=2694. Last modified 6 June 2013. Accessed 24 August 2013.

GCC Legal Network, "Law Number 24-1996 about Organizing High Education in Kuwait University, Public Authority for Applied Education & Training, and Private Schools." www.gcclegal.org/MojPortalPublic/LawAsPDF.aspx?opt&country=1&LawID=3682. Last modified 23 April 2013. Accessed 30 June 2013.

Dubai Islamic Bank, "The Manners and Approach of the Person Working in An Islamic Organization," Employee Manual of the Dubai Islamic Bank. No publisher, no date.

Islamic Constitutional Movement ICM (1991) "Al-Istiratijiyya al-Dusturiyyah alIslamiyyah Li Bina' al-Kuwait [Islamic Constitutional Strategy to Build Kuwait]," 31 March 1991.

Kuwait University, Official Website, "About the University." www.kuniv.edu/ku/ar/ABOUTKU/ABOUTKU/index.htm. Accessed 29 June 2013.

Kuwait National Assembly, Official Website, "Minutes of the Founding Assembly in Kuwait. Minute No. 19 (11-09-1962)." www.kna.kw/chapter1_meetings/0019.pdf. Last modified 2013. Accessed 24 August 2013.

Maududi, Abu L-Ala, *Islamic Law and Constitution*, Lahore: Islamic Publications, 1969.

Majmu'at al-Tashri'at al-Kuwaitiyyah (1): al-Dustur al-Kuwaiti wa Mudhakkiratih alTafsiriyyah [Kuwaiti Legislations Compilation (1): The Constitution of Kuwait and Its Explanatory Memorandum], Kuwait: Ministry of Justice, 2011.

Al-Marzuqi, Imad, "al-Ikhwan wa al-Salaf fi al-Kuwait," *al-Rai Newspaper*, 4 March 2012. http://www.alraimedia.com/Articles.aspx?id=316386. Accessed 17 March 2014.

Mylrea, Charles, and Stanley Gerland, *Kuwait Before Oil: Memoirs of Dr. C. Stanley G.Mylrea, Poineer Medical Missionary of the Arabian Mission, Reformed Church in America*, Translated by Muhammad al-Rumaihi, Kuwait: Dar Qirṭas, 1997.

Al-Mutawwa', 'Abdul'aziz. "Ila Abna' Watani [To the People of My Country]," *Al-Bi'tha Journal*, Kuwait: Center for Research and Studies on Kuwait, October 1953, 514.

Muslim Brotherhood, "General and International Codes of the Muslim Brotherhood," The Official Website of the Muslim Brotherhood. www.ikhwanonline.com/new/Article.aspx?ArtID=58497&SecID=211. Last modified 30 December 2009. Accessed 22 July 2012.

Nasih, Sa'ih, "Christianity Missionaries in Bahrain and Arab Land," *Majallat al-Manar*, No. 5 (May 1913): 379–383.

Official Website of ICM, "Dirasah 'An Majhudat al-harakah al-Dusturiyyah al-Islamiyya Athna' al-Ghazw al-Iraqi al-Ghashim [A Study about the Efforts of the Islamic Constitutional Movement ICM during the Iraqi Invasion]." www.icmkw.org/hadas/index.php/magazine. Last modified 2 August 2012. Accessed 26 August 2013.

Official Website of Jam'iyyat al-Islah, "'An al-Jam'iyyah [About the Society]." www.eslah.com/ah/?page_id=65. Last modified 2012. Accessed 24 December 2013.

Official Website of Kuwait National Assembly, "Qanun al-Intikhab [Election Law]." www.kna.kw/clt/run.asp?id=37. Last modified 2013. Accessed 26 August 2013.

Official Website of Kuwait Awqaf Public Foundation, "Waqf in Kuwait." www.awqaf.org.kw/English/AboutEndowment/EndowmentHistoryInKuwait/Pages/default.aspx. Last modified 8 May 2013. Accessed 30 June 2013.

Official Website of Kuwait Finance House, "Baituk.. Qissat Najah [Baituk .. Story of Success]." www.kfh.com/ar/about/news/ArchiveNewsDetails.aspx?q=M9tbDDFfYL0L2XuY DoRT3w==. Last modified 23 March 2010. Accessed 30 June 2013.

Official Website of Zakat al-Othman, "Know Us." http://othzk.com/page-1.html. Accessed 22 August 2013.

Interviews

Al-ᶜAtiqi, ᶜAbdulraḥman (Former Minister of Finance and a Private Advisor of the Emir), interview by Ali Al-Kandari, Kuwait, 5 May 2012.

Al-ᶜAtiqi, Yusif (The Third President of the Muslim Brotherhood after Abdulwahid Aman and Jassim Muhalhal), interview by Ali al-Kandari, Kuwait, 24 August 2010.

Al-Ashqar, ᶜUmar (Palestinian member of the Muslim Brotherhood a religious scholar and famous preacher), interview by Ali al-Kandari, Jordan, 1 October 2010.

Aman, ᶜAbdulwahid (The Founder of the Muslim Brotherhood Organization in 1968), interview by Ali al-Kandari, Turkey, 21 July 2010.

Al-Ghanim, Ali (the Chairman of the Kuwait Chamber of Commerce & Industry), interview by Ali al-Kandari, Kuwait, 25 September 2004.

Al-Hamad, Sulaiman (Palestinian member of al-Irshad), interview by Ali al-Kandari, Kuwait, 5 October 2010.

Al-Kandari, Jamal (MP in Kuwait National Assembly 1992–1996, 2006–2008), interview by Ali al-Kandari, London, 30 January 2013.

Al-Mutawwaᶜ, Abdullah. "Abdullah Al-Mutawwaᶜ in his Memoirs," interview by Rajab Damanhurī, *Al-Harakah Newspaper*, 3 September 2006.

Al-Ruwaishid, Ahmad (member of al-Irshad), interview by Ali al-Kandari, Kuwait, 3 August 2010.

Al-Rifaᶜi, Yusif (member of al-Irshad), interview by Ali al-Kandari, Kuwait. 8 August 2010.

Al-Rashid, Muhammad Ahmad (the developer of the Muslim Brotherhood organizational ideology), interview by Ali al-Kandari, Malaysia, 31 July 2010.

Al-Madhun, Hasan (Palestinian member of al-Irshad), interview by Ali al-Kandari, Jordan. 5 October 2010.

Al-Mutawwaᶜ, Ahmad (son of Abdulaziz al-Mutawwaᶜ, the founder of al-Irshad), interview by Ali al-Kandari, Kuwait, 25 August 2010.

Al-Nashmi, Ajil (Member of the Muslim Brotherhood and well-known religious scholar) interview by Ali al-Kandari, Kuwait, 30 August 2010.

Al-Nisif, Yusif (Member of al-Irshad), interview by Ali al-Kandari, Kuwait, 10 December 2010.

Archival Publications: UK and US Governments

"Administration Report for the Political Agency, Kuwait, 1912" in the *Annual Report of the Persian Gulf Political Residency for 1911*, IOR: R/15/1/711/2 (British Library, London), 113.

"Administration Report for the Political Agency, Kuwait, 1913" in the *Annual Report of the Persian Gulf Political Residency for 1912*, IOR: R/15/1/712/2 (British Library, London), 126.

"Administration Report for the Political Agency, Kuwait, 1941" in the *Annual Report of the Persian Gulf Political Residency for 1940*, IOR: R/15/5/206/135 (British Library, London), 135.

"Administration Report for the Political Agency, Kuwait, 1939" in the *Annual Report of the Persian Gulf Political Residency for 1938*, IOR: R/15/5/206/425 (British Library, London).

"Administration Report for the Political Agency, Kuwait, 1939" in the *Annual Report of the Persian Gulf Political Residency for 1938*, IOR: R/1/P. & S./12/3894 (British Library, London).

"Administration Report for the Political Agency, Kuwait, 1940" in the *Annual Report of the Persian Gulf Political Residency for 1939*, IOR: R/15/5/206/55 (British Library, London).

"Administration Report for the Political Agency, Kuwait, 1940" in the *Annual Report of the Persian Gulf Political Residency for 1939*, IOR: R/15/5/206/99 (British Library, London).

Extract from the *Mujallat ul Munar* of Cairo, Vol. 15, Part 7, dated Rajab 1330 (14 July 1913), 559, in IOR: 15/5/62 (British Library, London), 32.

U.S. Department of State (USDS). 1949. Confidential Central Files, Egypt, 1954, No. 564, Washington, DC.

Media

Youtube.com, "Mubarak al-Duwailah Yastathkir Dhikrayat al-Ghazw al-ʿIraqi wa Muʾtamar Jeddah [Mubarak al-Duwailah Recalls the Memories of the Iraqi Invasion and Jeddah Conference]," Web at www.youtube.com/watch?v=2lQPh3pAf5k. Posted 2 August 2012.

Youtube.com, "Muqtatafat min Muʾtamar Jeddah [Selections of Jeddah Conference]," Web at www.youtube.com/watch?v=QzR0KLbUYiY, Posted 10 July 2012.

SECONDARY SOURCES

Adams, Charles J., "Maududi and the Islamic State", in John Esposito (ed.) *Voices of Resurgent Islam*, Oxford: Oxford University Press, 1983.

Anon., "About Jamʿiyyat al-Irshad." *Majallat al-ʿIrshad* [al-ʿIrshad Journal], March 1957.

Asiri, ʿAbdulridha. *Al-Nizam al-Siyasi fi al-Kuwait* [Political System in Kuwait], Kuwait: al-Watan Prints, 1996.

Al-ʿAtiqi, ʿAbdullatif, "ʾInhiyar al-Fikr al-Yasari" [The Collapse of the Leftist Ideology], *Al-Qabas Newspaper*, 7 October 2010. www.alqabas.com.kw/node/397960. Accessed 23 August 2013.

Al-ʿAqil, Abdullah. Wikipedia of the Muslim Brotherhood, "Al-Waʿiz al-Muwaffaq.. Hasan Tannun [The Successful Preacher.. Hasan Tannun]." www.ikhwanwiki.com/index.php?title=حسن_طنون. Last modified 2011. Accessed 22 August 2013.

Al-ʿAqil, Abdullah, *Min Aʾalam al-Harakah al-Islamiyyah al-Muʿasirah* [Some Figures of Contemporary Islamist movement], Kuwait: al-Manar, 2001.

Al-ʿAqil, Abdullah, "ʿIsa ʿAbduh Ibrahim: Raʾid al-Bunuk al-Islamiyyah [ʿIsa ʿAbduh Ibrahim: The Pioneer of Islamic Banks]." http://www.odabasham.net/تراجم-117001/الدكتور-عيسى-عبده-ابراهيم-رائد-البنوك-الإسلامية. Last modified 25 April 2013. Accessed 30 June 2013.

Al-ʿAqil, Abdullah, The Official Historical Encyclopaedia of the Muslim Brotherhood, "ʿAbdulhakim ʾabdin." www.ikhwanwiki.com/index.php?title=عبد_الحكيم_عابدين. Last modified 8 May 2013. Accessed 30 June 2013.

Al-ʿAqil, Abdullah, The Official Historical Encyclopaedia of the Muslim Brotherhood, "Al-Daʿiyah Hasan ʾAshmawi." www.ikhwanwiki.com/index.php?title=حسن_العشماوي. Last modified 20 June 2012. Accessed 29 June 2013.

ʿAbdulhalim, Mahmud, *al-Ikhwan al-Muslimun: Ahdath Sanaʾat al-Tarikh* [The Muslim Brotherhood: Events that Made the History], Alexandria: Dar al-Daʿwah, 1994.

ʿAbdulʾati, Muhammad B. Aljazeera Channel, "Al-Afghan al-ʿArab." www.aljazeera.net/specialfiles/pages/119d2e8f-080d47e1-ad8b-82098360c304. Last modified 3 April 2004. Accessed 30 June 2013.

ʿAbduh, ʿIsa, *Silsilat Bunuk Bidun Fawayid: al-Faʾidah ʿAla Raʾs al-Mal Surah min Suwar al-Riba* [Banks without Usuries Series: Interest on the Capital is an Image of Usury], Cairo: Dar al-Fath, 1970.

Al-ʿAdsani, Khalid, "Tarikh al-Harakah al-Fikriyyah fi al-Kuwait [The History of Intellectual Movement in Kuwait]," Sijil al-Kuwait al-Yawm, 1951. 14–17.

ʿAntabli, Ashraf, Wikipedia of the Muslim Brotherhood, "ʾAhmad al-Sharabasi: Hayat wa Jihad [Ahmad al-Sharabasi: Life and Jihad]." www.ikhwanwiki.com/index.php?title=أحمد_الشرباصي. Last modified 2011. Accessed 8 September 2013.

Arjomand, Said Amir, "Islam in Iran vi., the Concept of Mahdi in Sunni Islam," *Encyclopaedia Iranica*, XIV (December 2007): 134–136. www.iranicaonline. org/articles/islam-in-iran-vi-the-concept-of-mahdi-in-sunniislam.

al-ʿAzamah, ʿAziz, *al-Almaniyya min Manthour Mukhtalif*, Beirut: Centre for Arab Unity Studies, 1992.

Baqir, Ahmad, *Dirasah ʿAn al-Maddah al-Thaniya fi Dustur Dawalat al-Kuwait* [A study on the Second Article of the Constitution of the State of Kuwait], No Publisher: 1994.

Bayat, Asef, "Islamism and Social Movement Theory," *Third World Quarterly*, 26, No. 6 (2005): 891–908.

Al-Bishri, Tariq, *Malamih ʿAammah lil Fikr al-Siyasi al-Islami fi al-Tarikh al-Muʿasir* [General Features of the Islamic Political Ideology in the Contemporary History], Cairo: Dar al-Shuruq, 1996.

Bin Bishr, ʿUthman, *ʿUnwan al-Majd fi Tarikh Najd* [The Title of Glory in the History of Najd], Riyadh: King Abdulaziz Foundation for Research and Archives, 1982.

Brown, Nathan, "Pushing Toward Parties Politics? Kuwait's Constitutional Islamist Movement," Carnegie Endowment for International Peace. No.79 (January 2007).

Center for Research and Studies on Kuwait, *History of Education in Kuwait: Documentary Study*, Kuwait: The Center for Research and Studies on Kuwait (CRSK), 2002.

Cleveland, William, *The Making of an Arab Nationalist: Ottomanism and Arabism in the Life and Thought of Sati' al-Husri*, New Jersey: Princeton, 1971.

Al-Dabbagh, Iman, "Jamʿiyyat al-Ukhwah al-Islamiyya fi Iraq: Dirasah ʿAn Nashʾat Harakat al-Ikhwan al-Muslimin fi al-Iraq [The Society of Muslim Faternity in Iraq: a Study of the Beginning of the Muslim Brotherhood in Iraq] 1949–1954," MA Thesis. University of Mousil. 2010.

al-Dayil, ʿUmar, *Safahat min Tarikh al-Daʿwah al-Islamiyya fi al-Zubair* [Pages from the History of the Islamic Daʿwah in Zubair], Unpublished-undated handwritten pamphlet.

Dekmejian, R. Hrair, *Islam in Revolution: Fundamentalism in the Arab World*, New York: Syracuse University Press, 1995.

Diwan, Kristin, "Islamic Finance beyond the State: The Renewal of Awqaf," MPSA Annual Conference, Chicago, 31 March – 3 April 2011.

Diwan, Kristin, "Islamic Finance and the Renewal of Awqaf," The Eighth Annual Harvard University Forum on Islamic Finance, May 2008.

Diwan, Kristin, "The Kuwait Finance House and the Islamization of Public Life in Kuwait," in *The Politics of Islamic Finance*, ed. Celement Henry, Rodney Wilson. Edinburgh: Edinburgh University Press, 2004.

Diwan, Kristin, "Culture and Capital: The Strategic Construction of Islamic Financial Institutions in the Gulf," International Studies Association, New Orleans, February 2010.

"Diwaniyyat al-Ithnain: al-Hadath Laisa Baʿidan wa la Yumkin Nisyanuh (1) [Monday Diwaniyyas: The Event Is Not Far and Could Not Be Forgotten (1)]," Al-Jarida Newspaper, 5 February 2009. www.aljaRida.com/news/index/309807/. Accessed 24 August 2013.

"Diwaniyyat al-Ithnain: al-Hadath Laisa Baʿidan wa la Yumkin Nisyanuh (3) [Monday Diwaniyyas: The Event Is Not Far and Could Not Be Forgotten (3)]," Al-Jarida Newspaper, 10 February 2009. www.aljaRida.com/news/index/310884/. Accessed 24 August 2013.

"Diwaniyyat al-Ithnain: al-Hadath Laisa Baʿidan wa la Yumkin Nisyanuh (6) [Monday Diwaniyyas: The Event Is Not Far and Could Not Be Forgotten (6)]," Al-Jarida Newspaper, 11 February 2009. www.aljaRida.com/news/index/311211/. Accessed 24 August 2013.

"Diwaniyyat al-Ithnain: al-Hadath Laisa Baʿidan wa la Yumkin Nisyanuh (7) [Monday Diwaniyyas: The Event Is Not Far and Could Not Be Forgotten (7)]," Al-Jarida Newspaper, 12 February 2009. www.aljaRida.com/news/index/311401/. Accessed 24 August 2013.

"Diwaniyyat al-Ithnain: al-Hadath Laisa Baʿidan wa la Yumkin Nisyanuh (8) [Monday Diwaniyyas: The Event Is Not Far and Could Not Be Forgotten (8)]," Al-Jarida Newspaper, 13 February 2009. www.aljaRida.com/news/index/311746/. Accessed 25 August 2013.

"Diwaniyyat al-ʾal-niyy: al-Hadath Laisa Baʿidan wa la Yumkin Nisyanuh (9) [Monday Diwaniyyas: The Event Is Not Far and Could Not Be Forgotten (9)]," Al-Jarida Newspaper, 15 February 2009. www.aljaRida.com/news/index/312058/. Accessed 25 August 2013.

"Diwaniyyat al-Ithnain: al-Hadath Laisa Baʿidan wa la Yumkin Nisyanuh (10) [Monday Diwaniyyas: The Event Is Not Far and Could Not Be Forgotten (10)]," Al-Jarida Newspaper, 16 February 2009. www.aljaRida.com/news/index/312433/. Accessed 25 August 2013.

"Diwaniyyat al-Ithnain: al-Hadath Laisa Baʿidan wa la Yumkin Nisyanuh (11) [Monday Diwaniyyas: The Event Is Not Far and Could Not Be Forgotten (11)]," Al-Jarida Newspaper, 17 February 2009. www.aljaRida.com/news/index/312673/. Accessed 24 August 2013.

"Diwaniyyat al-Ithnain: al-Hadath Laisa Baʿidan wa la Yumkin Nisyanuh (15) [Monday Diwaniyyas: The Event Is Not Far and Could Not Be Forgotten (15)]," Al-Jarida Newspaper, 22 February 2009. www.aljaRida.com/news/index/313758/. Accessed 25 August 2013.

"Diwaniyyat al-Ithnain: al-Hadath Laisa Baʿidan wa la Yumkin Nisyanuh (16) [Monday Diwaniyyas: The Event Is Not Far and Could Not Be Forgotten

(16)]," *Al-Jarida Newspaper*, 23 February 2009. www.aljaRida.com/news/index/314097/. Accessed 25 August 2013.

"Diwaniyyat al-Ithnain: al-Hadath Laisa Ba'idan wa la Yumkin Nisyanuh (19) [Monday Diwaniyyas: The Event Is Not Far and Could Not Be Forgotten (19)]," *Al-Jarida Newspaper*, 26 February 2009. www.aljaRida.com/news/index/314696/. Accessed 25 August 2013.

Diyab, Wafaʾi, *Wathaʾiq al-Ihtilal wa Haqaʾq al-Tahrir* [Documents of Occupation and Facts of Liberation], Lebanon: al-Muʾassasah al-Arabiyyah al-ʾUrubiyyah Lilsahafah wa al-Nashr, 1991.

Dusugi, ʿAbduh, Wikipedia of the Muslim Brotherhood, "Muhammad ʿAbdulhamid Ahmad... 'Aamid Tullab al-Ikhwan al-Muslimeen [Senior Student of Muslim Brotherhood]." www.ikhwanwiki.com/index.php?title=محمد_عبد_الحميد_أحمد. Last modified 2011. Accessed 21 August 2013.

Dusugi, ʿAbduh, Wikipedia of the Muslim Brotherhood, "Muhammad Najib Juwaifil: al-Lughz al-Mutheer" [Muhammad Najib Juwaifil: The Interesting Puzzle]. www.ikhwanwiki.com/index.php?title=نجيب_جويفل. Last modified 2011. Accessed 22 August 2013.

Esposito, John L., "Religion and Political Affairs: Political Challenges," SAIS Review: A Journal for International Affairs, 18, No. 2, 1998.

Esposito, John L., "Islamic Revivalism," Occasional Paper No. 3 of The Muslim World Today, Washington, DC: American Institute for Islamic Affairs, 1985.

Esposito, John L., *The Islamic Threat: Myth or Reality*, Oxford: Oxford University Press, 1992.

Esposito, John L., *Voices of Resurgent Islam*, Oxford: Oxford University Press, 1983.

Ernest Gellner, *Conditions of Liberty: Civil Society and Its Rivals*, London: Penguin Books, 1994.

El-Najjar, Hassan A., *The Gulf War: Overreaction & Excessiveness*, USA: Amazon Press, 2001. www.gulfwar1991.com/Gulf War Complete/Chapter 10, Palestinians in Kuwait, Terror and Ethnic Cleansing, By Hassan A El-Najjar.htm. Accessed 24 August 2013.

Elimam, Abdulghani A., Maurice Girgis, and Samir Kotob (1996), "The Use of Linear Programming in Disentangling the Bankruptcies of al-Manakh Stock Market Crash," *Operations Research*, No. 5 (1996): 665–676.

Eickelman, Dale F., and James Piscatori, *Muslim Politics*, Princeton, NJ: Princeton University Press, 1996.

Shafiq Ghabra, "Balancing State and Society: The Islamist movement in Kuwait," *Middle East Policy*, 5, No. 2 (May 1997).

Al-Ghunaim, Yaqoub. Kuwait News Agency (KUNA), "Nadi al-Muᶜallimin min Aqdam Andiyat al-Kuwait [Teachers Association One of the Oldest Associations in Kuwait]." www.kuna.net.kw/ArticleDetails.aspx?id=2189465&language=ar. Last modified 11 November 2011. Accessed 9 September 2013.

Al-Hajeri, Abdullah, "Citizenship and Political Participation in the State of Kuwait: The Case of the National Assembly (1962–1996)," PhD diss., University of Durham UK, 2004.

Al-Harbi, Marzuq, "Al-Haiʔah al-ᶜAalamiyya Liltadamun Maᶜa al-Kuwait [International Institution of Solidarity with Kuwait]," *Al-Watan Newspaper*, 25 February 2013. http://kuwait.tt/articledetails.aspx?Id=256740. Accessed 25 August 2013.

Hegghamer, Thomas, and Stephane Lacroix, "Rejectionist Islamism in Saᶜudi Arabia: The Story of Juhayman al-Utaybi Revisited," *International Journal of Middle Eastern Studies*, No. 39 (2007): 103–122. http://hegghammer.com/_files/HegghammerLacroix_-_Rejectionist_Islamism_in_Saᶜudi_Arabia.pdf. Accessed 23 August 2013.

Herb, Michael, "Kuwait Politics Database." http://www2.gsu.edu/~polmfh/database/DataPage1016.htm. Accessed 21 August 2013.

Hill, Allan, "Aspects of the Urban Development of Kuwait," PhD diss., Durham University, August 1969.

Hizb al-Tahrir, "Tarᶜif," Official Website of Hizb al-Tahrir. http://www.hizb-ut-tahrir.org/index.php/AR/def. Accessed 5 April 2014.

Hourani, Albert, *A History of the Arab People*, Cambridge MA: Belknap Press of Harvard University Press, 2002.

Al-Hudaibi, Hasan, "Duᶜat la Qudat," *Wikipedia of the Muslim Brotherhood*. http://www.ikhwanwiki.com/index.php?title=%D8%AF%D8%B9%D8%A7%D8%A9_%D9%84%D8%A7_%D9%82%D8%B6%D8%A7%D8%A9. Last modified 2011. Accessed 5 April 2014.

Hussain, ᶜAbdulᶜaziz, *Al-Mujtamaᶜ al-ᶜArabi fi al-Kuwait* [Arabic Society in Kuwait], Kuwait: Dar Qirṭas, 1994.

Al-Ibrahim, ᶜAbdulraḥmān. "Tatawwur al-Harakah al-Dusturiyyah fi al-Kuwait bayna 1938–1961 [Development of the Constitutional Movement in Kuwait Between 1938- 1961]," MA Thesis, University of Sharjah, 2011.

'Imara, Muhammad, "50 Sanah mundhu Istishhad Hasan al-Banna: al-Mashruᶜ al-Islami li Nahdat al-Ummah [50 Years since the Martyrdom of Hasan al-Banna: The Islamic Project for the Civilization Renaissance]," *Al-Mujtamaᶜ*, 9 February1999, 22.

Islamic Banker, "Murabahah." www.islamicbanker.com/education-resources/17. Last modified 2013. Accessed 8 September 2013.

Islamic Banker, "Musharakah & Mudarabah." www.islamicbanker.com/education-resources/15. Last modified 2013. Accessed 8 September 2013.

Ismail, Salwa, "Confronting the Other: Identity, Culture, Politics, and Conservative Islamism in Egypt," International Journal of Middle East Studies, 30, no. 2 (1998): 24.

"Al-Ikhtilat." Al-Mujtama^c, 4 April 1972, 4.

"Al-Itihad al-Watani li Talabat al-Kuwait Yantasir lil Huriyyat [The National Union of Kuwaiti Students Stands Up For Freedoms]," Sabr Electronic Newspaper, 13 February 2013. www.sabr.cc/m/inner.aspx?id=53192&cat=4. Accessed 24 August 2013.

Ibn Hanbal, Ahmad, Musnad Imam Ahmad, Riyadh: Dar Ihya' al-Turath al-Arabi, 1993. Jam^{c}iyyat al-Mu^{c}alimin [Teachers Society], Official Website, "About Us." www.moalem.org/aboutus. Last modified 2013. Accessed 24 August 2013.

Jamal, ^{c}Abdulmehsin, Lamahat fi Hayat al-Shi^{c}ah fi al-Kuwait [Glances at the Life of Shi^{c}a in Kuwait], Kuwait: Dar al-Naba', 2005.

Jamal, ^{c}Abdulmehsin, Al-Mu^{c}aradah al-Siyasiyya fi al-Kuwait [Political Opposition in Kuwait], Kuwait: Dar Qirtas, 2007.

Al-Jassar, Muhammad, "Constancy and change in contemporary Kuwait City: The Sociocultural Dimensions of the Kuwait Courtyard and Diwaniyya," PhD diss., University of Wisconsin, 2009.

Al-Jasem, Najat, Baladiyyat al-Kuwait fi Khamsin ^{c}Aaman [Kuwait Municipality in 50 Years], Kuwait: Baladiyyat al-Kuwait, 1980.

Al-Jasem, Najat, Al-Tatawwur al-Siyasi wa al-Iqtisadi fi al-Kuwait baina al-Harbayn 1914–1939 [Political and Economic Development of Kuwait Between the Two Wars 1914–1939], Kuwait: al-Majlis al-Watani Lilthaqafah wa al-Funun wa alAdab, 2002.

Juha, Shafiq, Al-Harakah al-^{c}Arabiyyah al-Sirriyya [Arabic Secret Movement], Beirut: alFurat, 2004.

Al-Khaldi, Abdullatif, Min A^{c}alam al-Fikr al-Islami fi al-Basra: Muhammad Amin alShanqiti [Some Intellectual Islamic Figures in Basra: Muhammad Amin alShanqiti], Baghdad: Awqaf Ministry, 1981.

Khaz^{c}al, Hussain, Tarikh al-Kuwait al-Siyasi [Political History of Kuwait], Vol. 1, Beirut: Dar al-Hilal, 1962.

Khusousi, Bader Aldin, Ma^{c}rakat al-Jahra': Dirasa Tawthiqiyyah [The Battle of al-Jahra': A Documented Study], Kuwait: That al-Salasil, 1983.

Kuwait News Agency (KUNA), "Hadath fi Hatha al-Yawm fi al-Kuwait [Happened in This Day in Kuwait]." www.kuna.net.kw/ArticleDetails.aspx?id=1887602&language=ar. Last modified 28 February 2008. Accessed 11 January 2013.

Kuwait News Agency (KUNA), "Dhikra Murur 20 ^{c}Aaman ^{c}Ala Ta'sis Bayt al-Zakat alKuwaiti [20 Years of Establishing Kuwaiti Bayt al-Zakat]." Last modified 15 February 2002. Accessed 24 August 2013.

Lacroix, Stéphane, *Awakening Islam: The Politics of Religious Dissent in Contemporary Saʿudi Arabia*, Translated by George Holoch. USA: Harvard Collage, 2011.

Lahoud-Tatar, *Carine Islam et Politique au Koweït*. Paris: Presses Universitaires France, 2011.

Lapidus, Ira M., "State and Religion in Islamic Societies," *Past & Present*, 151, No.1 (May 1996): 3–27. www.jstor.org/stable/view/651204. Accessed 14 December 2013.

Lutah, Saʿid, "Saʿid Lutah... Fikrat al-Masarif al-Islamiyyah [The Idea of Islamic Banking]," *Aljazeera Channel*, 8 March 2008. 30 June 2013. www.aljazeera. net/programs/pages/190b3512-df1a-4160-a620-eff9a9dcd492.

Mahmud, Ali, *Wasaʾ al-Tarbiyah ʿInd al-Ikhwan al-Muslimin* [Methods of Tarbiya of the Muslim Brotherhood]. Egypt: Dar al-Wafaʾ, 1989.

Al-Mansur, ʿAbdulʿaziz. Al-Kuwait wa ʿIlaqatuha bi ʿArabistan wa al-Basra [Kuwait and its Relationship with ʿArabistan and Basra 1896–1915], No Publisher, 1980.

"Marahil al-Tʿlim fi al-Kuwait [Stages of Education in Kuwait]," *Official Website of the Ministry of Education in Kuwait*, 2012. http://www.moe.edu.kw/SitePages/home.aspx. Accessed 16 March 2014.

al-Mdaires, Falah, *Jamaʿat al-Ikhwan al-Muslimin fi al-Kuwait* [Muslim Brotherhood in Kuwait]. Kuwait: Dar Qurtas, 1999.

Al-Mdairis, Falah, "Marhalat Taʾsis al-Ikhwan al-Muslimeen wa Buruzha fi al-Kuwait [The Episode of Founding the Muslim Brotherhood and its Appearance in Kuwait]," *Al-Qabas Newspaper*, 4 June 2006. www.alqabas.com.kw/ArticlePrint.aspx?id=173184&mode=print. Accessed 22 August 2013.

Miller, Judith, "CONFRONTATION IN THE GULF; Iraqi Pullout? Election in Kuwait? Prospects Worry Hawks," *The New York Times*, 8 October 1990. http://www.nytimes.com/1990/10/08/world/confrontation-in-the-gulf-iraqi-pullout-election-in-kuwait-prospects-worry-hawks.html. Accessed 17 March 2014.

Mitchell, Richard P., *The Society of the Muslim Brothers*, Oxford: Oxford University Press, 1993.

Al-Mutairi, Bader, *Al-Jamʿiyyah al-Khairiyyahh al-ʿArabiyyah*, Kuwait: The Center for Research and Studies on Kuwait (CRSK), 1998.

Al-Mulaifi, Ibrahim, "Al-Harakah al-Tullabiyyah al-Kuwaitiyyah fi 40 ʿAaman (1) [Kuwait Student Movement in 40 Years (2)]," *Al-Qabas Newspaper*, 4 October 2008. www.alqabas.com.kw/node/394316. Accessed 30 June 2013.

Al-Mulaifi, Ibrahim (2008), "Al-Harakah al-Tullabiyyah al-Kuwaitiyyah fi 40 ʿAaman (2), [Kuwait Student Movement in 40 Years (2)]", *Al-Qabas Newspaper*, 5 October 2008. www.alqabas.com.kw/node/395506. Accessed 24 August 2013.

Al-Mulaifi, Ibrahim, "Al-Harakah al-Tullabiyyah al-Kuwaitiyyah fi 40 ᶜAaman (3) [Kuwait Student Movement in 40 Years (3)]," *Al-Qabas Newspaper*, 6 October 2008. www.alqabas.com.kw/node/396445. Accessed 24 August 2013.

Al-Mutawwaᶜ, ᶜAbdulᶜaziz. "ᶜAn al-Nasharat [About the Brochures]," *Majallat al-Irshad* [al-Irshad Journal], August 1953, 66.

Al-Mutawwaᶜ, ᶜAbdulᶜaziz. "Manaᵓat al-umma [The Immunity of the Nation]," *Majallat al-Irshad* [Al-Irshad Journal], August 1953, 65–66.

Al-Mutawwaᶜ, ᶜAbdulᶜaziz. "Al-Banat wa al-Riyadah [Girls and Sports]," *Majallat al-Irshad* [Al-Irshad JOURNAL], March 1954, 92–93.

Munson, Ziad, "Islamic Mobilization: Social Movement Theory and the Egyptian Muslim Brotherhood," *The Sociological Quarterly*, 42, No. 4 (2001): 487–510.

Al-Nafisi, Abdullah, *"al-Harakah al-Islamiyya: Thagharat fi al-Tariq* [Islamic Movement: Apertures in the Path]," No Publisher: Kuwait, 1992.

al-Nasir, ᶜAbdulᶜaziz, *al-Zubair*, Saudi Arabiya; Wahj al-Hayat Communications, 2010.

Nasser, Muhammad, "Tarikh al-Mutalabat bi Taghiir al-Maddah al-Thaniya [The History of Demands to Change the Second Article]," *Al-Anbaᵓ Newspaper*, 16 February 2012.

Al-Nuri, Abdullah, *Qissat al-Taᶜlim fi al-Kuwait fi Nisf Qarn* [The Story of Education in Kuwait in Half Century], Kuwait: That al-Salasil, No date.

Al-Qinaᶜi, Yusif, *Al-Multaqatat*, Kuwait: Kuwait Government Press, No date.

Al-Qinaᶜi, Yusif, *Safahat min Tarikh al-Kuwait* [Pages from the History of Kuwait], Kuwait: No Publisher, 1960.

"Qissat Hayat Imraah Thairah ᶜala Hisar al-Unuthah [A Story of a Rebelled Woman Against the Siege of Feminism]," *Majallat al-Kuwait*, 22 November 2011, issue 337. http://kuwaitmag.com/index.jsp?inc=4&pid=2142&version=239. Accessed 16 March 2014.

Al-Rashid, Muhammad Ahmad, *al-Muntalaq* [the Start], Dubai: Dar al-Muntalaq, 1994.

Al-Rashid, Muhammad Ahmad, *al-ᶜAwaᵓiq* [the Obstacles], Dubai: Dar al-Muntalaq, 1994.

Al-Rashid, Muhammad Ahmad, *Al-Masar* [the Path], Cairo: Dar al-Nashr Liljamiᶜat, 2010.

Al-Rashid, Muhammad Ahmad, *Sinaᶜat al-Hayat* [the Making of Life], Damascus: Dar alFikr, 2005.

Al-Rayyis, Riadh, "Arab Nationalism and the Gulf," PhD diss., University of Exeter. 1986.

Al-Rumaihi, Muhammad, "Al-Harakah al-Islahiyyah fi al-Kuwait, al-Bahrain, wa Dubai [The 1939 Reformist Movement in Kuwait, Bahrain, and Dubai]," *Journal of Gulf and Arab Peninsula Studies*, No. 4 (1985): 34.

Al-Rushaid, ʿAbdulʿaziz. *Tarikh al-Kuwait* [History of Kuwait], Baghdad: al-Matbaʿah alʿAsriyyah, 1926.

Al-Rushaid, ʿAbdulʿaziz. "Introduction," *Kuwait Journal* (1928): 3.

Al-Rushaid, ʿAbdulʿaziz. "Shaikh Yusif bin ʿIsa al-Qinaʿi: The Reformer of Kuwait," [Shaikh Yusif bin ʿIsa al-Qinaʿi: Muslih al-Kuwait]. *Kuwait Journal* (January–February 1930): 330–332.

Rida, Muhammad J., *Maʿrakat al-Ikhtilat fi al-Kuwait* [The Battle of Mixed-Gender Education in Kuwait], Kuwait: Dar al-Rubaiʾān, 1983.

Al-Sharabasi, Ahmad, *Ayyam al-Kuwait* [Days of Kuwait], Cairo: Dar al-Kitab al-Arabi, 1953.

Al-Shammari, ʿAbdulmehsin. "Al-Masrah fi al-Kuwait... Khamsun ʿAaman min al-ʿAtaʾ [Theatre in Kuwait... Fifty Years of Giving]," *Majallat al-Kuwait*, 30 June 2013. http://kuwaitmag.com/index.jsp?inc=5&id=2531&pid=112&version=27. Accessed 29 June 2013.

Shamlan, Saif, *Min Tarikh al-Kuwait* [From the History of Kuwait], Kuwait: That alSalasil, 1986.

Shepard, William E., "Sayyid Qutb's Doctrine of Jahiliyya," *International Journal of Middle East Studies*, Vol. 35, No. 4 (November, 2003), 521–545.

Shihab, Saleh, *Tarikh al-Taʿlim fi al-Kuwait wa al-Khalij* [History of Education in Kuwait and the Gulf], Kuwait: Kuwait Government Press, 1984.

Al-Sadir, Muhammad B., *Iqtisaduna* [Our Economy], Beirut: Dar al-Tʾāruf, 1987.

Al-Sadir, Muhammad B., *al-Bank al-Laribawi fi Islam* [Non-Usuri Bank in Islam], Beirut: Dar al-Tʿaruf, 1994.

"Al-Taʿrif bil Jamʿiyyah [Introduction of the Society]," *Official Website of Jamʿiyyat Ihya al-Turath al-Islami*. http://www.altorath.org/main/define.htm. Accessed 17 March 2014.

ʾUlaiyyan, Hamzah, "Qissat al-Khumur fi al-Kuwait min al-Mamnuʿ Ila al-Masmuh [The Story of Alcohol in Kuwait from being Permitted to Be Prohibited]," *Al-Qabas Newspaper*, 26 January 2009. www.alqabas.com.kw/node/436874. Accessed 24 August 2013.

ʿUlaiyyan, Hamzah, "Al-Khamr fi al-Kuwait min al-Masmuh Ila al-Mamnuʿ [Alcohol in Kuwait from being Permitted to be Prohibited]," *Al-Qabas Newspaper*, 27 January 2009. www.alqabas-kw.com/AuthorArticles.aspx?id=62&page=20&date=28032012. Accessed 29 June 2013.

Al-Wehaib, Walid, "Al-Ikhtilat fi Kulliyat al-Tijarah [Mixed-Gender Education in Business School]," *al-Siyasah Newspaper*, 28 September 1973, 28.

Wahbah, Hafiz, *Jazirat al-ʿArab fi al-Qarn al-ʿIshrin* [Arabian Peninsula in the Twentieth Century], No Publisher: No date.

Al-Wuqayyan, Khalifa, *al-Thaqafah fi al-Kuwait: Bidayat, Ittijahat, Riyadat* [Culture in Kuwait: Beginnings, Trends and Pioneers], Kuwait: al-Faisal Press, 2010.

Yakan, Fathi, "Fiqhiyyat Tanzimiyya: About Shura [Fiqh of Organization: About Shura]," Official Website of Fathi Yakan. www.daawa.net/display/arabic/efuqh/efuqhdetail.aspx?eid=144. Accessed 23 August 2013.

"Ya ḥukkamana [O Ye Our Rulers]," *Majallat al-Irshad*, December 1953.

Jasim Al-Yasin, *Lildu'at Faqat: Da'waht al-Ikhwan Haqa'iq..Shubuhat..Tamaniyyat* [For Preachers Only: The Muslim Brotherhood; Facts, Misconceptions and Hopes], Kuwait: Dar al-Da'wah, 1990.

Zaki, Muhammad, *Al-Ikhwan al-Muslimun*, Cairo: Wahbah, 1954.

Zaidan, 'Abdulkarīm, *Usul al-Da'wah* [Principles of Da'wah], No Publisher, 1976.

Zuhailī, Muhammad, "Mulkiyyat A'yan al-Waqf baina Maqasid al-Tashri' wa Mathalib alSaitarah [The Ownership of Waqf Properties between the Philosophy of Islamic Law and the Fault of Seizing them]," Waqf Conference III, Medina, January 2010, 645–681.

Zollner, Barbara H. E., *The Muslim Brotherhood: Hasan al-Hudaybi and Ideology*, London: Routledge, 2009.

Al-Zubaidi, Mufid, *Al-Tayyarat al-Fikriyyah fi al-Khalij al-'Arabi 1938–1971* [Intellectual Trends in the Arabian Gulf 1938–1971], Beirut: Markaz Dirasat al-Wihdah alArabiyya, 2000.

Al-Zumai, Ali, "The Intellectual and Historical Development of the Islamist Movement in Kuwait 1950–1981," PhD diss., University of Exeter, 1988.

INDEX

Note: The page numbers followed by 'n' represents footnotes

A. A. Alkandari, *The Muslim Brotherhood in Kuwait*, Contemporary Gulf Studies, https://doi.org/10.1007/978-981-99-3050-0

Printed in the United States
by Baker & Taylor Publisher Services